YALE STUDIES IN ECONOMICS: 5

MAINSPRINGS OF THE

GERMAN REVIVAL

by HENRY C. WALLICH

PROFESSOR OF ECONOMICS, YALE UNIVERSITY

NEW HAVEN: YALE UNIVERSITY PRESS, 1955

LONDON: GEOFFREY CUMBERLEGE, OXFORD UNIVERSITY PRESS

To M. W.

PREFACE

THE REVIVAL of Western Germany has been one of the spectacular economic performances on the postwar scene. This book tries to discover the mainsprings that gave it momentum. The approach is deliberately selective; I have focused on what seemed to me the important causal factors, and have made no attempt to present a complete historical record. I have tried, moreover, to view the German achievement not only as a recovery but also as a process of growth. Since 1950 or 1951 the revival has increasingly represented new growth, and growth at a very fast rate. Germany, in fact, is an outstanding example of a highly developed economy in process of further rapid development.

To bring into perspective the circumstances and policies that seem to me responsible for this growth, I have tried to place the German experience in the framework of a more general theory of development. This theory is presented in Chapter 2. Readers not especially interested in basic problems of economic development may skip this chapter without loss to the readability of the rest of the book.

It is a cause of sincere regret to me that I have found so little to say about my native city of Berlin, which is still undergoing severe hardships. In a general history of the German revival the struggle to keep Berlin going would deserve a larger place. But though Berlin's political and moral importance is a matter of record, economically the city has made no positive contribution to the West German revival.

I am greatly indebted to a large number of public servants, businessmen, and economists both in Germany and in the United States, who have given generously of their time and

vii

thought to make this book possible. Especially I want to thank Dr. Eduard Wolf of the Bank deutscher Länder and his able staff, particularly Miss Dreissig, Dr. Gleske, and Dr. Schlesinger, and the members of the "Inselkreis," with whom for many months I shared the stimulation of a weekly luncheon discussion. Miss Ruth Metzger rendered valuable help as research assistant for the last chapters. To the Rockefeller Foundation an expression of thanks is due for its financial contribution. Responsibility for the contents of the book naturally falls upon the author.

A German translation of the original English text is being published by Fritz Knapp, Frankfurt.

H. C. W.

New Haven, Connecticut
February 15, 1955

CONTENTS

CHAPTER 1

The "German Miracle"—A Summary View

TEN YEARS AGO Germany was a defeated and broken country, seemingly ruined beyond resurrection in our time. Today the West German economy is among the healthiest in Europe. Though the scars of wartime bombing are still visible in the cities, the standard of living is well above prewar. A rapid expansion of production and exports continues unabated since 1948. Unemployment, which was for some years the darkest spot in the picture, has been reduced to a tolerable level. Germany's currency reserves are almost equal to those of Great Britain. Her public finances, with their succession of surpluses in the face of tax reductions, are the envy of Europe. If there is anyone who forecast this ten years ago, the record of his prediction has not been preserved.

Germany has confounded not only the prophets but to some extent also the economists. Had a poll been taken shortly after the war it is a fair bet that a considerable majority of economists would have regarded the maintenance of fairly tight controls as advisable. But as soon as the Germans regained some measure of influence over their affairs they threw off a large part of the existing controls. They chose instead to rely upon tight money and balanced budgets as the means to keep the currency sound, prices stable, and the economy in order. They reduced the role of the government and gave private business the scope and the incentives to do most of the work of reconstruction. These "orthodox" policies did not go all the

1

way to a laissez-faire paradise—far from it. A substantial amount of government intervention remained. But measured against the contemporary climate of opinion, and compared with what most other European countries were doing, they were orthodox enough to be strikingly novel.

This book is an attempt to come to grips with the "German miracle." The term is regarded with disfavor in Germany, and rightly insofar as it seems to imply that the revival was a phenomenon surpassing all understanding. But it would be equally wrong to see in the revival nothing more than the inevitable result of the famous German *Tüchtigkeit,* their ability to get things done. A great many circumstances and events beyond German control helped, and the respective roles played by good management and good luck are not easy to unravel. Besides Tüchtigkeit there was foreign aid, the Korea boom, and a host of other factors. That all these things came together at the right time and place is the real German miracle.

Though the German experience is historically unique, it nevertheless carries some broader lessons. If the stock of conservative monetary and fiscal policies has risen in the world, it is in part due to the German example. Countries seeking rapid development of their economies are likely to be interested in the German policies. Whoever believes that a free economy can produce such development will find the German experience heartening. Insofar as the past can supply clues to the future, Germany's postwar history may throw light upon questions such as those posed by the country's rearming, by pressure for reunification, and by the struggle over Germany between West and East.

Tourist-eye observers of Germany's performance sometimes stress some one factor as *the* cause of revival. Hard work, the tax system, labor discipline, and Marshall aid are among the things most frequently singled out for this distinction. Each such observation points to an important element, but all "single-cause" explanations are doomed to inadequacy by the obvious multiplicity of causal factors. Of course there is bound to be disagreement as to the relative importance of these factors. People exist—though they seem to be harder to find in the last few years—who assert that Germany recovered despite and not because of her policies. One may disagree, one can present evidence, but one cannot disprove. One must beware also of the facile enthusiasm of those who, by diagnosing every event and circumstance as an important contribution to the German revival, end up by overexplaining the phenomenon. The fact is that many things had to come together to make Germany's spectacular revival possible. But there is no need to compound a whole series of submiracles to explain the central one.

The factors which the author regards as the mainsprings of the German revival center in three broad fields. One set has its origin in current history, the momentous events of the postwar years culminating in the East-West split. They have affected the life of every nation, but none more profoundly than Germany. A second set of factors resides in Germany's economic and human geography, if that term is permissible to describe the favorable industrial and resources structure of the country together with the immigration of refugees and the inherent qualities of the German people. The third and last set comprises the policies that have been pursued, initially by the Allied Occupation but later in growing measure by the Germans themselves.

History

To ask ourselves how the world would look today if the East-West split had not occurred is almost like wondering what would have happened if Eve had never eaten the apple. The possibilities being infinite, opinions are likely to differ. As for Germany, however, the guess is easy: The united Allies would still be sitting on top of a united Germany, holding her down politically and economically. The initial severities would have worn off, no doubt, but there would scarcely have been a 180 degree reversal. It is largely thanks to the East-West split that things have worked out so very differently for Western Germany: the rapid mutation from foe to friend, the shift of occupation policy from holding down to building up, the flow of Marshall aid. For all this Germany has had to pay the heavy price of partition. This is a national tragedy and may become the cause of trouble in the future. But economically West Germany has suffered surprisingly little from partition, as we shall see presently.

Foreign aid of 4.5 billion dollars was a very material factor in the revival. It is true that the Allies took as they gave, by imposing upon Germany burdens that in the aggregate exceeded this sum, in the form of reparations, occupation costs, restitution, coal exports, recognition of old debts, and others. But the weight of these burdens was carefully adjusted by spreading them over long periods, or by making them payable in German instead of foreign currency, and in other ways. Foreign aid, on the other hand, supplying foreign exchange and investment funds from the very beginning, came in a form and at a time that made it decisive.

The Korea boom, another fruit of the East-West conflict, also played a vital role in helping Germany to her feet. Up to that time things had been going well enough, but it was widely felt that the harder part of the recovery job was still ahead. Few people believed that by the end of the Marshall Plan Germany would succeed in lifting her exports—then little more than one-third their 1954 volume—to a level that would make her self-supporting. The world-wide Korea splurge set off some remarkable fireworks in the German export industries. These industries specialized in machinery and other capital equipment, just the things that were most in demand, and they had excess capacity. Their competitors in other countries were for the most part solidly booked and now had to load up their production schedules further with urgent military orders from their own governments. German exporters, with prompt delivery dates and good, reasonably priced equipment, took full advantage of the unique situation. Within little more than a year they had pushed exports to a level that made further aid unnecessary.

Aside from the East-West split two more gifts of history to the German revival deserve to be recorded: Germany's remarkable political stability since the war, and the fact that this stability meant government by the conservatives instead of by the socialists. After World War I German politics had been marked by repeated threats of internal upheaval, by external conflict, and by a succession of weak governments. For the economy little stimulation was to be derived from any of this. After World War II domestic extremism and external pressure were held in check by the Allied Occupation. Stability of government, in the hands of the conservative coalition led by Dr. Adenauer's Christian Democrats, is traceable to certain stabilizing provisions of the German constitution and to popular satisfaction with the Adenauer-Erhard policies. The continuity of this probusiness administration was enormously important.

It is true that members of the opposition sometimes claim that they would have followed the same policies of rapid decontrol adopted by the Adenauer administration. If so they seem to have had peculiar difficulty in expressing this intention in their many speeches during 1948 and 1949. These contain little but attacks upon Erhard, the author of these policies. A more convincing reading of the record of party politics is that, while both parties were against total rationing of the precurrency-reform type, even the Christian Democrats had considerable doubts about Erhard's bold policies until their success had become manifest.

Economic and Human Geography

When the partition of Germany came to be understood as one of those provisional arrangements that tend to become permanent, it looked to many like a coup de grâce to the prospects of recovery. A closely integrated system of industries and markets was being broken up. The industrial West was being cut off from its main source of foodstuffs. At the very best, it seemed, Germany would gradually evolve an economic pattern like that of Belgium at a lower level, with a heavy dependence on foreign trade for her livelihood. Adding to these obstacles the damage believed to have been inflicted by Allied bombing and that still to be inflicted by dismantling, one arrived at what looked like a really desperate situation.

Industrial structure and foreign trade. These calculations proved to be as wrong as they had seemed plausible. The partition, if it had to happen, could hardly have gone much better from the point of view of the West. The area that before the war had had 56 per cent of the population retained about 61 per cent of industrial capacity. For most industries the cut came very close to that average. There were some, of course, where it did not: The electrical equipment industry, for instance, had only 38 per cent of its capacity in the West; the leather industry on the other hand had 72 per cent and suffered from excess capacity. Some smaller industries were lost 100 per cent. These losses, however, were made up rather easily. For a country with Germany's investment potential the rebuilding of a hosiery industry or a textile machinery industry presented no great problem. Excess capacity, on the other hand, usually was absorbed by the rapid expansion of the whole economy.

Even the loss of the bread-basket provinces proved to be much less damaging than had been expected. In fact so long as German exports were flowing smoothly the loss of the eastern provinces might even be accounted a gain. Where previously West Germany had bought tariff-protected high-priced grain from East Germany, she now obtained her foodstuffs cheaply in world markets. In either case she had to pay with industrial products, but the world market offered better terms of trade than East Germany, traditionally a subsidy area, might have provided.

The amount of war damage likewise proved to have been greatly overrated. Successive surveys brought successive reductions of the estimated results of bombing. After allowing for such repairs as could be made within the plant, the amount of capacity knocked out probably was less than that constructed during the war, so that Germany found herself with slightly better than prewar capacity. With regard to dismantling, too, the ultimate bite was not nearly so bad as the first bark. The Allies' timely change of heart brought rapid cuts in the number of plants to be removed. Many of those dismantled would have been useless for peacetime purposes in any case. Though dismantling did hurt in many places, it often led to the replacement of an old plant by one of the latest design and to an increase in Germany's power to compete.

In the end, therefore, Germany again found herself with the same well-rounded industrial structure that she had before the war. The main characteristic of this structure was its strength in the capital goods industries. Partition and subsequent investment intensified this concentration. At certain times in the past, when markets were lacking, these industries had been more of a liability than an asset. To the postwar world, however, they were as tailored to order. Capital goods were urgently needed for Germany's own reconstruction, and the entire world was clamoring for them. While countries relying more heavily on exports of consumer goods were running into protectionist trade restrictions abroad, Germany was supplying the machines for the new protected industries. In the contemporary international climate Germany discovered that she possessed a quite remarkable export potential.

Meanwhile a second discovery was made that is less easily explained. Though exports were booming, imports were not. Despite growing liberalization the German economy refused to assume the predicted shape of a larger Belgium. Despite the loss of the eastern bread basket, despite partition, population growth, war damage, and dismantling, Germany's import needs remained modest. Whereas Belgium's imports equaled 40 per cent of her national income in 1952, and whereas during the liberal twenties Germany's import ratio had been well over 20 per cent, in 1952 they were only 16 per cent. This was a ratio almost as low as that of self-sufficient France.

The low level of imports and the consequent balance of payments surplus are really the most miraculous phase of the German miracle. Numerous contributory factors can be cited, of course—the decline in prices of foodstuffs and raw materials after the Korea boom, the diminishing import content of German production, changes in social structure and consumption habits, the low-grade German diet, the benefits of Dr. Schacht's autarchy program, the productivity gains made by the German farmer, and the protection which agriculture nevertheless continues to enjoy. Whether they all add up to a full explanation of the lag in imports is doubtful. It would therefore not be altogether surprising if this part of the miracle proved to be temporary.

Meanwhile the ease with which the consequences of partition have been overcome raises rather curious questions about two famous economic doctrines: about the popular one of the need for European economic integration, and about the less popular but not altogether dissimilar old German idea of *Lebensraum.* All the evidence is not yet in, and in any case there is nothing in the German experience to make us doubt the importance of an expanding foreign trade. Trade expansion has been vital to the recovery. But it is remarkable how smoothly it has proceeded without the benefit of special arrangements for integration or absorption of the trade partners. We cannot pursue this train of thought, but the German experience is suggestive.

Refugees. When Germany was at its lowest, hungry, bombed out, and saved from starvation only by Allied aid she received a fantastic visitation: millions of destitute refugees streaming in from the East. Ethnic Germans expelled by the Czechs and the Poles, national Germans expelled by the Poles and the Russians, and plain fugitives from Russian Zone communism, all crowded into West Germany. By 1948 there were 8.5 million of them. By 1953 the stragglers had brought the total to over 10 million.

A country that had not enough food and housing for its own people could hardly have been saddled with a more disastrous burden. So at least it appeared at the time, and in discussions of Germany the integration of the refugees always figured as one of the knottiest problems.

But the refugees did not remain a burden exclusively. It is hardly possible to increase the population of a country by 25 per cent without making some impact on production. As time went on the refugees were absorbed into the gathering German boom. They were willing to work hard, for low wages, and on the roughest jobs. Starting from scratch, they were under desperate pressure to make good. Some of them were aided by special skills, and a few succeeded in quickly rebuilding the enterprises they had lost in their home countries. In the aggregate they greatly raised German national income above what it would have been without them.

From the point of view of the original inhabitants of West Germany the refugees probably remained a burden. Without them the housing shortage might today have disappeared; social security burdens would be lower; and much of the capital that went to create jobs for the refugees could have been used to improve the equipment and raise the productivity of the local people. The balance of payments, too, might have reached equilibrium earlier than it did, though today that is not much of a consideration. One may say, therefore, that although in terms of total national income the refugees have made an enormous addition, in terms of per capita income they have been a negative influence. But if one is inclined to feel, as some German observers do, that without the almost insatiable needs of the erstwhile paupers the German boom might not have lasted, it would follow that they deserve credit also for helping to keep up per capita income.

Population structure. Another phase of the population picture where earlier appraisals have proved unduly alarming is the age and sex distribution. Shortly after the war there was much talk of "biological destruction." This has proved premature, to say the least. It is true that the German population pyramid, which ought to look like a well-grown Christmas tree, has a badly weatherbeaten appearance, with deep gashes marking the two wars. The predominance of women and old people means much individual human grief. But the economic damage to date seems to have been minor. The percentage of the population that is of working age (15–65) has dropped only moderately below prewar. The reason is that while there are now more old people there are also fewer children. The percentage of people actually in the labor force has also declined only very moderately. More women have taken jobs, some old people work a little longer. Meanwhile the large crop of Hitler babies has reached working age. When one considers that the difference between a 48- and a 40-hour week means more for productive capacity than almost any conceivable distortion of the population structure, the German problem falls into better perspective.

There remains the qualitative damage that no percentages can measure. The generation of men that now occupy top jobs (40–65) has been thinned out by the losses of two wars. The younger generations have suffered neglect in their training. There is a noticeable scarcity of men qualified to carry high responsibilities and of competent technicians, the latter a very unusual situation for education-minded Germany. But although those who must stand in the breach complain of overwork, and with reason, there is no evidence that the revival has been held up. The survivors of the wars, together with the old men and the women, have pulled Germany up again.

Labor's performance. Hard work ranks high on the list of tourist-eye explanations of the German miracle. And indeed no visitor to Germany can help being impressed with the sight of the German workingman's steady pace nor with the evidence, easily audible from his hotel room, of construction work at all hours of the night. It comes as something of a shock to find that the statistics do not seem to support the case. Working hours per week during most of the recovery years were below the high levels of the Hitler period, and no higher than in Holland or Switzerland. Labor intensity as measured by productivity—admittedly an uncertain procedure—likewise showed no discernible increase. It is to extrastatistical activities, therefore, that one must look for evidence of unusually hard work. In some trades, for instance, especially construction, workers frequently did double shifts, only one of which was counted. Many businessmen and public servants virtually worked themselves to death during the first years following the currency reform. Most importantly, perhaps, a great many people spent their spare time repairing war damage to their homes and their belongings. To the head of an American household operating on the "do-it-yourself" principle this may not seem very extraordinary, yet the apparent intensity with which it was done in Germany must have counted for a good deal.

With all that there was to be done and all that was accomplished it may seem peculiar to raise the question of whether this hard work was really necessary. But we must not forget that most of the time Germany had from one to two million unemployed who might have shared the work. It is true that only part of them could at any time have joined those already employed, because unemployment was concentrated away from the industrial centers. Yet in some degree it would have been possible. Balance of payments considerations forbade an expansionary policy that would have produced such an absorption of unemployment. One cannot help wondering whether it is more meaningful to say that Germany recovered because of her hard work or despite her unemployment.

One other thing besides their toil and skill the German workers contributed to the revival: their willingness to accept low wages and forego strikes. They thereby made possible a high level of profits, savings, and investment that greatly aided the build-up of industry. A conscious decision by the rank and file as well as the unions not to rock the boat and to let reconstruction take precedence over wage hikes was largely responsible for this restraint. The decision was aided no doubt by the rapid and continuous improvement in labor's standard of living and, on the part of the unions, by the initial lack of strike funds. The unions' concentration on the somewhat esoteric goal of codetermination—participation in management—may also have played a role. After the Korea boom labor pressed its case more aggressively, and the gap between prices and wages, whence had come the big profits, started to narrow. Labor then began to get an increasing share of the rapidly rising national income. As the years went by, the irritation born of continued political opposition and isolation gradually sapped the unions' cooperativeness and appeared to be pointing toward more vigorous wage action in the future. But the old class belligerency of the German worker with his strongly Marxist orientation seemed to be giving way to a more moderate line. German sociologists began to talk of the absorption of labor into a new middle class.

Policies

At the end of the war, when the countries of Europe first faced up to the immense task of reconstruction, two schools of thought emerged as to the best way of doing the job. It is a great oversimplification, of course, to squeeze the infinite variety of national policies into a couple of small boxes. But that is the pattern in which posterity, with the unfairness of history, may well remember them. One school held that the way to get maximum performance out of an economy was to push production agressively through credit, large government expenditures, and strong central planning of investment and foreign trade. The inflationary repercussions of such expansionary or full-employment policies would be blocked by means of price control, rationing, and tight regulation of foreign trade. The same measures, combined with sharply progressive taxation, would also serve to realize the social aspirations usually associated with this point of view, fair shares, social security, avoidance of unemployment at all cost. Great Britain under the Labor government was the foremost exponent of these doctrines, which were popular also in the Scandinavian countries. The other school held more or less the opposite view on most of the points mentioned. It was less concerned with injecting fuel into the economic machine in order to push production and employment, and more with improving the functioning of the machine. It stressed decontrol, stable currencies, and freer foreign trade. It was less emphatic about social values and more willing to accept inequalities of income and consumption. Belgium was the first country to develop this approach. There is perhaps no need to add that the political complexion of the second school was on the whole more conservative than that of the first.

Germany's choice. Germany during the 1930's had conducted an economy that exemplified the extreme of the first type. No Western country has had more thoroughgoing experience with peacetime planning and control. Her natural bent toward order and organization would seem to predispose her in favor of a controlled economy. That she chose the other way after the war is therefore not without wider significance. It is true that some of the reasons for her choice were not directly related to the merits of the case. The incredible three years before the 1948 currency reform, when everything was rationed and nothing was available, had given controls a very black eye. That this was only a caricature of a planned economy, in no way comparable to the orderly conditions in England and the Scandinavian countries, did not prevent its being used as a scare exhibit. The decisiveness of Germany's choice of a free economy, moreover, was in some measure due to the personal convictions of the leading personalities. Finally, the extreme sensitivity of the German people to any hint of inflation imposed a restraint that policy makers in other countries did not feel so strongly. But when all is said, it remains interesting that the country with the most intimate experience of full-scale planning and controls turned its back upon them so deliberately.

There was no lack of contemporary criticism. When Germany took the first step toward decontrol—removing price and other controls on a broad front after the currency reform —a great many expert eyebrows were raised. Even though in principle one inclined toward free markets and private enterprise, the action seemed premature for a country in Germany's desperate position. When prices shot up temporarily there was an international chorus of "I told you so." During the following period of rather slow progress and mounting unemployment, official pressure was exerted by the Allies for an expansionary policy. Time and again the lack of over-all planning was criticized. It was not until after the end of the

Korea boom that the German policies were generally recognized as successful.

Tight money and balanced budgets. The two basic problems with which Germany had to cope were those facing every country in Europe: to increase investment in order to produce more, and to even up the balance of payments by exporting more and importing less in order to become self-supporting. The attainment of these goals seemed more remote for Germany, however, because she started from so much lower. In addition Germany was afflicted with heavy unemployment and a catastrophic housing shortage.

To do the job with an economy relying on market forces and incentives, without the forced draft and controls of a planned economy, required above all a sound currency. The basis for it was laid by the currency reform of June 1948, very largely of American design. To keep the currency sound meant giving priority to stable money and international balance over domestic expansion and full employment. It called for tight money and a balanced budget. The Bank deutscher Länder and Finance Minister Schäffer were united in their determination to block inflationary financing. In the face of heavy unemployment they sometimes found that position difficult to maintain, but where they yielded ground they yielded very little. At the time one might have wondered whether financial virtue was not being carried a little too far, and whether on occasion they should not have been a little more ready to rise above principle. During the following Korea boom, however, the previous restraint proved to have been extremely fortunate. And although an easy money policy was consistently avoided, monetary restraint was sufficiently flexible to permit the volume of money to expand with and ahead of the economy, its amount doubling within a period of five years.

Decontrol. Anti-inflationary policies and a sound currency permitted the rapid dismantling of price ceilings, rationing, and materials controls. This was the bold policy of Economics Minister Erhard, initiated without the requisite prior approval of the Allies but accepted by General Clay. But though decontrol went much further and faster than most people would have thought feasible, it was by no means complete. Most manufactured consumer goods were freed immediately after the currency reform, but basic foods and basic industrial materials like coal and steel remained under control for a long time. Full decontrol might have put too much pressure upon the still precarious monetary and fiscal balance. Too sharp an initial price rise might have provoked irresistible demands for new price ceilings. What was actually done seems to have represented a wise mixture of freedom and control.

Saving and investment. If private investment was to be encouraged without easy money, other sources of finance had to be available. Decontrol had produced very generous profit margins as a result of the initial advance of prices. Mounting evidence that the currency could be trusted brought about a gradual revival of consumer saving, mainly in the form of savings deposits. To channel profits into investment and to stimulate savings in general the regular income tax rates, savage by American standards, were modified in favor of savers and investors. Handsome tax exemptions were available for investment in business, in housing, in shipbuilding, in public securities, and in savings deposits. Whoever was able to save could thereby reduce his taxes. Businesses ploughing back their profits could rebuild their decimated equity. For those who knew their tax law the real burden of taxation became quite bearable. By these devices the German economy financed its revival despite a totally dead securities market and tight though expanding bank credit.

In this field, too, the principles of a free economy were not carried to any unrealistic extremes. German policy did not favor public investment and public planning, but it employed both where it seemed convenient. The government's own investments, including those from the counterpart generated by United States aid, were substantial. The tax privileges themselves, in fact, amounted to a general form of planning insofar as they channeled money into specific areas like housing and shipbuilding.

Foreign balance. It was the international field, however, where Germany's sound finance, free market policies paid off best. Most countries after the war discovered that it is relatively easy to produce and hard to export. Germany's need to export was greater than the others', because she started from scratch and had to make up a three-year head start which the rest of Europe had gained between the end of the war and the currency reform. In this plight conservative financial policies worked wonders. Tight money and balanced budgets created buyers' markets and avoided the excess demand that in other countries had increased imports and absorbed potential exports. German industry, finding the capacity of the domestic market limited, was forced out into the world market. Stable or falling domestic prices helped push sales. Imports, being kept within bounds by market forces, could then be liberalized without excessive risk.

Liberalization on a multilateral basis did in the foreign sphere what decontrol did at home. It provided flexibility and permitted the markets to breathe. By freeing other European countries' exports to Germany it encouraged reciprocal concessions and became a stimulus to exports. By exposing the German domestic market to foreign competition it stimulated competition at home. Although the freeing of her foreign trade created some tense situations and one or two minor upsets, it became the keynote of Germany's policy. For the country that had given birth to Schachtianism this was an interesting change of approach.

It must be added that liberalization did not measure up to

the highest standards of purity. German agriculture continued to enjoy strong protection, while it was also shielded against price fluctuations at home. In her export promotion, too, Germany employed some methods that were at variance with liberal trade principles, such as her system of bilateral agreements with a number of countries, mainly overseas. The same can be said of other promotion devices, among them central bank export credit and tax concessions on foreign sales, although their importance has been much overrated by Germany's competitors. Here as in all other fields actual policy was a mixture of freedom and control. The accent everywhere was sufficiently far on the side of freedom to regard freedom as the dominant characteristic of the German economy. Those, however, whose principle is "the freer the better" and who reject any admixture of control as an adulteration cannot claim Germany's success as proof of their doctrine.

Conclusion and outlook. The outstanding aspect of the German system was the wide range of the incentives it offered. Some of them were built-in—the urge to overcome the consequences of the lost war, to re-establish one's personal status, to recover material possessions. From the incentive point of view a lost war seemed to be much more effective than one barely won. Other important incentives were aided by policy. Free markets gave freedom of action. Tight money stimulated competition, combining the stick of penalty with the carrot of reward. In buyers' markets large profits were not guaranteed, but whoever made money was allowed to keep most of it under a tax system that forgave taxes to those who saved and invested. Labor had a motive to perform, since overtime earnings were tax exempt and the stores were filled with the essential luxuries that had not been seen there for ten years. On the other side there was the threat of unemployment for the laggards.

The system produced severe inequalities of income, partly at the expense of labor but more particularly at that of the

large population of pensioners, old people, refugees, and unemployed. But the concentration of income was the price of
high saving and high investment.

The system gave freedom of action to the strong. It was
hard on those who could not make their way. There was
ostentatious luxury consumption, though quantitatively it
probably did not amount to much. At the same time there
was heavy unemployment, and there were refugees, the war
victims, and the old people. The very comprehensive German
social security system put a floor under these pensioners so
that they could not go under completely. But that was a far
cry from the "fair shares" of the British. It was a harsh system,
but it was in keeping with the situation. The war had ended
in crushing defeat, and there was no illusion that peace would
be enjoyable. Fair shares might have overburdened the strong,
and all might have sunk together. By being allowed to save
their own skins first, they were put in a position where they
could pull the rest after them. The rapid advance of the
economy helped everybody. Though at a painful distance,
wages and pensions followed profits. The gap between them
permitted investment which accelerated the advance. The
rapid rise of income took the place of redistribution. It is in
this sense that the *Soziale Marktwirtschaft,* the social free
market economy, which on the face of it was neither completely free nor outstandingly social, produced socially positive results.

The success of German policies must not cause us to lose
perspective. It does not prove that a laissez-faire economy produces the most rapid growth, because it was far from being
such an economy. Neither does it prove that an economy of
the German type provides insurance against depressions or
stagnation. It is true that German policy makers, on more than
one occasion when slump or stagnation seemed to threaten,
rejected expansionary advice and were in each case proved
right by events. But Germany was operating under the excep-

tional stimulus of postwar reconstruction and at times developed remarkable luck, as in the case of the Korea boom. Again one is reminded of the concatenation of good fortune and good management. There is no stabilizing magic in the German system, and some day depressive tendencies will no doubt have to be met. It would be tragic if the great success so far should then become an obstacle to flexible action.

In looking toward the future, however, it is not only economic problems that give the observer pause. The Germans themselves, indeed, have since the war paid attention to little but economic pursuits. Their needs and efforts in that field have absorbed them so completely that politics, for instance, has received only marginal attention. The partition and occupation of the country, which has given German politics a slightly artificial air, may have contributed to this lack of popular participation. So may the forced politicization of all aspects of life under the Nazis—there is a strong yearning to forget and cultivate one's garden. A psychological element of repression may enter into this. Artistic and cultural pursuits have encountered a similar lack of interest. The great flowering of art and literature that was expected to follow the demise of the Nazis has not materialized. The soul-searching, the exploring of new directions, the intense creative activity that should accompany the rebirth of a nation is lacking. An emotional and intellectual vacuum goes hand in hand with the preoccupation with money-making and creature comforts.

For a nation of Germany's tradition this state of affairs is disquieting. It is understandable perhaps as a reaction to Hitler and the war, but one wonders how long it will last. It is conceivable, no doubt, that the successive failure of monarchy, democracy, and dictatorship has left the Germans permanently disillusioned, without ideals, and skeptical toward all nonmaterial values. But it would take more time than has passed since the war to establish that as a believable fact. In the past the Germans have generally felt the need to attach themselves to some ideal or idea, using those terms without moral connotation. The present seems to be an interregnum, and one cannot help asking what may eventually fill the vacuum.

It would be pleasant to think, of course, that the Germans might revert to being the people of poets and thinkers that they were in the past. German observers of the contemporary scene seem to discount this possibility. Another alternative might be some new political enthusiasm. Of those that today can be discerned on the horizon none seems to have strong probabilities. There are no doubt still a great many unreconstructed Nazis about, and their resurgence is not out of the question. Yet their activities to date have been noisy rather than significant. Reunification presents a ready-made handle for a revival of nationalism. But though the subject is on everybody's lips there seems to be less drive and more caution and hesitancy, in some cases perhaps induced by self-interest, than the foreign observer would have expected. A deal with Russia and defection from the West is another obvious danger. The Russians seem to hold all the trumps, while the Allies have already given what they had to give. Yet the German fear of Russian domination is so great, and to the Russians themselves the risk inherent in playing their trumps is so serious, that it is hard to envisage a basis for such a deal. A new man on horseback proclaiming a nationalistic dictatorship is still another possibility, particularly if a serious depression should supervene. As of today, however, most Germans seem to be so thoroughly immunized to hollow phrases that his appeal would be slight.

The present political and cultural vacuum in Germany compels one to speculate what might fill it. None of the possibilities mentioned seems very likely. Yet the existing condition appears unstable and in danger of being displaced by some new enthusiasm. God help Germany and the world if it is again the wrong one.

CHAPTER 2

Some Principles of Economic Development

GERMANY'S RESURGENCE from wartime destruction is in many respects a phenomenon *sui generis*. In some of its aspects, however, it can also be regarded as a special case of a rapidly growing economy. Since the war the world has become growth-conscious to an unprecedented degree. Many countries have made vigorous efforts to accelerate their economic development. A good deal of recent economic writing has revolved around problems of development, both of underdeveloped and more advanced countries.

Before entering into a detailed account of Germany's recovery, therefore, it seems worth while to view it more broadly in terms of the general problem of economic development. I shall draw, for this purpose, upon some ideas that I have presented in greater detail elsewhere.[1]

Reconstruction versus Growth

To begin with it is perhaps advisable to consider how far growth theory can be applied to postwar Germany. Was what happened in Germany only reconstruction or was it also growth? If both then in what proportions? Is it at all possible to draw such a distinction in the German experience?

It is clear that reconstruction is a very much easier job than new development. Minor repairs are sufficient in many cases to bring large productive units back into operation. Relatively large increases in output can be obtained, therefore, with a small amount of additional capital. The economic pattern is already there—the channels of production and distribution, the knowledge of methods, markets and people, the skills and discipline of the labor force. The participants are likely to work much harder in order to get back to their old living standards than they would to raise themselves further. The problem of capital accumulation and financing finds make-shift solutions that cannot easily be applied to new development.

In postwar Germany a clear-cut isolation of elements of growth is impossible. The main question is whether growth was an important component, or whether the whole process so far must be regarded mainly as one of reconstruction. Comparing per capita income—the most frequently used measure of growth—for 1953–54 with 1936, one finds no more than a 16.5 per cent increase in real terms, which is modest in comparison with many other European countries. But this is the reflection of the 25 per cent increase in population for which Western Germany has had to provide. Comparing aggregate income for 1953–54 with 1936, there is a 55 per cent advance. If one considers further the quite abnormal nature of the population increase one can hardly deny that the increase in total income indicates real growth. The length of the period during which income expanded uninterruptedly, from 1948 to the present, would certainly be sufficient to warrant speaking of growth and not simply of a cyclical upswing.

Throughout this period, moreover, major shifts in the structure of production were going on. Industries lost in Eastern Germany were rebuilt from scratch. Export production had to be adapted in some measure to new markets. New products and new methods of production were introduced. The relative importance of existing products changed. Capacity lost by some firms was replaced by new capacity in others. Even where in an aggregate sense there was only a recovery of previous per capita output levels, great qualitative changes occurred.

During the early period, say through 1951, the recovery element undoubtedly predominated heavily. This is evident, among other things, from the extraordinarily high annual increments, showing income gains from 13 to 20 per cent (Table 2, p. 36). It is confirmed by the very low (marginal) capital-output ratios, which were of an order ranging from 1.5:1 to 2:1 (Table 9A, p. 56). In 1952–54 annual increases amounted to only 7 to 8 per cent, with capital-output ratios of 2.5 to 3.5:1. The 1952–54 figures are not unusual for rapidly growing countries, even though they are above the European average. They could represent equally well a tapering off of reconstruction or a continuing growth trend.

The question whether the German experience was mainly one of recovery or whether it also contained a strong element of growth is important not only for the analysis of the past but also for an appraisal of the future. If one believes that what we have witnessed was mainly recovery, one must conclude that with the end of this phase Germany is likely to advance much more slowly. The opposite view implied above—that a strong growth element has been present all along—suggests that further annual increases of 5 to 8 per cent are possible. This, however, is a broader matter. Enough has been said to make the use of doctrines relating primarily to economic development seem permissible in connection with postwar Germany. This can be said with the more confidence because in some of their aspects these theories would be applicable also to reconstruction pure and simple.

Orientation toward Production or Consumption

Important aspects of economic growth become apparent when one contrasts the development process that the now industrialized countries experienced during the 19th century with the current development drive of the underdeveloped countries. The key feature of the earlier development was the entrepreneur. His drive for profit and wealth carried the economy forward. He saw the great possibilities offered by new techniques and markets, and he made the investments required to exploit them. The desire of the masses for greater welfare was not an initiating factor, although greater welfare was achieved in the process.

In the interplay by which production and consumption reciprocally stimulate each other the initiating impulses thus came predominantly from the side of production. In the interaction between investment and income growth emphasized by modern theory the causal chain tended to run predominantly from investment to income. That is to say, investment was in good part of the kind referred to as "autonomous," based on innovation, speculation, and broad hopes, contrasted with investment "induced" by rising consumption. Consumption and demand played a dependent role; the motive forces were mainly on the side of production and supply.

In all these respects today's underdeveloped countries present a striking contrast. Many of these countries are now driving ahead vigorously. But it is not the entrepreneur, or at least not he primarily, who is powering this drive. The entrepreneur in those countries had his chance for many decades and has been slow to take it. Now other forces have come to life that deny him the role of leadership. Broad masses of people have had an opportunity to become impressed with the existence of living standards far above their own—the much discussed demonstration effect. Governments have learned that there are many things they can do to speed up progress. In these countries, therefore, popular desire for higher consumption, expressed to some extent through government action, has become a major—perhaps the major—force making for development. Here then it tends to be consumption that stimulates production. In the absence of a large group of bold entrepreneurs investment tends to be less autonomous and more predominantly induced. One may say that under these conditions the chief initiating impulses come from the side of consumption and demand.

It will have been noted that these characteristics apply in

some measure also to the advanced countries that have gone, as most have, a greater or lesser way toward the welfare state. The entrepreneur has lost much of his earlier predominance; profit and wealth no longer enjoy broad social approval as prime goals of economic activity. Popular desire for higher mass living standards has become articulate and to a large extent determines the course of the economy. Investment tends to become cautious, nonspeculative, induced. Consumption and demand dominate the scene.

The contrast here described, primarily a contrast in economic climate, can be traced also in the changes that economic doctrine has undergone. There has been a secular shift of emphasis away from the originally predominant concern with production and supply and toward greater interest in consumption and demand. The early classical writers, when discussing the determinants of the value of goods, regarded cost of production as the chief factor. In the analysis of factors determining the level of national income they also stressed elements of production like natural resources, capital, labor, and technology. Demand was largely—not always—taken for granted. Schumpeter's theory of economic development— mainly applicable, in his own words, to 19th-century capitalism—put the entrepeneur and innovation in the central spot. In the second half of the 19th century these things began to change. With the advent of marginal utility emphasis tended to shift to demand as a factor in the analysis of value. Eventually, Keynesian economics made aggregate demand the key concept in national income determination. Economic analysis today is strongly, though not uniquely, consumption oriented.

The distinction between an economy oriented toward production and one oriented toward consumption is reflected in many characteristics of these economies. The production-oriented economy was built upon powerful incentives. Few things were to be had free, but the rewards to effort and luck were great. It was a harsh system. There was freedom for the strong and little consideration for the weak. Sound money was the rule because labor had little chance to push wages up beyond productivity, the property instincts of the dominant groups opposed inflation and the law was solidly on the side of property. The distribution of income tended to be governed by marginal productivity (excepting cases of monopoly) with little correction of the "verdict of the market" by progressive taxation or government pressure. Private savings were usually high, stimulated by entrepreneurial self-financing and uneven income distribution. Buyers' markets predominated, deflation was more of a danger than inflation. The otherwise remarkable effectiveness of the system as a generator of growth was, therefore, to some extent weakened by periodic depressions.

In consumption-oriented economies, including the modern welfare state, conditions are in many respects reversed. Individual success in the economic struggle is no longer the only means of advancement. Progress is expected to come in large measure through the action of the government or the labor union. The nexus between personal effort and economic betterment is weakened. In consequence the supply of productive factors diminishes. Working hours are shortened while living standards are still low; early retirement laws and restrictive practices of various sorts have the same effect. The supply of savings is kept low because entrepreneurial activity, originally its main source, has only limited scope, and because progressive taxation makes saving more difficult while social security makes it less necessary. Marginal productivity ceases to be the final arbiter of income distribution.

Meanwhile large demands are made upon the national product by consumers, investors, and the government. Since the market cannot effectively distribute resources when demand tends to overexhaust the national product, political processes are likely to take the place, to some extent, of market processes, and government influence spreads. The general climate tends to be inflationary, employment overfull except where there is structural unemployment or underemployment; sellers' markets predominate. Incentives are weak, because rewards and penalties alike are not firmly tied to economic performance. The negative implications of this for economic development are compensated to some extent, however, by the relative freedom from internally generated depressions which the constant excess demand seems to insure.

It goes without saying that the economies here described are ideal types which we cannot expect to find in actuality in pure form. Every historical economy has had features of both types, but usually with one or the other predominating. Nineteenth-century economic development was not exclusively entrepreneurial, and entrepreneurship is by no means totally lacking in present day underdeveloped countries or welfare states. What can be asserted, I believe, is that entrepreneurship and what goes with it was the dominant feature of most 19th-century development, and that so far at least it has not been dominant in most of the newer development.

Obviously, too, the distinction made is not primarily a statistical proposition. Supply and demand, production and consumption must always balance *ex post*—the amount bought is the same as the amount sold. The distinction depends basically upon the spirit that pervades the economy. It is social values that count: the approval bestowed upon thrift, profit, and business success or upon welfare, social security, and equality of income. The nature of the distinction is best expressed by the word "orientation"; all aspects are represented, but on balance an economy leans in one or the other direction.

The distinction between production- and consumption-oriented economies runs parallel to an important conceptual pattern that underlies much of contemporary dynamic growth theory—the body of theory associated with the names of Harrod, Domar, and Fellner.[2]

This theory centers upon the reciprocal relationship of investment and income growth. One side of the relationship is given by the fact that investment increases capacity and thereby makes possible an increase in output and income. The other side is given by the tendency of rising income to induce new investment.

Of these two chains of causation, that running from increases in capacity to higher output and income involves a variety of questions mainly dealing with problems of production. How much output can be expected from a given increment of capital? How is this calculation affected by additions to the labor force? What new inventions and methods of production are available?

The second chain of causation, that by which rising income induces new investment, involves questions dealing mainly with consumption and demand. How is a given increase in income divided between consumption and saving? How much can individual firms expect their markets to benefit from higher consumption? If savings are large, how can the gap in aggregate demand be filled? If they are small how can excessive claims upon the national product be satisfied?

At any time, in any economy, both relationships and their attendant problems are present. But they are not always of equal importance. In an economy where for any reason a high volume of investment can normally be expected, the problems surrounding the effect of this investment upon income will be the important ones. Such a situation would exist in a well-functioning capitalistic economy with active entrepreneurs, a good supply of innovations, and free markets. It would be an economy with a high proportion of autonomous investment. This entrepreneurial economy corresponds in its characteristic features to the production-oriented economy. One might say in Harrod's terminology that it follows the "natural" rate of growth, i.e., the rate made possible by the availability of productive factors and technology.

Another kind of economy that in a sense must be called production oriented, though it has little of the entrepreneurial about it, is the Russian communist system. It is clear from all reports that the Russians concentrate on production and are little interested in consumption and demand except in how to keep them down. It is not surprising that this attitude has led to the creation of a system of incentives and a degree of income inequality which seem to go beyond what many capitalist countries regard as socially tolerable.

The other aspect of the investment-income relationship, a rise in income inducing investment, is likely to predominate under different conditions. These conditions are given, for example, when autonomous investment is small, innovations scarce, entrepreneurs sluggish or discouraged. Prospects for growth of capacity and maintenance of full employment then rest mainly upon the ability of rising income to induce investment. If such increases in income as take place fail to induce enough investment, savings will not be absorbed and income will slump again. This is the case of the stagnating economy with large unemployment. The Keynesian analysis and much of the current growth dynamics were evolved out of concern over this situation.

There is another instance in which this aspect of the investment-income relationship predominates. It is different in its outward manifestations but not altogether in its meaning. Where excessive demands converge upon the national product, with broad consumer groups seeking higher standards of living and making their desires felt through political action, the key problem is how to translate this form of demand into an increase in capacity. This may happen in the advanced welfare state or in the underdeveloped country. The essence of the problem is again the effect of income on investment.

Both cases, the stagnant economy as well as the inflationary, correspond in characteristic respects to the consumption-oriented economy. In both cases the production-oriented elements are weak—incentives dulled, innovation lagging, entrepreneurship dormant. In the stagnant economy consumption and demand are also weak. They are the key factors, nevertheless, to the businessman who fixes his eyes on stagnant markets instead of on expanding technological opportunities, to the government that seeks to combat stagnation by creating purchasing power, and to the economist who does not altogether reject the Keynesian analysis. As for the inflationary economy, the reasons for calling both the extreme welfare state and many underdeveloped countries consumption oriented have already been mentioned. Reverting to Harrod's terminology, one might say that for these economies the "warranted" rate of growth is of special importance—the rate of growth which induces enough investment to absorb available savings. If they fail to stick to it they suffer depression or inflation.

A *caveat* is in place once more. The significance of these parallelisms must not be overstressed. It is not claimed that the Harrod-Domar-Fellner model and that implicit in the production-consumption orientation analysis are coextensive in all respects. Yet a common denominator clearly exists.

The reason for presenting this theoretical framework is that it seems to fit the German case remarkably well. We may hope, therefore, that it may give us some help toward understanding the nature of Germany's recent growth experience. When we attempt to interpret what has happened in Germany in terms of the above framework it immediately becomes evident that Germany's recovery and growth since the currency reform shows most of the earmarks of a vigorously production-oriented economy. Entrepreneurs were active and politically powerful. There was elbowroom for the strong and only a minimum of social consideration for the weak. Incentives were tremendous for entrepreneurs and workers alike, and much investment seems to have been strongly autonomous. Government policy sought to intensify incentives and relied upon them in preference to planning and controls; it kept the economy lean, through tight money and conservative budgets, and provided a degree of competition high in comparison with past German practices.

Various traits that clearly denote production orientation can be traced in special fields. One such instance is the financing of the revival. Despite the almost complete lack of capital market facilities German business achieved a high rate of investment by means of internal financing. The production-oriented aspect of this performance is to be found not in the fact of internal financing as such but in the successful effort to overcome financial obstacles instead of giving in to the seeming impossibility of raising money.

Another instance appears in the field of foreign trade. Once world markets were again open to them, German exporters proceeded with extraordinary aggressiveness. Within a few years they had built up a large export surplus for an economy whose viability had been seriously questioned a few years earlier. The search for foreign markets and the tendency toward export surpluses seem to be as characteristic, other things being equal, of a production-oriented economy as foreign trade deficits are of the consumption-oriented type.

Still another instance is the attitude of labor. German labor made no strong drive for a higher share in the national income. Wages went up rapidly, but this was a by-product of a rise in income that was sparked by entrepreneurial activity. The contrast with labor action in consumption-oriented economies is striking.

Yet one cannot deny that there also were strong impulses on the side of consumption. In a starved-out country this could hardly have been otherwise. There was little consumer saving prior to 1953. Successive waves of consumer purchases, centering first on food, then on clothing, then on home furnishings, swept over the economy. Consumer credit, previously almost unknown in Germany, began to spread. These consumption impulses, however, did not have the consequences that were predicted above for consumption-oriented economies. Both government and labor unions adopted policies that prevented them from gaining the upper hand. Wages were held down, social security and war damage payments were kept to a minimum (though very considerable in the aggregate), monetary and fiscal policy remained tight, a considerable amount of unemployment was allowed to continue. The incentives that had been restored by the currency reform and the freeing of markets remained unaffected.

Thus the production elements clearly predominated, but a certain mixture of forces resulted that was beneficial. The propensity of the production-oriented economy to periodic depressions was in part compensated by consumption impulses. During a period in which other countries suffered repeated setbacks in their growth German income expanded from year to year. Those who pinned their faith to the inherent dynamics of the German economy instead of to expansionary monetary and fiscal measures were proved right time and again.

The argument of this chapter may now be summarized briefly. We have tried to view the German revival as an instance of economic growth. We have argued that while the revival was in good part a recovery it also contained enough of a growth element to permit analyzing it from that point of view. We found that Germany exhibited in many respects the characteristics of a growth pattern that we have called production oriented. This is a pattern that has made great contributions to the growth of the now industrialized countries but that in most parts of the world has yielded to a consumption-oriented pattern. From the latter Germany borrowed a few elements without, however, weakening her basic production orientation. We have expressed the view that this constellation has been particularly helpful for the revival. The following chapters will throw further light upon this thesis.

CHAPTER 3

The Comeback of Production and Income

To GET A SUMMARY picture of the German revival the best though perhaps not the most colorful method is to look at the national income statistics. We shall survey these here—the growth of income; its origin, utilization, and distribution; and the investment that powered the advance. The account of the often dramatic events accompanying the rise of income must be reserved to the next chapter.

The Growth of Income

The extent and speed of recovery and growth since the war are shown by (1) the index of industrial production and (2) the gross national product data. For the precurrency-reform period the production index is our only source of information.

The rate of growth. The index (Table 1) shows the desperately low level of economic activity during the three immediate

TABLE 1: *Index of Industrial Production*

	1946	1947	1948	1949	1950	1951	1952	1953	1954
January	27	31	49	81	93	124	135	142	155
April	31	39	56	85	103	137	141	158	172
July	38	42	60	87	111	131	138	154	172
October	40	46	76	97	132	144	160	173	193
Annual average	34	40	63	90	114	136	145	158	176

Sources: 1940–47, *Monthly Report of the Military Governor,* August 1948, p. 98; bizonal area only, excluding food processing and construction. 1948–54, *Statistisches Jahrbuch; Wirtschaft und Statistik;* all industry.

postwar years and the slow recovery prior to currency reform. With currency reform (June 1948) comes a rapid upsurge which carries the index forward some 50 per cent in five months. There follows a period of relative stagnation, leading into a renewed upswing by early 1950. This upswing is further intensified by the world-wide Korea boom and exhausts itself only in late 1951. A new period of dullness then sets in, which blends into progress less spectacular but still well above the European average from 1952 on. The two periods of semistagnation since the currency reform, as well as the first two boom phases, will become the chief topics of the next chapter.

The gross national product data, available only since the currency reform (Table 2), confirm this picture, although the

TABLE 2: *Gross National Product*
(*in billions of DMark*)

Year	Current Prices Half year at annual rates	1936 Prices Half year at annual rates	Per cent of increase over corresponding period of previous year
1936 full year	48.0	48.0	
1948 2d half	70.7	41.7	
1949 1st half	76.5	44.5	
2d half	82.3	49.5	18.7
1950 1st half	82.1	50.5	13.5
2d half	97.4	59.2	19.6
1951 1st half	106.6	60.7	20.2
2d half	120.6	64.8	9.5
1952 1st half	121.1	64.3	6.0
2d half	131.0	69.0	6.5
1953 1st half	127.1	67.9	5.6
2d half	140.3	75.2	9.0
1954 1st half	136.8	73.4	8.1

Sources: Statistisches Jahrbuch; Wirtschaft und Statistik.

advance was more moderate. During the earlier years, it showed annual rates of increase of up to 20 per cent. Later, as recovery turned into new development, the growth rate settled down to lower though still very respectable annual increases of the order of 5 to 8 per cent.

Per capita growth. When one examines the growth of the national product on a per capita basis rather than in the aggregate the achievement is not quite so impressive.

Thanks mainly to the influx of refugees, Western Germany's population in 1954 had increased by more than 25 per cent over 1939 and its labor force by more than 15 per cent. The impressive increase in output is the result, therefore, of the labor of a much greater number of people. By 1949, for instance, the national product (in constant prices) was back to its 1936 level, but on a per capita basis was still 20 per cent below 1936. For a large part of the population this was aggravated by an intensified unevenness in the distribution of income, upon which we shall have to comment presently. By 1953 the national product was 49 per cent ahead of 1936, but per capita it was only 16 per cent above 1936, about 5 per cent below 1938, and 12 per cent below 1939.

The difference between the global and the per capita performance of the German economy reminds us that "growth" has more than one dimension. Germany's income has grown, but welfare has not grown commensurately (brushing aside such hairs as one might feel tempted to split over the comparability of two periods with different income distributions). Eventually, no doubt, the growth in total product may become the cause of further welfare gains. This might happen, for instance, through the greater economic and political bargaining power that economic growth has given the country, or through the higher productivity made possible by the larger market. In that sense it could perhaps be argued that growth in the aggregate also tends to produce growth per capita, despite simultaneous population increases.

Some peculiarities of the data. The data we have discussed so far, especially the index of production, have some peculiarities of which the reader must be warned.

First, the index is based upon census data assembled in 1936. It represents the physical output of thousands of products weighted according to the prices of that year. If it were weighted according to current prices the increase in output over 1936 would probably appear somewhat smaller.

Second, the index covers a range of economic activities accounting for about 58 per cent of the total product in 1954, but for only 39 per cent in 1948. The fact that the index has grown so much faster than the national product shows that industrial output, as might be expected, has advanced more rapidly than some other forms of production. One must beware of assuming—a mistake sometimes made in popular presentations—that increases in the index imply equal, all-round increases in national output.

Third, the index serves also as a basis for computing the industrial component of the gross national product. This makes it easy to calculate this product at prices of 1936, the year by whose prices the index is weighted. To arrive at its value at current prices, however, the 1936 figures have to be inflated by the corresponding price indexes, with the consequent danger of error.

The reliability of the index for the years prior to currency reform is subject to considerable doubt. Allied statisticians began to compute a production index almost immediately after the end of hostilities. The chaotic state of the economy, however, with trade between zones and often between counties severely inhibited, made the job a rather heroic one. As the currency reform approached the collecting of data became easier, but the data themselves quite likely became worse. An increasing share of production went into gray or black channels or was held back altogether, so that the figures shown in Table 1 may represent a substantial understatement of true output. The gain after currency reform is overstated to that extent.

The choice of 1936 as a base year deserves some comment. The fact that census data are available only for 1936 is the main reason for the practice of basing the index as well as most prewar-postwar comparisons upon 1936. To make such a comparison it is necessary to recompute the old Reich statistics for the much smaller area of the Federal Republic (excluding West Berlin). An uncertain job at best, this recomputation becomes almost impossible for any but a census year. The use of 1936 for prewar-postwar comparisons, instead of the year 1938 which is employed by most other countries, has a decisive influence upon the result of the comparison. National product in 1938 was about 23 per cent above 1936, private consumption 17 per cent; industrial production alone probably was up by an even wider margin. Comparisons based upon 1938, insofar as they are technically feasible, do not look nearly so good as those based upon 1936.

There is some justification, however, for using 1936 even aside from statistical convenience: It was a year of reasonably high activity but not one overstimulated and distorted by large-scale arms production and consumer shortages. Moreover, the use of 1938 as a base would not make for a more meaningful comparison between Germany and other European countries, because for most other countries 1938 was not a year of outstandingly high activity. But apart from these statistical considerations the choice of a base year has had its political side. The permissible level of industrial production (fixed by the occupation authorities as a percentage of 1936), Germany's need for foreign aid, and her ability to contribute to the European Defense Community all look different depending on whether a given postwar output is interpreted as 120 per cent of prewar or as 100 per cent. In these debates the Allies and Germans have sometimes found themselves involved in curious shifts of preferences.

Origin of Income

The main single source of income, as might be expected, is industrial production (Table 3). In 1953–54 it accounted for 34 per cent. To this must be added part of the output of artisans whose activity in many cases amounts to manufacturing. The share of agriculture and forestry (8.5 per cent) is small but not insignificant. Domestic agriculture supplies, in fact, 65 to 70 per cent of total food consumption. Rental income, representing largely the services of housing (not shown in

TABLE 3: *Origin of Gross National Product*
(in per cent)

	1936	1949		1953–54	
		Current prices	1936 prices	Current prices	1936 prices
Agriculture and forestry	10.6	9.5	9.3	8.5	7.9
Industry, excluding construction	31.0	30.5	28.6	34.3	33.1
Construction	4.3	4.7	4.0	5.2	4.5
Artisans, excluding construction	3.8	4.2	4.2	3.4	3.2
Public administration	7.7	7.4	10.2	7.0	7.8
Services for occupation authorities	—	2.0	2.7	.9	1.1
All other services	21.7	21.2	23.9	18.1	20.8
(Subtotal: national income)	(37.9)	(63.1)	(39.1)	(103.7)	(56.3)
Plus indirect taxes, minus subsidies	12.5	12.7	10.2	15.0	14.8
Plus depreciation	8.4	7.8	6.9	7.6	6.8
Total: gross national product	100.0	100.0	100.0	100.0	100.0
Gross national product in billions of DMark	48.0	79.4	47.1	139.0	74.3

Sources: *Statistisches Jahrbuch; Wirtschaft und Statistik.* Discrepancies are due to rounding.

Table 3) is noteworthy for its extraordinarily low level equal in 1953 to 1.2 per cent of the national product.

Of particular interest from the viewpoint of growth are shifts in the relative importance of the various sources of income. According to a widely accepted theory a rise in per capita income tends to be accompanied by shifts following a clearly defined pattern.[1] The share of agriculture (and of raw materials generally) tends to shrink, that of services to expand; the share of industry expands as long as the country is still comparatively undeveloped, while in a more advanced country, such as Germany, it tends once more to decline. Such a pattern would follow from the normal elasticity of demand for different forms of consumption when income per head rises. There is little doubt, for instance, that demand is more elastic for luxuries, such as many services and durable consumer goods, than for essentials like food.

The German data confirm this theory only in part, for reasons that will soon become apparent. The share of agriculture has indeed undergone a slight shrinkage. This is true whether one compares the latest year with 1948–49 or with 1936. The shrinkage is particularly noticeable in terms of constant prices. Services, too, however, have shrunk as a proportion of national income, at least in terms of current prices. The share of industry has increased sharply.

What does this somewhat unorthodox behavior mean? The relative drop suffered by services since 1948–49 is probably due to their tendency to adjust themselves fairly rapidly to changes in population. By 1948–49 Western Germany's population had increased more than 20 per cent over prewar levels. Services like retail distribution and transportation were capable of rapid expansion to meet the added needs and hence started off after currency reform at a high level. Manufacturing industry required more time to expand; its gradual growth later ate into the share of services. The great increase in exports of manufactured products gave industry an added fillip. The growth pattern of the various sources of German income does not, therefore, do much to refute the theory mentioned before. What the pattern shows is mainly that German postwar growth was a special case and that, in its early stages at least, it had in it more of recovery than of new development. At the same time, however, the experience does suggest that special cases of this kind may be rather frequent. The theory may have to admit a good many exceptions.

Income Utilization

The utilization of income (Table 4) presents two striking features: (1) the low share of private consumption and (2) the high share of investment. These two facts contain a good part of the explanation of Germany's rapid recovery. Beginning with the currency reform and until 1951–52 gross investment rose in relative as well as absolute terms; since then it has de-

TABLE 4: *Utilization of Gross National Product*
(in per cent)

	1936	1949		1953–54	
		Current prices	1936 prices	Current prices	1936 prices
Private consumption	62.2	65.2	61.8	56.3	59.3
Government consumption	19.9	18.3	22.1	16.1	17.1
(Occupation cost, current)		(4.9)	(5.3)	(2.9)	(2.8)
(Occupation cost, investment)		(.8)	(.6)	(.8)	(.5)
(Salaries and pensions)		(7.2)	(9.8)	(6.8)	(7.4)
(Purchases)		(5.4)	(6.3)	(5.4)	(6.1)
Gross Investment *	17.9	19.8	17.6	24.4	20.95
(Replacements)	(7.0)	(7.8)	(6.8)	(7.6)	(6.7)
Foreign balance †	0	—3.3	—1.5	3.3	2.65
Total: gross national product	100.0	100.0	100.0	100.1	100.0
Total in billions of DMark	48.0	79.4	47.1	139.0	74.3

* Including government investment but excluding occupation investment.
† Excluding shipments to West Berlin and the Russian Zone.
Sources: Statistisches Jahrbuch; Wirtschaft und Statistik.

clined slightly in relative terms. Only a few European countries, notably Norway, Iceland, and Luxemburg, have had higher investment ratios; some of these, moreover, are the result of different statistical techniques. Net investment, which takes account of depreciation, has of course been lower. The depreciation of equipment allowed for, however, is in part actuarial rather than real. Much of German equipment is of recent origin, so that annual replacement needs are less than the depreciation charged on the books.

A warning about the investment data is in order, however. In the first place, they include public investment (which in Germany is considerable), with the exception of occupation investment. This is fairly standard practice in Europe but not in the United States; it makes German and American figures not fully comparable. In the second place, the part of investment represented by industrial equipment is computed not from balance sheets of businesses but on the basis of the output of investment goods, with extra allowance for installation costs, deductions for exports, etc. This is obviously a rough procedure which can easily lead to an overestimate of investment. In the third place, the data on changes in inventories are quite rough. They rely on private surveys as well as official material. A check of the investment data from the the side of savings is possible only to a very limited extent at the present time. All this casts a measure of doubt upon the impressive investment picture. The doubt does not affect equally, however, the data on level and growth of income presented earlier, which would be all the more remarkable if investment should have been overestimated.

If investment is high, private consumption is correspondingly low. Germany has had to keep her belt tightened in order to reach high investment levels. The standard of living that the Germans have drawn from their income is therefore somewhat lower than what other nations might have permitted themselves. For the great mass of consumers this is all the more true because of the relatively uneven distribution of income.

A detailed breakdown of consumer expenditures (Table 5) shows several interesting facts. Food expenditures were high-

TABLE 5: *Personal Consumption*
(*in per cent*)

| | 1936 | 1950 | | 1953–54 | |
		Current prices	1936 prices	Current prices	1936 prices
Food	32.6	33.8	33.4	32.5	30.2
Stimulants	14.2	15.5	9.4	15.9	11.4
Clothing	13.5	16.8	14.8	14.7	13.9
Home furnishings	5.5	7.2	7.5	8.1	7.7
Heat, light	3.6	3.2	3.9	4.3	4.8
Health	4.7	3.1	3.9	4.1	5.0
Housing	13.8	8.2	13.0	7.7	12.0
Transportation	3.9	4.7	4.8	5.2	5.5
Cultural activities	5.3	5.7	6.9	5.8	7.2
Household services	2.2	1.3	1.8	1.3	1.8
Other services, including banking and insurance	0.7	0.5	.6	.4	.5
Total	100.0	100.0	100.0	100.0	100.0
Total in billions of DMark	29.0	57.3	33.3	78.2	44.1

Source: Wirtschaft und Statistik.

est during the early days of the recovery, then diminished relatively while income increased. Expenditures for clothing and furniture grew in relation to income as people found themselves able to replace their wartime losses and move into new homes. The share of housing diminished throughout, reflecting controlled rents. Compared with 1936 it was down almost 50 per cent in 1936 prices. Transportation rose significantly, also against prewar, as a result of higher expenditures on travel and on vehicles.

How has the pattern of consumption expenditures changed in the face of rising per capita income? The same principles apply that were mentioned above in connection with the pattern of production. One would expect the most urgent expenditures, principally on food, to advance less than relatively postponable ones, such as clothing and furniture, while luxuries might be expected to rise more than any. The behavior of expenditures on food, clothing, household furnishings, and transportation are in line with this expectation. The remarkable constancy of stimulants in the consumers' budget (tobacco, alcoholic beverages, coffee, and tea) is unexpected, unless the (plausible) conclusion is accepted that these things are no longer luxuries. The decline of expenditure on education and entertainment also disappoints expectations. Some of these shifts, however, have alternative explanations: the relative speed with which food, clothing, and housing, respectively, became available after currency reform; the differential price movements of various classes of goods; and the "derived demand" for items like household furnishings (from residential construction) and transportation (from the mushrooming of suburbs).

The breakdown of investment expenditures is likewise illuminating, provided the data prove accurate (Table 6). On this latter point German statisticians have strong doubts, and the data would probably never have been allowed to see the light of day had they not been required for the use of international agencies. With appropriate caution, therefore, we may say that the composition of investment appears to have undergone several inherently plausible shifts. There seems to have occurred an extraordinary increase in inventories and in their share in aggregate investment. Given the totally "empty" state of the German economy at the start of the period, this is not surprising. Lesser increases appear to have taken place in the share of mining, utilities, and housing. The first two of these found it hard to attract capital during the early period of recovery; the improvement is therefore only a relative one. Manufacturing and construction, after starting out with a lion's share of total investment, lost ground considerably as time went on. The rapid upsurge of industrial production is partly explained by the high initial share of investment in manufacturing.

TABLE 6: *Gross Investment*

(in per cent, at current prices)

	1949	1950	1951	1952	1953
Agriculture	9.7	9.7	9.8	8.9	8.7
Mining	4.7	4.3	4.6	5.6	6.1
Manufacturing and construction	29.7	29.4	28.2	26.3	25.3
Electricity, gas, and water works	8.1	8.3	9.3	10.1	9.7
Transportation and communication	13.6	12.2	11.6	10.5	9.7
Housing	18.2	21.6	23.0	24.9	26.4
Public administration	6.75	6.2	5.3	5.3	5.8
Other service trades	9.25	8.3	8.2	8.2	8.3
Total domestic investment	100.0	100.0	100.0	100.0	100.0
Total domestic investment in billions of DMark *	14.8	18.0	22.5	24.7	27.7

* Excluding increase in inventories.
Source: Federal Ministry of Economics.

The Distribution of Income

Ever since the currency reform Germany has had the reputation of a high degree of inequality in its income distribution. For a number of years this reputation rested largely upon circumstantial evidence, but it has on the whole been confirmed by the income pyramid for the year 1950 finally published in 1954.[2] This income inequality has probably been an essential condition of Germany's rapid advance. Without it, savings and investment and consequently the rate of growth would very likely have been lower.

The adverse social effects have at least in part been compensated by the very rapidity with which high investment pushed ahead the income of even the less favored groups.

They have been further mitigated by the way in which the swollen ranks of war victims, refugees, and old people were taken care of, which has required a certain redistribution of income through taxation. But this redistribution has covered at best the barest needs of these pensioners. It has left the inequality of incomes probably a good deal more pronounced than it is in most Anglo-Saxon countries.

Distribution of income in 1950. The main characteristics of the postwar income distribution can be observed by studying the income pyramid shown in Table 7. It indicates that at the

TABLE 7: *Comparison of Income Distributions,* *
1913, 1928, and 1950

Per cent of recipients	Per cent of income received by each group		
	1913	1928	1950
0–50	24.5	23.2	16.0
50–90	34.8	39.6	48.3
90–95	9.3	10.0	8.7
95–98	8.4	9.5	9.2
98–99	4.3	4.8	3.2
99–100	18.7	12.9	14.6
	100.0	100.0	100.0

* Excluding pensioners.

Sources: "Das deutsche Volkseinkommen vor und nach dem Kriege," *Einzelschriften zur Statistik des Deutschen Reichs* (Berlin, 1932), no. 24, p. 108 ff.; "Zur Frage der Einkommensschichtung," *Wirtschaft und Statistik*, June 1954, p. 265. For 1928, Paul Jostock, *Die Berechnung des Volkseinkommens und ihr Erkenntniswert*, "Schriften der deutschen wirtschaftswissenschaftlichen Gesellschaft" (Stuttgart and Berlin, W. Kohlhammer Verlag, 1941), p. 115.

bottom of the pyramid 57 per cent of the income receivers got 23 per cent of the income; at the top, 5 per cent got 27 per cent of the income. The highest annual income for the bottom 57 per cent was 2,400 DMark, while the top 5 per cent started at 6,000 DMark.

Main attention centers on the very populous lowest group. Its situation, it must be pointed out, looks a good deal worse than it is. Its low average income does not mean that wage scales for a large part of the population were substantially below 200 DMark per month. A great many incomes in that bracket are the product of part-time or vacation work by women, students, apprentices, temporarily unemployed, new entrants into the labor force, and the like. Many of those falling into the lowest bracket were not fully dependent upon their own earnings, being contributing members of a household. It has been estimated that in 1952 for every 100 households of two persons or more there were 90 contributing income receivers, who supplied about 30 per cent of the households' total income.[3]

On the other hand, the bottom bracket does not contain a large number of people who really belong there: the pensioners of various kinds, whose incomes, being derived from the taxes and contributions of income producers, were not included in the computation. It has been estimated that 10 to 12 million people receive pensions of one sort or another, from old-age benefits to Equalization of War Burdens payments and unemployment relief. Probably more than half of these are wholly dependent upon this income. It is this group that has really been at the short end of the distribution scale.

The concentration at the top is probably understated by the data of Table 7. In 1950 there were large corporate profits but few dividends, which served to keep taxable incomes down. So did the widespread practice of charging personal expenditures for travel, entertainment, automobiles, and even housing to business expenses. Finally, a certain amount of tax evasion no doubt took place. The incomes accounted for in the tax statistics fall short of total national income by almost 30 per cent. While there are many legitimate factors contributing to this result, evasion cannot have been altogether absent.

Comparison with 1913 and 1928. A comparison of the 1950 pyramid with that of 1928 confirms the impression that the degree of inequality has increased at the bottom and at the very top. The lower 50 per cent of income receivers in 1950 had to get along on approximately 17 per cent of total income, against 23 per cent in 1928. The top 1 per cent had 14.6 per cent of income against 12.9. It is true that in 1950 the lowest bracket may have been made to look unduly bad by the unsettled state of the economy, which probably produced an unusually high number of "occasional" small incomes. The top incomes for 1950, on the other hand, are considerably understated, for reasons already mentioned.

In the center of the distribution, meanwhile, a great evening up has taken place. The 40 per cent falling between the 50th and the 90th percentile had 48.3 per cent of income in 1950, against 39.6 in 1928. These are the skilled workers and the better paid of the unskilled, whose gains are quite visible, of course, even to the naked eye.

In comparing 1950 with so remote a year as 1913—a rather bold statistical undertaking—the same results are obtained except at the apex of the pyramid. The lowest group (0–50 per cent) did much worse in 1950 than in 1913. The middle group (50–90 per cent) did very much better. The top groups came off worse in 1950 than in 1913. This instance of greater equality—if it is not a statistical mirage produced by the peculiarities of the 1950 data—seems to reflect the decimation by two lost wars and two inflations of the great pre-World War I fortunes.

A comparison of the 1950 pyramid with one of the Hitler period cannot accurately be made, because the available data, covering the year 1936, include the income of pensioners, while the others exclude it. In broadest outlines, however, the 1936 distribution seems to confirm the story told by the others: the lowest group never did worse than in 1950, the middle group never seems to have done so well. For the top 5 per cent, the 1936 and the 1950 figures both hover somewhat above the 25 per cent mark. In this connection it is worth noting that in the United States the share of the top 5 per cent fell from 24.6 per cent in 1919–28 to 19.4 in 1939–48.* [4]

The degree of redistribution through taxation. The comparisons made above are of income before taxes. Did taxation even things out appreciably? There can be no doubt that it did so between income producers and nonproducers, for without the pensions provided by the producers via taxes and contributions the nonproducers would have nothing at all. Total benefits of 16 to 17 per cent of national income represent a rather substantial redistribution, although part of these benefits goes to people who are also income producers. Moreover, a good part of total pensions were paid for by the beneficiaries themselves in the past years through contributions to the social security funds. This puts a somewhat different face on the question of "who supports whom," although it does not alter the fact that the pensioners must be taken care of out of the current national income produced by the active population.

Granted, however, that the income of the producers is redistributed in significant measure among the nonproducers, there remains the other question: Is there much of a redistribution among the income earners themselves? How do they share in the tax burden and in government services? The answers to these questions involve a complicated and on the whole rather inconclusive consideration of tax problems. Weighing the evidence as best one can, one comes to the conclusion that a somewhat greater amount of redistribution among income producers is probably achieved today as compared with prewar years. This seems to follow because, even

* If "economic income" is taken as a measure, which however presents a more refined concept than that of the German statistics, the change was from 29.5 per cent in 1919–28 to 23 per cent in 1939–48.

if the tax system has not become more progressive—some observers think that it has become less so, at least over certain ranges—the total tax burden has increased in relation to national income. Such redistribution as occurs would therefore affect a larger fraction of income. Furthermore, government expenditures since the war have probably gone to benefit more predominantly the lower income groups, particularly through subsidized low-cost housing.

It seems clear, however, that this redistribution from high to low income earners is not very large even today. By way of illustration it may be mentioned that the income-tax burden on incomes averaging 250,000 DMark in 1950 was only 55 per cent of taxable income. Since taxable income is well below economic income, owing to large allowable deductions and other factors, the true burden even after certain surcharges was probably well below 50 and perhaps even below 40 per cent. Rates have been reduced repeatedly since that time.

The meaning that these facts hold for Germany's recovery potential is evident. They imply that the high savings of the upper income groups have been left relatively undisturbed by the tax collector and that the money-making incentive has not been dulled very much by high tax rates. We shall see this in greater detail in later chapters.

The pensioners. The adverse social implications of an unequal income distribution have to some extent been compensated, as we saw before, by rapid growth of per capita income and by the social security system. Since in this book we shall repeatedly have to note conditions and policies that may appear harsh, it is only fair to say in advance that Germany cares for its old, sick, and handicapped on a comprehensive if not generous scale. Social security benefits since the currency reform have absorbed about 40 per cent of public revenues and 16 to 17 per cent of the national income. The majority of the

10 to 12 million recipients, excluding retired civil servants, are old people and widows; the remainder: war victims, unemployed, and Equalization of War Burdens beneficiaries.[5] With dependents, the number of people partly or wholly supported by social security benefits may be 14 to 17 million. The coverage achieved by the social security system is evidently very wide.

Less impressive is the level of most of these benefits. Their average runs well below 100 DMark per month, with wide variations, of course, in individual cases. Even allowing for the fact that many pensioners receive more than one type of benefit, the median receipt per pensioner is estimated at no more than 100 DMark. For anyone wholly dependent upon this income (many pensioners are employed or are members of larger households) a monthly allowance below 100 DMark is desperately little. Even so, these modest levels are in many cases reached only because local relief supplements the basic benefits. The general level of benefits has been raised since 1950, but the pensioners—sometimes referred to by impatient Germans as "social baggage"—nevertheless remain a socially and financially submerged group that forms the lowest layer of German society. Here are the real stepchildren of the German recovery.

Changes in the income distribution since 1950. The severe inequality evident in the 1950 income pyramid has probably been evened up somewhat in the intervening years. That is the conclusion to be drawn from semiannual information on the share of wages and salaries in the national income (Table 8).

The trend of these data shows a sharp decline in the share of wages and salaries in late 1950 and early 1951, reflecting the upsurge of prices and profits during the Korea boom. Thereafter wages and salaries gradually regain and then surpass their earlier share.

In appraising this evidence it must be remembered that the number of wage and salary earners has continued to increase quite rapidly, while that of self-employed (in good part farmers) has advanced only moderately. In particular, this makes it impossible to compare meaningfully the postwar share of wages and salaries with that of 1936. The absolute level of this share is moreover probably understated throughout because the data do not include certain fringe benefits paid by many

TABLE 8: *Shares in the National Income*
(*in per cent*)

		Wages and salaries *	Profits and all other income †
1936	full year	61.0	39.0
1949	full year	64.2	35.8
1950	1st half	64.6	35.4
	2d half	61.7	38.3
1951	1st half	60.1	39.9
	2d half	61.4	38.6
1952	1st half	61.9	38.1
	2d half	63.5	36.5
1953	1st half	64.8	35.2
	2d half	65.6	34.4
1954	1st half	65.2	34.8

* Wages, salaries, and civil service pensions, excluding voluntary social benefits paid by enterprises to labor, which may amount to 3 to 5 per cent of the wage bill.
† Privately and publicly owned enterprises, farmers, professions, property income, and voluntary social benefits.
Source: Bank deutscher Länder, *Monthly Report,* May 1954.

employers, often in the form of pension funds, which for labor as a whole may account for 3 to 5 per cent of total wages. The international comparability of the data is likewise doubtful, owing to peculiarities of the German economy as well as of German statistics. Nevertheless, the pronounced upward trend in the share of wages and salaries since 1951 may probably be taken as an indication that the inequality of incomes is diminishing, at least where labor incomes are concerned.

The Relation between Investment and Income

We have seen that in Germany the rate of investment and the rate of growth of income have both been high. Gross investment has run as high as 25 per cent of the gross national product, net investment close to 20 per cent. Annual growth of income has been as much as 20 per cent, and present rates of 5 to 8 per cent are still above the European average. It is clear that there is a causal relation between high investment and rapid income growth. Can one go beyond this statement, can one perhaps say that a given investment can be expected to produce a given increase in income?

The question is one with which a businessman has to deal every time he considers adding to his firm's equipment. Economists, in the past at least, have approached the matter only under highly restrictive assumptions. They have concentrated on the increase in output that occurs when additional capital is employed while other productive factors are held constant, which gives us the marginal productivity of capital. But the characteristic feature of a growing economy is that the other factors do not remain constant. The labor force increases, technology improves, new natural resources are discovered or old ones exhausted. Under such realistic conditions the marginal productivity theory does not apply.

To cope with the problem, which the mounting interest in economic growth has pushed into the foreground, another concept has been developed—the capital-output ratio. It is a crude device; it says no more than that in certain observable instances a given increase in capital equipment was accompanied by a certain increase in output. (More accurately, this should be called the *marginal* capital-output ratio, since we are dealing with *increases* in the stock of capital and output.)

The new concept does not say that the increase in equipment was the sole cause of the rise in output, for this rise is the joint product of changes in all factors together. One cannot argue, therefore, that because under certain circumstances in the past a given investment has been accompanied by a given income rise further investment will produce proportionate increases. However, if the other factors—steady growth of labor force, flow of inventions, etc.—can be expected to behave in the future as they did in the past one can perhaps use the capital-output ratio as a guide to the prospective yield of future investment at least for a few years ahead.

In many countries that are now intensely concerned with their economic development, this very imperfect device has been found helpful. It gives at least a tentative answer to a question of paramount importance: how much capital the country must save up or borrow to attain a certain rate of growth or, alternatively, how much growth it can expect from the capital available. Our present knowledge of historical capital-output ratios is still very limited, but at least it permits conclusions as to orders of magnitude. Current literature about underdeveloped countries abounds with estimates of capital-output ratios, perhaps not always seasoned with the necessary grains of salt.

In postwar Europe calculations of this sort have been rare. One might have thought that in an enterprise like the Marshall Plan, designed to lift European production, the question might have been profitably raised as to how much capital it would take to achieve a given increment of income. But the Marshall Plan was in good measure geared to recovery rather than new development, so that normal experience with capital-output ratios was not applicable. The balance of payments approach, moreover, which the Marshall Plan stressed, tended to lead away from thinking in terms of such ratios. Nevertheless it seems possible to put the concept to work in Europe.

By applying it to Germany we may hope to throw some light on the recent recovery and to provide a clue to the prospects for future growth.

The annual capital-output ratios for Germany are shown in Table 9*A* for gross investment as well as for net. A lagged version is also shown, relating income growth of a given year

TABLE 9 A: *Capital-Output Ratios*
(*in billions of DMark at 1936 prices*)

Year	Gross national product (1)	Growth (2)	National income (3)	Growth (4)	Gross invest- ment (5)	Net invest- ment (6)	Gross ratio $(7) = \frac{(5)}{(2)}$	Net ratio $(8) = \frac{(6)}{(4)}$
1948 *	41.8		35.8		n.a.	n.a.		
1949	47.1	5.3	39.1	3.3	8.3	5.1	1.57	1.55
1950	54.8	7.7	44.6	5.5	10.8	7.3	1.40	1.33
1951	62.7	7.9	49.7	5.1	13.6	9.7	1.72	1.90
1952	66.7	4.0	52.6	2.9	13.0	8.7	3.25	3.00
1953	71.6 †	4.9	56.3 ‡	3.7	14.6	9.8	2.98	2.65
1954 1st half	36.7	2.8 §	28.6	1.9 §	7.8	5.2	2.79	2.74

* Second half at the annual rate.
† Gross domestic product.
‡ Domestic income.
§ Computed against the first half of 1953.
Source: Wirtschaft und Statistik, various issues.

to the investment of the preceding year (Table 9*B*). Postponing comment on the many inadequacies of this computation, we may note their chief results. During the first two or three years of the recovery all ratios were of the order of 2:1 or less. In 1952 and 1953 they tend to jump, sometimes to twice their previous level, and average around 3:1. From all that we know about similar data in other countries ratios of 2:1 or less are quite exceptional. The German ratios therefore confirm the view that the early growth of income represented mainly recovery and that investment was in good part repair and rehabilitation of existing capacity. For 1952 and 1953, however, this can hardly have been true, and even for 1951 the low ratio is probably the result of an income surge made possible by excess capacity.

TABLE 9 B: *Lagged Capital-Output Ratios* *
(*in billions of DMark at 1936 prices*)

Year	Gross national product (1)	Growth (2)	National income (3)	Growth (4)	Gross invest- ment (5)	Net invest- ment (6)	Gross ratio $(7) = \frac{(5)}{(2)}$	Net ratio $(8) = \frac{(6)}{(4)}$
1948 †	41.8		35.8		n.a.	n.a.		
1949	47.1	5.3	39.1	3.3	8.3	5.1		
1950	54.8	7.7	44.6	5.5	10.8	7.3	1.08	.93
1951	62.7	7.9	49.7	5.1	13.6	9.7	1.37	1.43
1952	66.7	4.0	52.6	2.9	13.0	8.7	3.40	3.34
1953	71.6	4.9	56.3	3.7	14.6	9.8	2.65	2.35
1954	36.7	2.8 ‡	28.6	1.9 ‡	7.8	5.2	2.43	2.37

* Ratio of investment in 1948 to income growth in 1949, etc.
† Second half at the annual rate.
‡ Computed against the first half of 1953.
Source: *Wirtschaft und Statistik*, various issues.

The apparent tendency of the figures to settle down around 3:1 in 1952 and 1953 raises the question whether a similar performance can be expected for the future. The figures developed by Fellner for the United States show that the average there for long periods has fluctuated between 3.5:1 and 5:1.[6] The question is highly speculative of course, and no more than a speculative answer can be attempted. Even this needs to be prefaced with some critical comment on the applicability of the capital-output ratio to postwar Germany.

The following observations seem in order.

1) The use of annual ratios, made necessary by the short and nonhomogeneous period under review, is of doubtful propriety. Averages for decades would be much better. The

investment of a given year naturally does not achieve its full effect in raising capacity and income during that year, nor even in the next (as implied in the lagged figures). Even the direct effects—those relating to the specific output produced by the added investment—may in the case of a large plant take several years to reach their final level. The indirect effects—the stimulus to further investment and output given by investment in power, transportation, and basic industries, for instance—may take decades to mature. It will be remembered, however, that the German investment of the recovery period contained relatively little of such basic investment.

2) Neither the gross nor the net ratios are conceptually quite satisfactory. The gross ratio fails to show whether net investment is taking place or merely replacement (an unnecessary concern in the case of Germany). The net ratio disregards the increases in capacity and improvements in quality that may come from mere replacement. In a growing economy it also understates the true increase in capacity that is being brought about, because it makes the erroneous assumption that the annual wearing out of capacity is equal to the depreciation that is being charged on the books. In Germany, where so much equipment now is quite new, depreciation charges undoubtedly much exceed the volume of equipment taken out of operation each year.

3) German postwar growth, during and after the "repair" phase, has been accelerated by increases in employment averaging 400,000 per year. These added workers have helped to keep the capital-output ratio low, but this advantage cannot be expected to last indefinitely. American ratios shown by Fellner have of course been similarly kept low by immigration. To purge the capital-output ratio concept of the influence of changes in labor supply one would have to operate with a ratio of *increase in capital per worker: increase in output per worker,* but in practice this would probably lead back to the unreality of the marginal productivity reasoning.

4) The German economy has had to do a large amount of technological catching up since the war, drawing mainly upon American experience. This unusual rate of innovation has probably constituted another nonrecurring shot in the arm which has helped to keep the capital-output ratio low.

5) The price of capital equipment in relation to other prices influences the capital-output ratio. Since the war, in Germany and elsewhere the price of equipment has been relatively high. This has probably raised the capital-output ratio and has adversely affected the reconstructing countries. One cannot know, of course, whether in consequence of the changed price relationship a smaller amount of equipment was bought with an unchanged volume of saving, or whether saving adjusted upward so as to make possible the financing of an unchanged amount of equipment. Presumably both adjusted and met somewhere in the middle. The lower rate of return resulting from higher costs must in any case have acted as a deterrent to investment.

6) Movements in the terms of trade have affected the capital-output ratio in Germany. The growth of income has been enhanced by an almost continuous improvement in those terms after the top of the Korea price wave was passed.

7) The intensity with which equipment is used is of course important for the capital-output ratio. Night shifts and round-the-clock operations are not customary in Germany, but overtime has been frequent during the reconstruction period. It has contributed to a low capital-output ratio.

8) The endowment with natural resources, which has done much to keep the capital-output ratio low in the United States, has not been a positive factor in Germany. The country has no major resource of outstanding volume except coal. This consideration argues for the prospect of a higher ratio in Germany than in the United States over the long run.

9) Finally, the composition of investment is of course decisive for the kind of capital-output ratio that emerges. Some

kinds of output are capital intensive, i.e., are produced with relatively little labor and much capital. Here we have the industries with high capital ratios, except where annual depreciation of capital is very large. Among them are housing and certain highly mechanized manufacturing industries, not necessarily or even usually the so-called heavy industries.[7] Other forms of production tend to be labor intensive, i.e., labor is their main cost item; they have a low capital-output ratio. Among them are backward forms of agriculture, many service industries, and a large part of manufacturing industry.

German concentration of investment upon industries with low capital-output ratios (manufacturing, agriculture) during the early recovery period helps to explain the rapidity of the early advance. Since then, as the data of Table 6 suggest, a shift has been taking place toward investment in lines with high ratios (utilities, housing) or with slow maturation (coal mining). This shift fits in with the trend toward a higher ratio that we have observed. What does it suggest for the future?

In Germany one frequently hears the view expressed that the time of the big annual increments of income is over and that Germany will now fall in line with the growth rates of other European countries. Were this to happen Germany would have to accept a rather modest position among European nations, well below the per capita incomes of England, Belgium, and probably other countries. This halt in growth would be especially hard, given the existing distribution of income, not for the working classes but for the pensioners and the white-collar groups. From a national point of view it would imply that the success of postwar policies was after all a relative one and that the stamp left by two lost wars has been too deep to be erased.

Whether the Germans who view future growth prospects pessimistically are fully alive to these implications for their country or not, the facts presently known bear them out only in part. It is certainly not likely that sustained annual growth rates of 10 to 20 per cent will recur. But if investment and saving continue at recent rates (gross 25 per cent, net 18 to 20 per cent) would Germany have to resign herself to growth rates of 2 to 3 per cent?

The answer depends on how far the capital-output ratio will rise from its present level of (net) 3:1. The expected slower growth of the labor force and the shift toward more capital-intensive forms of production, as well as some lesser factors enumerated above, point toward a higher, i.e., less favorable ratio. This trend could be slowed, though perhaps not stopped, by the large volume of technological catching up that the German economy still has to do. But even at a capital output ratio of 5:1, a savings ratio of 20 per cent would permit an annual growth of 4 per cent. Capital-output ratios within the range of 3.5:1 to 5:1 would permit annual growth rates of 4 to 6 per cent. That the actual ratio at times of stable full employment should long go much outside this range seems unlikely in the light of past experience.

In addition to the capital-output ratio it is of course the savings ratio that is decisive for continued rapid growth. For 1951–53 gross savings (including depreciation) ranged around 25 per cent of gross product, net savings around 18 to 20 per cent of national income (bearing in mind that these savings figures are based upon estimates of investment, and hence are as uncertain as the latter). Strong forces pulling upward as well as downward are now working on the ratio. Higher per capita incomes, increasing satisfaction of pent-up demand, and greater confidence in the currency and in the general outlook tend to raise the savings ratio. So does the reduction in personal and corporate income-tax rates which went into effect at the end of 1954. On the other hand reduced capacity of business for self-financing owing to lower profit margins, a gradual tendency toward a more even distribution of incomes, and the pending repeal of special tax concessions for savers tend to push the savings ratio down. On balance the outlook seems good for continued high savings.

A high savings ratio is of course also an element of danger. It provides the makings of a boom and bust economy, for unless the high savings are absorbed by high investment there will be a depression. High investment and a consequent high rate of growth of capacity must be maintained. This in turn calls for a high rate of growth of consumption. Otherwise the savings ratio would rise rapidly and an implausibly large volume of investment would become necessary to absorb savings. One may conclude with some plausibility that a high rate of income growth will not only be possible but even necessary for Germany.

CHAPTER 4

Monetary Policy and Fiscal Policy

A TIGHT MONETARY and fiscal policy, coupled with reliance upon free markets and free enterprise, has been the chief characteristic of German economic policy during the recovery period. The history of the actions and events in the monetary-fiscal field, therefore, is in large measure the history also of the recovery. The present chapter in giving an account of financial policies will likewise seek to present a broader view of economic events.

The Precurrency-reform Period (May 1945–June 1948)

With the end of the war organized economic activity in Germany came to a near halt. Over large areas production and distribution all but ceased. There was no railway transportation. In many localities there was no electric power, no gas, no water. There was no telephone and no mail. Large masses of people, bombed out or expelled, were tramping the highways in search of food and shelter. Widespread starvation was avoided only through the intervention of the occupying armies. Under Allied administration—all German public authority had vanished with the surrender—essential functions were gradually restored.

Some basic services, mainly power, water, and gas, came back fairly soon. Others took longer. For months many towns did not see a locomotive. Practically all bridges were down, traffic moved only over short stretches, and journeys took days that used to be made in hours. Trade at first was controlled at the county level and often ended there. Intercounty and later interstate connections were re-established very gradually; interzonal operations were on a trade-agreement basis. Industrial production limped along at a quarter or a third of its 1936 pace.

The only economic magnitude that did not drop below past norms was the volume of money. The inflationary war finance of the Nazis had pushed the money supply to dizzy heights, and at these it remained up to the currency reform. The exact total for the three Western zones will probably never be known; it must, however, have been well above the 118.7 billion Reichsmark registered by private holders during the currency reform (currency and all types of deposits).[1] After the reform one-tenth of the earlier amount proved sufficient to conduct a larger volume of business at higher prices.

The disproportion between money and goods was so great that one should have expected large-scale black markets to develop immediately. That this did not happen was a source of surprise to the Allies. What held black markets in check for a while was the extraordinarily rigid pattern of prices and wages with which Germany had lived for a decade and the effective control system of the Nazis that the Allies had to take over much as they found it. For a while, therefore, most goods continued to move through legal channels, although in very inadequate volume.

Gradually, however, nature began to take its course. A growing proportion of goods found their way into gray or black markets. It became increasingly difficult to do business and even merely to exist strictly within the limits of the law. Firms selling all their output through legal channels could not replace their stocks of raw materials nor hold their labor. Individuals could scarcely survive on daily rations of 1,100 calories that often were not met,[2] and on coupons for one pair of shoes every fifteen years if available. Each side supplemented its resources by more or less frequent forays into illegal territory.

Grotesque conditions resulted. Each day, and particularly on weekends, vast hordes of people trekked out to the country to barter food from the farmers. In dilapidated railway carriages from which everything pilferable had long disappeared, on the roofs and on the running boards, hungry people traveled sometimes hundreds of miles at snail's pace to where they hoped to find something to eat. They took their wares— personal effects, old clothes, sticks of furniture, whatever bombed-out remnants they had—and came back with grain or potatoes for a week or two. Many who lacked the strength to provide for themselves in some such way succumbed to their hardships.

Businessmen had to engage in similar uneconomic pursuits. Firms producing readily usable goods like shoes or light bulbs paid their workers in kind, in addition to their regular wages. Firms in less convenient lines would try to shift part of their output so as to have something barterable. If that was not possible they would trade part of their output against consumer goods or give their workers coal. An even more complicated system of barter had to be carried on to secure raw materials, spare parts, and fuel. Only a part, eventually perhaps no more than half, of total output continued to be sold subject to official controls at legal prices.

These conditions finally led to an almost complete repudiation of the currency. In legal transactions money was of secondary importance compared to the ration coupons that went with it. In gray or black dealings, where fears of currency reform and of the tax collector made large money hoards especially unwanted, barter was the prime form of operation. The general goal of business was to buy as much and sell as little as possible, to build up physical assets in plant, equipment, and inventory, and to preserve substance by not selling against paper money. The cigarette became standard money

over large sectors of the economy, both as a means of payment
and as a measure of value—a curious commentary on the text-
book view that durability is an essential characteristic of the
money stuff.

That large-scale starvation was avoided was primarily the
result of American and, on a smaller scale, British aid. This
aid was given consistently from the start, totalling 64 million
dollars in 1945, 468 million in 1946, and 600 million in
1947.* ³ In other respects Allied economic policy underwent
considerable shifts during that period.⁴ Until July 1947 it was
governed by Joint Chiefs of Staff's Directive 1067, which reflected many of the ideas of the Morgenthau Plan. Reparations, dismantling, limitation of industry, forced coal exports,
decartelization and deconcentration of industry were the chief
manifestations of Allied economy policy during the early occupation period.

The widening East-West split, however, together with the
natural subsidence of wartime emotions and the high cost of
these policies to the United States, led to an early stoppage of
reparations to Russia and a reduction in the dismantling program, and to repeated increases in ceilings on steel and other
industrial output. A more positive attitude toward German
reconstruction began to replace the original emphasis on holding the country down. During the second half of 1947 prepara-
tions were made for Western Germany's participation in the
Marshall Plan.

In the monetary and fiscal fields the outstanding measure
was a very stiff income-tax law passed by the Control Council
early in 1946. The law's aim was to prevent inflationary deficits in state budgets and to reduce, insofar as possible, the
monetary overhang. In outward appearance this was probably
the fiercest piece of income taxation ever inflicted on a Western country.⁵ It reached an incremental rate of 50 per cent

* The data give the value of aid-financed imports and do not include aid
given by individual military units, which is believed to have been considerable.

at the 2,400 DMark level and of 70 per cent at 13,200 DMark. In reality the burden was not so heavy as it seemed. Most people were not living on their nominal incomes, and compared to black-market prices the income tax was still cheap. The incentive-killing effect that one might have supposed the tax to have was likewise not very significant, because legal wages and salaries held out little incentive in any case. As for reducing the monetary overhang, the disproportion between tax revenues and volume of money was too great to permit noticeable effects. The tax did, however, achieve the minor miracle of balanced budgets in a ruined economy.

Monetary policy in the ordinary sense was out of the question as long as the economy remained in its inflated state. A complete currency reform was clearly required, both as a first step toward a revival of monetary policy and, more importantly, as an essential condition of more rapid economic recovery. Plans for a reform had been worked out by a group of American economists as early as the spring of 1946.* Under the Potsdam Agreement the reform would have had to be carried through equally in all four zones. Protracted negotiations with the Russians, however, led nowhere. That the Western Allies preferred to let two years drag by rather than to proceed unilaterally attests to their realization that the splitting of the currency also meant the final splitting of Germany. When the currency reform was put through in June 1948 these unhappy expectations were fully realized, and the introduction of the new currency in West Berlin touched off the blockade of the city.

The delay in the reform by two years undoubtedly delayed the recovery of Germany substantially, but the time was not altogether lost. While living standards improved very little, production did move up from the level of one-quarter of 1936 to about one-half—and this is probably an understatement. Through repairs, and some investment and accumulation of

* Referred to in the press as the Dodge-Colm-Goldsmith Plan.

stocks, the basis was laid for the rapid upsurge after the reform. Investment probably represented a high proportion of the very low income of the period, although there are no data to prove it. At the human level a similar process of accumulation was going on: Frustration helped to store up energies that burst into action once productive effort acquired meaning again. Meanwhile the difficulties of the period impressed upon many Germans a deep-seated prejudice against "planning." Caricature as it was of a planned economy, the spectacle did much to predispose people in favor of the system soon to be established by Minister Erhard.

The Currency Reform

The main features of the currency reform proper were: (1) the contraction of the money supply and (2) the reorganization of the public and private debt structure. The currency reform was accompanied by a tax reform and by a progressive removal of price and rationing controls. A scheme for the equalization of war damages, which was to have been a sequel to the reform, did not materialize until 1952.

The measures. There was general agreement that the way to remove the disproportion between money and goods was to cut the money supply to fit the volume of goods at existing prices. The alternative method, theoretically conceivable, of letting prices rise to fit the money supply found few supporters. As to the details of the reform, innumerable proposals were made from various German sources. The most authoritative of these was the Homburg Plan of April 18, 1948. [6] The plan eventually put into effect by Allied law in June 1948 was the expression mainly of Allied views but also contained some German contributions.[7]

The contraction of the money supply was the most conspicuous element of the reform. All currency and bank deposits owned by individuals and firms had to be registered. They were to be converted into the new Deutsche Mark at a rate of 10:1, in other words, scaled down to 10 per cent of the original amount. Of this 10 per cent one-half was placed at the owners' immediate disposal, i.e., as quickly as the necessary computations could be ground out and checked by the income-tax office. The other half was again split, one-fifth (equal to 1 per cent of the original amount) being made freely available later, while one-tenth was set aside for investment purposes in a blocked account. The other seven-tenths were canceled when it became clear that release would endanger the success of the reform. The net effect of all these percentages was a conversion rate of 100:6.5 (with some qualifications for smaller amounts). This severe scaling down applied to savings deposits as well as demand and time deposits, a fact that became a source of much bitterness and social distress.

To provide people with cash during the conversion period a per capita "allowance" was given to each individual, totaling 60 DMark. Of this, 40 DMark were available on the day of reform, 20 DMark two months later. The allowance could be obtained against old Reichsmark at a rate of 1:1. But to the extent that the applicant's funds exceeded 60 Reichsmark, the DMark allowance was charged against them at the 10:1 rate. Businesses were allowed 60 DMark per employee on the same terms, to avoid a complete stoppage of wage and other payments. State and local governments and other public authorities were given an allowance equal to one month's revenue. Their old funds were canceled in toto.

The sharp reduction in liquidity made necessary a reorganization of debts. People whose cash holdings had just been scaled down to 6.5 per cent of their previous level could not be expected to meet short-term obligations 100 per cent. All debts were therefore devalued in the ratio of 10:1. For long-term debtors, particularly in the case of mortgages on unbombed property, such virtual debt extinction promised a tremendous windfall. To prevent enrichment of this kind the "devaluation profit" was absorbed into a fund from which war damage compensation payments were to be made later.

The banks found their balance sheets thrown into even greater disorder by these measures than had been occasioned previously by the default of the Hitler government debt. To restore their solvency they were given new government obligations sufficient to bring their assets to the level of their (greatly diminished) liabilities plus a modest allowance for capital. These equalization claims (*Ausgleichsforderungen*) bore interest at 3 per cent, which was below any market rate likely to establish itself in the near future and made the securities de facto nonnegotiable. To restore liquidity the banks were given reserves equal to 15 per cent of the demand deposits and to 7.5 per cent of the time and savings deposits arising out of the conversion. The reserves took the form of deposits with the central banking system; they were 50 per cent above the minimum reserve requirements fixed by the system. The resulting excess liquidity, which soon was further swelled by the gradual flow of the various initial allowances into the banks, was to prove a source of trouble.

Simultaneously with the currency reform new personal and business tax rates were introduced. They reduced sharply the rates imposed by the Allies in 1946, but not as sharply as the German administration had wished. As a compromise the occupation authorities agreed to a series of concessions that exempted from taxation income saved and invested. These concessions, which in effect eased mainly the burden on the upper brackets and favored independent businessmen, later played an unexpectedly important part in financing the recovery. The initial deficit produced by these tax cuts proved to be temporary, owing to the rapid rise of the national income.

Finally, a series of decontrol measures was introduced following the currency reform (somewhat later in the French Zone). They centered on the price of manufactured consumer goods. Some foodstuffs were likewise freed, but most basic foods, rents, and basic materials remained under control for some time. This decontrol action does not seem to have been planned as an integral part of the measures accompanying the reform. It was introduced amid considerable skepticism, but was probably in good part responsible for the remarkable success of the operation.

The spirit of the reform. One comment stands out above all others, favorable or unfavorable: The German currency reform was a tremendous success. No other financial operation in German history has had such an immediate and profound impact. Observers, left wing as well as right wing, agree that it transformed the German scene from one day to the next. On June 21, 1948, goods reappeared in the stores, money resumed its normal function, black and gray markets reverted to a minor role, foraging trips to the country ceased, labor productivity increased, and output took off on its great upward surge. The spirit of the country changed overnight. The gray, hungry, dead-looking figures wandering about the streets in their everlasting search for food came to life as, pocketing their 40 DMark, they went on a first spending spree. That there were dark spots in this bright picture will become apparent from the further unfolding of the tale. The dominant fact, however, was the great success of the reform in getting the German economy back into operation.

The main characteristic of the reform was its toughness. In putting the monetary system in the best possible shape for recovery it made few concessions to social equity. No great effort was made to temper the economic wind to shorn creditors and savers. The cut in the volume of money of 93.5 per cent was high in comparison to most current proposals. The treatment of savings deposits as money instead of debts was harsh. So was the 10:1 cut in the value of debts. Earlier proposals had sought to couple with the reform a plan for equalization of war damage and losses from the reform itself. This would in some measure have compensated for the harshness of the operation. The Allies were agreed on the need for such a plan but refused to see it grafted on the reform. The Germans were asked to produce a scheme within six months; it took a great deal longer, however, before it was implemented.

The counterpart of the toughness of the reform was the aid it gave to the active forces of the economy. It raised production incentives by keeping down the burden of carrying the unproductive part of the population—pensioners, owners of savings, old people, people unable to fend for themselves. By wiping slates clean it favored entrepreneurs, businessmen, and debtors at the expense of fixed-income receivers and creditors. Broadly speaking, the reform and its consequences were hard on the economically weak. Only the extraordinarily comprehensive German social security system, which distributes over 15 per cent of the national income, kept the reform from being unbearable by putting a floor under those who otherwise would have fallen into an economic void.

The basic features of the currency reform were intensified through the policies pursued thereafter by the German authorities. Even though the reform was imposed by the Allies, and could almost certainly not have been put through with equal severity by a parliamentary German government, one may say that its spirit was in harmony with the hard, go-getting mentality that has pervaded the German economy ever since.

On the purely technical side the success of the reform was a credit to the good judgment of its authors. Many of the technical decisions were difficult, and most of them were confirmed by the results. On a few points subsequent events revealed what may have been errors of judgment. The initial DMark quotas allowed to individuals, businesses, and public authorities turned out to be on the high side when added to the new DMark arising from conversion of Reichsmark at the 100:6.5 rate. The continuing increase in money supply and bank reserves resulting from the gradual conversion of Reichsmark defied central bank control. An unexpectedly rapid expansion of credit was further facilitated by the fact that the initial quotas were all in the form of central bank money and added to the already high liquidity reserves of the banks as soon as they were deposited. These factors combined created an inflationary environment that the technicians had not anticipated and that for a while seemed to jeopardize the entire undertaking.

The Post-reform Inflation (June–December 1948)

The ultimate success of the currency reform, from the point of view of monetary stability, was not assured until the beginning of 1949. This must be said despite the rapid normalization of the distorted economy that the reform and its associated measures brought about, and despite the rise in the production index of 50 per cent in six months (Table 10). Gratifying as these results were, they coincided with an increase in money, credit, and prices that for a while seemed in danger of getting out of hand. For monetary and fiscal policy, therefore, the period was one of intense struggle against inflation.

The plan of the reform had been to keep business very short of funds in order to force the sale of hoarded stocks to consumers, who had been endowed with relatively generous cash allowances. To limit the use of bank credit for continued inventory hoarding, new current account credits (which in Germany ordinarily represent the bulk of short-term bank loans) had been prohibited for the first two months, leaving bills (a more formal and less flexible type of credit) as the only major form of bank financing. Despite these restrictions expansionary forces gained the upper hand.

The reliance that the authors of the reform had placed on hoarded stocks proved a sound speculation. The initial monetary tightness—ten days after the reform the total money supply (currency and demand deposits) did not exceed 6 billion DMark—brought these stocks out in volume. But business showed a surprising capacity for getting along temporarily with next to no cash balances. Very soon, moreover, various inflationary factors began to make themselves felt. Bank credit rose from almost zero at the time of the reform to 5.2 billion in December; the conversion of old balances provided large additional amounts; and the second installment of the 60 DMark per capita allowance became payable. All this combined to lift the money supply to 12.3 billion in September and 14.3 billion in December. ERP (European Recovery Program) goods, which had been counted upon to help meet the situation, came in disappointingly slowly. The tax cuts which accompanied the currency reform produced initial deficits. Personal saving was very small, since pent-up consumer demand was intense. The upward trend of prices led to renewed inventory hoarding. The fate of the new currency seemed to hang in the balance.

One powerful anchor to windward remained: Wages continued virtually stable. Despite bitter protests on the part of union leadership over the rise in prices and the growing in-

TABLE 10: *Economic*

Month	Industrial production 1936 = 100	Employment (millions)	Unemployment (% of labor force)	Basic materials prices 1950 = 100	Factory prices 1950 = 100	Cost of living 1950 = 100	Gross hourly wages 1950 = 100
June	54	13.5	3.2		n.a.	98	76.6
July	60			77	103	102	
August	65			83	106	104	
September	71	13.5	5.5	87	108	107	83.5
October	76			91	109	112	
November	81			92	105	111	
December	79	13.7	5.3	93	106	112	88.1

Sources: Bank deutscher Länder, *Monthly Reports; Wirtschaft und Statistik,*

equality of incomes, serious strike action was not resorted to. The reasons for this restraint seem to have centered around (1) a general reluctance on the part of the leadership as well as the rank and file to interfere with the recovery; (2) the relatively satisfactory living conditions compared to the pre-currency-reform period; (3) the fact that many basic necessities remained under price control or rationing, which caused living costs to lag behind the rise in industrial prices; (4) the appearance of some unemployment; and (5), last but not least, the total impoverishment of the unions through the currency reform.

As the production index shot upward from 54 in June (which, however, understates true activity) to 79 in December, prices of basic materials rose by 21 per cent, factory prices by 14 per cent, and living costs by 14 per cent. Part of this increase was no doubt inevitable now that normal economic relationships were being re-established. Labor productivity had greatly diminished in relation to prewar, and with wages constant costs could not be covered without higher prices. But the movement that took place went much beyond the needed adjustment, as evidenced by the very substantial profits that

Indicators, June–December 1948

Currency and demand deposits (billions of DM)	Time and savings deposits (billions of DM)	Bank loans (short and long term) (billions of DM)	Redis- counts (billions of DM)	Discount rate	Exports (millions of $)	Imports		Net foreign exchange reserves (millions of $)
						Total (millions of $)	Commer- cial (millions of $)	
n.a.	n.a.	1.3						173
n.a.	n.a.	2.4		5				146
n.a.	n.a.	3.2			60.4 av.	165.9 av.	59.3 av.	164
12.3	4.2	3.8						186
13.2	3.4	4.5						224
14.0	3.0	4.6		—	70.1 av.	120.1 av.	47.1 av.	243
14.3	3.2	5.2		—				283

various issues.

appeared. Demands for a renewed price freeze began to spread.

Such was the situation that monetary and fiscal policy had to face. With fiscal operations tightly circumscribed by previous tax and expenditure legislation, the burden of flexible adjustment fell largely upon the monetary authorities. Monetary action was also made difficult, however, by the steady influx of converted balances and by the excessively large bank reserves inadvertently created by the currency reform. General credit restraint was further inhibited by the special and justifiable need for bank credit on the part of certain industries. Businesses whose output remained under price control could not, like most others, finance themselves through retained earnings. Export industries were regarded as specially deserving of credit and had to be sheltered against credit tightness. Selective controls seemed indicated to take account of such cases.

The Bank deutscher Länder took three steps:

1) It increased reserve requirements from 10 to 15 per cent.
2) It refused to discount bank acceptances except for the financing of exports and of public storage of foodstuffs and certain raw materials.
3) It requested all banks to limit their total loan volume to the level of October 31, 1948, except in special cases and after consultation with the respective Land Central Bank. The discount rate was left at its original level of 5 per cent, because an increase would have been unavailing with respect to the many banks that did not need to rediscount, and burdensome for many industries whose expansion was desirable.

These measures were probably not without effect. It is hard to believe, however, that they deserve more than a minor share of the credit for the final defeat of the inflation.

The first measure, higher reserve requirements, was the only *general* credit control action, as contrasted with the other measures which were *selective*. It could not mean much, however, in a banking system where many banks had ample reserves and most others had easy access to central bank credit via rediscounts.

The second measure, limitation of acceptances rediscounted, affected seriously only those banks that needed central bank credit and had no other paper to offer. In practice this meant mainly a number of small banks which, for lack of deposits, were financing most of their operations by means of acceptances. As for the selective effect of this measure, it suffered from the fact, familiar from early Federal Reserve experience, that the nature of the credit instruments offered to the central bank does not indicate the use which the bank will make of the money. Banks with well rounded portfolios were usually able to find enough eligible paper so as not to be hamstrung by the central bank's rejection of certain instruments. However, in view of the greater specialization of the German banking system, the "eligibility approach" may not have been quite so futile as it had proved in the United States.

The third measure, finally, limitation of total credits to the October 31 level, had to be handled extremely flexibly. In an expanding economy, with business clamoring for credit and the banks anxious to rebuild their decimated portfolios, it could never have been made very firm. The measure is noteworthy in two respects, however: First, the Bank deutscher Länder had no legal authority to impose a credit ceiling. Yet the traditional authority of the central bank was so strong that the action was not seriously questioned. Second, the action, which was itself derived from earlier Reichsbank practices, set a pattern for similar unorthodox measures in the future.

From this initial trial of strength the main technical problems with which monetary policy would have to wrestle in the future became apparent. The tools in the hands of the Bank deutscher Länder were few and most of them did not bite very sharply. The discount rate was of limited effectiveness as long as business paid 10 per cent for short-term credit and anticipated large price fluctuations. Open market operations had little scope while the money market was narrow and the capital market nonexistent. They would have been fruitless, moreover, even if feasible, so long as the German banks felt no reluctance to rediscount and were able to do their lending in a way that gave them plentiful supplies of eligible paper. Increases in reserve requirements were stymied by the same factors. The unrestrained use of rediscount facilities gave an open-end character to the credit system. Exceptional devices, such as loan freezes or rediscount ceilings, became necessary to keep credit in bounds.

The inflationary trend came to a halt around the end of 1948, half a year after the currency reform. The main forces contributing to its demise, besides monetary restraint, were (1) the growing gap between prices and consumer purchasing power created by wage stability; (2) the end of the influx of converted balances; (3) the emergence of budget surpluses resulting from rising revenues due to higher national income; and (4) the incipient downturn in world markets. The role played by monetary restraint must to some extent remain a matter of opinion. The actions of the Bank deutscher Länder deserve some of the credit for the reduction in the rate of expansion of short-term bank credit. From a monthly rate of 800 to 900 million during the third quarter the monthly increment declined by about 100 million during each month of the fourth quarter. But the slowing down of the boom would by itself have reduced the demand for credit. The rate of credit expansion therefore is no very clear indicator of the effectiveness of monetary restraint.

For the recovery and further growth of Western Germany the six months of the currency reform boom were of extraordinary importance. It was a period during which the base was laid and the pattern set for what was to follow. Enormous profits on hoarded stocks were made thanks to the price rise, and wide margins established promising future profits. Extraordinary opportunities opened up for aggressive entrepreneurs. Firms starting on a shoestring had a chance of getting a solid foothold. Large business profits could be ploughed back with the benevolent approval of the otherwise heavy-handed tax collector. As a result of the rapidly growing inequality of incomes, savings and investment rose to levels one would have thought out of reach of an improverished country.

At the same time, the basis was laid for future spurts of consumption. One of several successive consumer "waves" was on its way—the "food wave." Conspicuous luxury consumption began to obtrude itself and to irritate the broad public as well as many foreign observers. But many small luxuries, unknown even during the late Nazi period, could be had at relatively modest prices. Most people bought them and worked overtime to pay for their fling. The incentives were strong on the side of consumption as well as production.

Slow Growth and Rising Unemployment (*January 1949–March 1950*)

The currency-reform boom, which lasted perhaps six months, was followed by a period of fifteen months during which the advance slowed down considerably. It was a period of relative stagnation of output—if one may call a 23 per cent gain by that name; prices fell, and unemployment increased rapidly (see Table 11). By precurrency-reform standards the performance was still a very satisfactory one, particularly since during this period the soundness of the currency became increasingly established. But the loss of the earlier momentum and the alarming growth of unemployment, which reached 2 million in early 1950, created concern. From this ensued a bitter debate over what not a few observers considered the unduly restrictive policy of the Bank deutscher Länder.

Various factors contributed to this turn of events. In part they were those which had been responsible for the end of the boom: prices too far ahead of wages, accumulation of budget surpluses and later also of ERP counterpart funds, and the recession in the United States. In the second half of the year came the relative appreciation of the DMark against sterling and other European currencies that were devalued further than the DMark. A positive reduction in money and credit was not among the retarding factors, since bank credit increased by 8.6 billion and the volume of money by 3.0 billion during these fifteen months. The downturn of the price movement, however, was itself a powerful deflationary force. In any event, after the great initial advance it was not unnatural that there should be a certain period of consolidation. The question was whether what was taking place meant more than

TABLE 11: *Economic Indicators,*

Month	Industrial production 1936 = 100	Employment (millions)	Unemployment (% of labor force)	Basic materials prices 1950 = 100	Factory prices 1950 = 100	Cost of living 1950 = 100	Gross hourly wages 1950 = 100
1949							
January	81			92	106	110	
February	84			91	105	109	
March	83	13.4	8.0	90	105	108	90.1
April	85			89	104	107	
May	87			91	104	107	
June	88	13.5	8.7	92	102	107	93.3
July	87			92	102	106	
August	89			93	101	104	
September	94	13.6	8.8	93	101	105	94.8
October	97			96	101	105	
November	104			95	100	106	
December	98	13.6	10.3	94	100	105	95.5
1950							
January	93			95	100	102	
February	96			95	100	101	
March	99	13.3	12.2	95	99	100	96.5

Sources: Bank deutscher Länder, *Monthly Reports; Wirtschaft und Statistik,*

that, meant real stagnation or perhaps even an incipient depression. And there was the further question whether in the face of mounting unemployment Germany could afford such a breathing spell. What were the social and political dangers, and what was the economic cost of the waste of man power? These were the key issues of the debate.

The extreme case for a vigorous full-employment policy, including central bank expansion and budget deficits, could be stated something like this. Unemployment, in addition to the human misery it caused, was a serious political threat. Hitler had been helped to power by the unemployment of the thirties. The unemployed, moreover, represented productive capacity that should be put to work. More production, more

January 1949–March 1950

Currency and demand deposits (billions of DM)	Time and savings deposits (billions of DM)	Bank loans (short and long term) (billions of DM)	Redis- counts (monthly average) (billions of DM)	Discount rate	Exports (millions of $)	Imports		Net foreign exchange reserves (millions of $)
						Total (millions of $)	Commer- cial (millions of $)	
14.2	3.5	5.5	1.5	5	74.4	114.7	32.7	333
14.4	3.8	5.9	1.5		84.2	165.7	93.5	338
14.6	4.0	6.3	1.6		96.1	166.9	52.9	359
15.0	4.2	6.6	1.6		88.3	163.3	68.9	402
15.1	4.5	6.9	1.5	4½	101.4	222.8	155.1	434
15.6	4.3	7.8	1.2		94.2	208.8	137.4	401
15.8	4.5	8.3	1.3	4	100.9	179.0	122.7	367
16.1	4.7	9.0	1.6		97.6	219.1	121.0	337
16.4	4.7	9.6	2.0		102.0	161.0	98.8	295
16.9	4.8	10.6	2.5		80.9	190.7	99.5	253
16.9	5.0	11.3	3.3		87.9	169.0	109.1	204
19.6	5.2	11.9	3.6		115.1	275.7	189.3	151
17.1	5.5	12.6	3.6		104.4	230.1	172.3	27
17.1	5.9	13.2	3.7		112.4	168.3	134.3	2
17.3	6.1	13.8	3.9		139.7	195.5	158.7	−6

various issues.

investment was the way to get Germany on her feet and off the American taxpayer's back. If the expansionary policies should, despite higher production, increase Germany's external deficit, direct import controls could be used to keep the drain within bounds. To seek balance of payments equilibrium by tight monetary policies meant to aggravate unemployment and ran counter to modern democratic principles. That expansionary policies should lead to inflation and renewed currency trouble was not likely, given the presence of idle labor. In any case, mild inflation was a calculated risk that would have to be taken. Price controls could be resorted to if the case arose.

In a more moderate vein it was argued that there were a number of special deflationary factors that ought to be counteracted: the passive balance of payments, the overvalued exchange rate, the budget surpluses and counterpart accumulation. It was also observed that full-employment policies might not increase imports as much as their opponents feared; because the import content of much German industrial production is low, and because the unemployed were to some extent eating imported food anyhow. The measures suggested to carry out a policy of expansion were increased public spending and stimulation of private investment. Both would have to be financed by the Bank deutscher Länder, since other sources of funds were inadequate.

The conservative case countering these views might be summarized in a similar list of key propositions. For a country like Germany, with two inflations behind it, the need for a stable currency had to take precedence over all other considerations. This meant achievement of external balance and avoidance of inflationary risks at home. External balance would have to be reached very quickly, moreover, because of the scheduled rapid decline of American aid. The way to raise exports and reduce dependence on imports was not to push production by inflationary financing but to create a buyers' market at home by tight monetary and fiscal policies. German businessmen, having so long been cut off from the outside world, would not willingly seek new markets abroad if selling was made easy for them at home. Domestic price increases would further jeopardize Germany's ability to compete internationally, particularly with those European countries which, in the fall of 1949, had devalued more than Germany.

The possibilities of bringing idle man power into production, it was further argued, were much smaller than the expansionists supposed. Total employment had hardly declined; in fact, industrial employment was up, although not enough to offset reductions in agriculture and elsewhere. The bulk of the new unemployment was due to growth of the labor force, mainly through refugees. Much of this unemployment was structural. Its causes were of a kind that could not be quickly remedied: the insufficient capacity of industry, especially in view of shortages of coal, steel, and power; the concentration of the unemployed in the agricultural states where the refugees had first found shelter, combined with the shortage of housing in industrial areas; the lack of the required industrial skills and the physical handicaps of many unemployed. While unemployment could no doubt be reduced by expansionary financing, this was not the way to deal with the structural part of it.

The prospects for enduring recovery and progress, the conservative case concluded, were better if monetary stability were given priority over short-run efforts to push production. The inherent dynamics of the German economy, where so much remained to be done, were strong enough to remove the fear that a rigorous sound money policy might lead to lasting stagnation. Inflation was a much more immediate danger. Finally—a novel and interesting thought to which little weight was attached at the time but which gained significance later—a country without exchange reserves and with little elasticity in its economy was well advised to retain certain reserves of productive capacity. These could be employed to absorb sudden spurts of demand that might occur in a politically unstable world.

The various parties to the dispute subscribed to a greater or lesser number of the respective propositions with greater or lesser vigor. An aggressive full-employment policy was favored by the Social Democratic party, the trade unions, and, it was said, by some elements within the British Military Government. A more moderate expansionary policy was recommended by the representatives of the Economic Cooperation Administration, with growing urgency as time went on. There is no evidence that other United States government agencies lent support to aggressive expansionary plans. The West German government leaned toward the conservative view and was quite reluctant to go in for employment-creating projects until late during the period.

Most conservative of all was the Bank deutscher Länder, whose position as "financier of last resort" made its view fairly decisive. The expansionary actions of the Bank deutscher Länder, once the inflationary spurt had ended, were far from precipitous. It lifted the credit ceiling (March 1949), removed the restrictions on the rediscounting of acceptances (May), cut the discount rate by successive steps from 5 per cent to 4 per cent (May to July), and reduced reserve requirements to approximately their initial levels (July and September). It allowed the inflow of exchange reserves during the first half of the year to have its full liquidity-increasing effect. During the second half, when the balance of commercial payments (excluding American aid) turned against Germany, it allowed rediscounts to rise from 1 billion to 3.6 billion without hindrance. In connection with an intensified public investment program in the summer and fall of the year, the Bank made certain stand-by commitments. These consisted of arrangements to finance particular export and investment projects, on a strictly temporary basis, through the purchase from banks of some of their holdings of compensation certificates, up to the modest amount of 300 million.

Throughout this period the Bank was under pressure from many sides to move more boldly and rapidly. Its own basic tendency was different. Even as it was easing up on credit it managed to convey an atmosphere of restraint and financial austerity. The volume of its commitments seemed to reflect the concept of "stingy finance" which was the intellectual legacy of the currency reform. Its over-all policy plainly gave expression to the primacy of currency stability and balance of payments equilibrium over full employment.

In the fall of 1949 the conflict between these two goals became extraordinarily acute. While unemployment rose by 600,000 above the preceding year, the balance of payments turned sharply passive. The latter development was provoked by generous import liberalization, as recommended by the Organization for European Economic Cooperation (OEEC), and put Germany into the red with most of her European trade partners. The resulting drain on bank reserves counteracted the Bank deutscher Länder's mild measures to increase liquidity. The fear of aggravating the external deficit made the Bank even more reluctant to engage in bold expansionary action.

Nevertheless, at the beginning of 1950 the rise of unemployment to the 2 million level forced the government and the Bank into more determined action. The foreign trade picture, though somewhat improved, was still uncertain, and the level of industrial production, 15 per cent above 1949, was not such as to demand urgent stimulation, but the social and political implications of mass unemployment could no longer be resisted. Action was initiated on a broad front, with fiscal policy taking an important role. A new round of tax cuts was scheduled, to become effective in June. A work-creation and housing program was started or rather planned. The Bank deutscher Länder promised its financial support; the total amount potentially committed was 2 billion DMark, which, however, was unlikely to be outstanding at any one time.

But the execution of these programs was slow. The familiar difficulties of most anticyclical public-works schemes showed themselves—disagreement over how and where to spend, delays in programming, bottlenecks in execution. Three months later, before the program had got well underway, the economic weather had changed once more as the consolidation period gave way to a new upswing. Another three months later, with the program not yet in full swing, the Korea boom had broken out, and whatever had been right in planning became a source of embarrassment in execution.

It is difficult to appraise the policies of these fifteen months without reference to the Korea boom, which could not then be foreseen. The basic policy of putting stable money and external balance ahead of employment stimulation has proved justified by the strong position eventually achieved by the German economy. The revival in the spring of 1950 has shown also that the monetary authorities were right in trusting to the natural dynamics of the economy to lift output without central bank prodding. But had Korea not occurred there might have been reason to wonder, nevertheless, whether conservatism had not been carried a little far.

In the light of what actually happened after the Korean invasion, however, the previous policies proved extremely fortunate. Like other countries Germany experienced a sharp rise in activity. Unlike most other countries Germany had excess capacity. This capacity reserve enabled Germany not only to avoid a major domestic price rise but also to take advantage of the spurt in foreign demand. Exporters in other countries were at a disadvantage because they often were fully booked and had to compete with rising domestic arms production. This ex post facto justification of past policies was of course a stroke of luck, but it was not all luck. The German monetary authorities had framed their policies with the thought in mind that a capacity reserve could come in handy, although this had been by no means a decisive consideration. Like many events in Germany's postwar history, the outcome was a remarkable combination of good luck and good management.

Revival and Korea Boom (April 1950–June 1951)

As a result of the Korean War German monetary and fiscal policy abruptly found itself confronted with the second boom in two years. This time, however, it was not domestic inflation that had to be controlled. It was the external deficit, generated by panicky purchases of raw materials at rising prices and financed through EPU (European Payments Union) credit, that threatened to wreck Germany's precariously maintained balance.

The period of consolidation had given way to a more rapid resumption of the upward trend during the spring of 1950. Exports, stimulated by the lack of demand in the domestic market, increased by about 50 million dollars per month over the previous year. The world-wide improvement in prices and production also provided a lift. The initially severe pressure of foreign competition, which the 1949 liberalization had permitted to become effective in the domesitc market, had been largely absorbed. The easing of credit and the expansionary fiscal measures were beginning to have some effect. All this, aided by the consolidation that had taken place and by seasonal factors, made for a more vigorous forward movement which carried the production index from 99 in March to 110 in June 1950. Then came the invasion of South Korea. Within five months the index shot up another 23 points. Prices of basic materials moved up 13 per cent during the same period, and a further 14 per cent by March 1951. Factory prices rose 19 per cent by the latter date. The cost of living, however, rose only 7 per cent. The balance of commercial trade (excluding aid-financed imports), which had been mildly active, in the spring turned passive to the extent of 133.6 million dollars during the second half of 1950, and the balance of payments was considerably more unfavorable. Bank credit expanded by 5.3 billion DMark from June 1950 to March 1951. The rise in the money supply, counteracted by the passive balance of payments, came to only 0.6 billion.

The brusqueness of the upswing and of the accompanying run on imports was largely the result of the sensitiveness of German businessmen and consumers to the threat of inflation and shortages. Apprehensions frequently voiced in this respect by the monetary authorities proved well founded. Businessmen rushed into raw-material markets to stock up,

TABLE 12: *Economic*

Month	Industrial production 1936 = 100	Employment (millions)	Unemployment (% of labor force)	Basic materials prices 1950 = 100	Factory prices 1950 = 100	Cost of living 1950 = 100	Gross hourly wages 1950 = 100
1950							
April	103			95	98	100	
May	109			95	98	99	
June	110	13.8	10.0	96	98	99	97.5
July	111			98	98	99	
August	117			100	99	99	
September	125	14.3	8.2	105	100	100	100.6
October	132			106	101	100	
November	133			108	102	100	
December	131	14.2	10.7	111	106	101	105.3
1951							
January	124			116	111	102	
February	130			119	115	103	
March	133	14.2	9.9	121	118	106	109.0
April	136			121	119	107	
May	138			118	120	107	
June	136	14.7	8.3	118	119	108	117.2

* Temporarily the figures for deposits were only reported by maturities as at
Sources: Bank deutscher Länder, *Monthly Reports; Wirtschaft und Statistik,*

with the fortunate incidental result that on the whole they bought earlier and more cheaply than their less nervous competitors in other countries. Consumers started hoarding to beat the shortages and restrictions that seemed imminent. Their action is reflected in the sudden drop in the rate of saving, as shown by the slowing down in the growth of savings deposits. During the first quarter of 1951 there was even a slight drop in savings deposits.

The spree was enlivened, of course, by the fiscal and monetary measures which had been decided upon during the preceding winter to overcome the then existing slackness. Expenditure programs as well as tax cuts and refunds had just

Indicators, April 1950–June 1951

Currency and demand deposits (billions of DM)	Time and savings deposits (billions of DM)	Bank loans (short and long term) (billions of DM)	Rediscounts (monthly average) (billions of DM)	Discount rate	Exports (millions of $)	Imports		Net foreign exchange reserves (millions of $)
						Total (millions of $)	Commercial (millions of $)	
17.6	6.4	14.2	3.7	4	127.7	177.7	144.3	31
17.9	6.7	14.5	3.5		140.3	161.1	128.8	66
18.0	7.0	15.1	3.4		153.9	187.9	149.2	126
*	*	15.6	3.3		171.6	225.4	165.7	116
*	*	16.2	3.1		177.1	205.3	174.3	86
18.9	7.5	17.2	3.6		165.2	239.1	210.1	−6
*	*	18.2	4.5	6	214.1	311.9	263.2	−106
18.9	7.9	18.8	4.6		233.0	286.6	248.9	−144
19.2	8.2	19.5	5.1		241.1	314.8	273.5	−158
18.4	8.5	19.9	4.7		218.9	295.3	257.8	−184
18.6	8.7	21.0	5.0		232.7	290.6	253.6	−229
18.6	8.8	20.4	4.8		259.2	299.0	250.9	−182
18.6	8.9	20.4	4.4		273.5	256.4	206.4	−107
18.8	9.0	20.7	4.3		272.9	249.5	193.3	4
19.6	9.3	21.3	4.3		297.2	255.0	209.7	77

the quarter.
various issues.

begun to take effect when the crisis struck. The rising volume
of bank credit added fuel to the flames.

The main part of the external deficit thus generated was
incurred vis-à-vis member countries of the EPU. About 75
per cent of Germany's trade was with these countries. Imports from them, moreover, were liberalized to the extent of
60 per cent. The restrictions that protected Germany's dollar
import sector could therefore not be applied effectively to the
EPU sector unless the liberalization policy was to be breached.
In October 1950, four months after the start of EPU, Germany was within a few million dollars of exhausting her full
quota of 320 million dollars with the organization. From then
on the struggle with the Korea crisis became in the main a
struggle with the EPU deficit.

The Bank deutscher Länder opened its anti-inflationary
campaign in October, somewhat late as it would seem, with
the following measures:

1) A 50 per cent increase in reserve requirements, bringing
   the top rate to 15 per cent.
2) Refusal to rediscount acceptances for banks who allowed
   their total acceptance credit to exceed its level as of the
   date of the announcement.
3) An increase in the discount rate from 4 to 6 per cent.
4) An attempt to reduce rediscounts by 10 per cent.

Further measures, taken by the government in cooperation
with the Bank deutscher Länder, involved:

5) A combing out and substantial reduction of outstanding
   import licenses, insofar as import contracts had not been
   signed under them.
6) A requirement that importers must deposit 50 per cent
   of the DMark value of the foreign exchange applied for.

Demands for direct controls over raw materials, which came
from many sides, including the American occupation authorities, as well as for consumer rationing and price controls, were
vigorously fought by Minister Erhard. Only belatedly certain

allocation measures were introduced to satisfy American demands. In practice the measures remained virtually without effect. Meanwhile the EPU, in order to give the German measures time to work themselves out, granted Germany a special short-term credit of 120 million dollars. It did so in view of the corrective program submitted by the German government and of a report rendered by Dr. Per Jacobsson of the Bank for International Settlements and by Professor Alec Cairncross, then of the OEEC. The rapid subsequent repayment of the credit justified the EPU's confidence, although events in the meantime brought some rough moments and things did not work out quite as planned.

The action which the Bank deutscher Länder had taken in October, though severe by ordinary standards, was only moderately so under the prevailing conditions. It suffered, moreover, from two weaknesses already observed during the 1948 inflation: (1) Many banks possessed or could generate enough eligible paper to meet higher reserve requirements and get around restrictions placed on particular types of rediscounts; and (2) panicky inventory hoarders were not greatly impressed with the rise in the cost of credit.

The credit control measures did succeed in forcing down the rate of credit expansion from 1 billion in October to 0.6 billion in November and 0.7 billion in December. Together with the other actions mentioned they might even have turned the tide had a new flood of inflationary demand not been unleashed by China's entry into the war. The ensuing scare purchases once more pushed up the German EPU deficit. Therewith the measure of last resort which Germany had struggled so hard to avoid became inevitable. Upon advice by the Bank deutscher Länder the German government suspended the liberalization of its EPU imports and reverted to administrative import restriction.

This action put an end to the external deficit, although at the cost of sacrificing the liberal trade principles to which the

government stood committed. Commercial imports during
the second quarter of 1951 dropped 20 per cent below the
level of the first quarter. Exports meanwhile caught up and
closed the time gap that had arisen between rapidly expan-
sible imports of raw materials and slowly maturing exports of
industrial goods. Repayment of the EPU credit was completed in May 1951.

In view of the fact that the change in the German position
coincided with the turning point of the world-wide raw-
materials boom, one may ask whether this downturn did not
contribute a good deal to the German improvement. German
sensitivity to price movements had shown itself to be high.
Falling world prices undoubtedly acted to discourage imports.
Quite possibly, therefore, the crisis could have been weathered without deliberalization. At the time the decision was
taken, however, the impending reversal of world markets
could not have been foreseen.

Even while it became necessary to fall back upon direct
trade controls, the Bank deutscher Länder continued its restrictive monetary policy with a series of new measures. These
were:

1) Establishment of "guiding rules" for banks to govern
   certain balance-sheet ratios, such as the ratio of secondary reserves to deposits, that of short-term loans to
   capital funds, and the ratio of certain assets to total
   assets. These rules were to exert pressure upon overex-
   tended banks to bring their loans and deposits into a conservative relation to liquid reserves and capital funds.
   For many banks the adjustment to the new ratios did involve some credit restriction. But because the adjustment
   was bound to be painful, arrangements had to be made to
   spread it over a reasonable period. No immediate strong
   credit restraint could be expected nor was intended. The
   measure was essentially for the long-run.

2) Imposition of a new credit ceiling, limiting each bank's loan volume to the level prevailing at the end of January. Long-term loans and credits for exports and for official storage operations were excluded.

3) One month later this ceiling was rolled back by one billion, the reduction to be completed within three months.

These measures were effective to the extent of producing a small reduction in short-term bank credit which had been rising steadily since the currency reform. Credit repayment, however, brought no real curtailment in business liquidity. The active turn in the balance of payments, and especially the decline in import applications with their 50 per cent deposit requirement, counteracted the effects of credit restriction. The growth in the money supply was halted but not reversed. The latter no doubt would have been too much to expect. Nevertheless, the restraint exerted was sufficient to prevent a major increase in prices despite continually growing business activity.

The measures taken by the Bank deutscher Länder, like their predecessors during the 1948 boom, were unorthodox. They were direct controls of the kind that do not work through market forces as traditional central bank measures do. Monetary policy had become more powerful between 1948 and 1951, but it still had to rely on techniques considerably less than ideal.

By June 1951 the boom had on the whole run its course, and it was possible to add up the profit and loss. On the positive side Germany had experienced another great rise in output, had doubled her exports, and had come out of the emergency with a relatively small increase in prices and wages. Her domestic free market policy had weathered the crisis successfully. On the negative side Germany bore the scars of a critical balance of payments struggle. She had had to suspend liberalization and thus to undo some of the earlier progress toward rational and cooperative relations with the world economy. The ground lost here was not recovered until January 1952. On balance one may say that Germany had come through very well, with the fundamentals of her economy greatly strengthened and her liberal principles dented but not broken.

For this outcome monetary policy deserves its share of praise, although the score was not perfect. Credit restraint had helped to avoid serious inflation but had not quite succeeded in holding the line against the external deficit, as some observers thought it ought to have done. The Bank deutscher Länder argued that this would have required an unbearable tightening of credit that would have done much harm to production and employment. In this view one must, I believe, concur. The central bank cannot undertake to become the "restraint of last resort" in the way it is the lender of last resort. If it were to allow itself to become the residuary legatee of all the pressures and disequilibria that other agencies have failed to cope with, it would clearly endanger its existence as an independent institution. During the 1950–51 crisis, for instance, monetary policy not only failed to receive the support of an active fiscal policy but found its task made more difficult by the 1950 tax cut. It was in the nature of Germany's —and most other countries'—fiscal arrangements that desirable tax increases could not be made at short notice. The resulting extra pressure, however, could not be contained altogether by monetary policy acting alone.

On the other hand, the Bank deutscher Länder's action disavowed another group of observers who held that any monetary restraint was inappropriate under the circumstances. Their view was that the external deficit should be combatted by direct trade restrictions. They welcomed deliberalization, though in their opinion it came too late. This action having been taken, however, they felt that there was no further reason for severe credit restraint. The Bank deutscher Länder, by introducing a second series of restrictions, showed its disagreement with this view. In part the Bank deutscher Länder's motive appears to have been the desire to help create conditions that would permit a quick return to freer trade. More importantly, however, the direct controls that stopped the trade deficit were regarded not as a shield behind which credit expansion could go on with impunity but as an added inflationary threat (foreign supplies being reduced) which demanded counter measures.

Credit goes to monetary policy not only for what it did *during* the emergency but also for what it had done *before*. The "capacity reserve" which had been created through the much criticized earlier lack of open-handedness contributed a great deal to maintaining relative stability. That this concatenation of circumstances held an element of luck, and that nevertheless there was merit in the ability to exploit this luck, has already been remarked.

The Lull after the Korea Boom (*July 1951–June 1952*)

The Korea boom of 1950–51, like its predecessor of 1948, was followed by a period of relative stagnation. Output continued to rise, but no longer by leaps and bounds. The controversy over the relative merits of expansionist and restrictive monetary and fiscal policies flared up again, although less publicly than before. Again the conservative side won out. The episode ended when, about the middle of 1952, natural forces created a new upswing.

The period was, in the main, a reaction from the excesses of the Korea boom. Consumer goods output especially was affected, as consumers found leisure to repent of their hasty overstocking and dealers sought to reduce inventories. Capital goods output continued to do well on a rising tide of exports. Once more a process of consolidation set in. The bottlenecks in coal, steel, and power, which had been felt during the boom, were gradually broken. The balance of payments improved, through both a rising volume of exports and a strongly favorable trend in the terms of trade. Liberalization of imports from EPU countries was reintroduced in January 1952; this step in effect ended the emergency situation. Employment continued to mount, unemployment fell slightly. Factory and basic materials prices continued to rise moderately, and there was a further small gain in wage rates. The cost of living, nevertheless, began to decline. Bank credit and money supply continued to increase, stimulated by an active balance of payments and growing bank liquidity.

On the whole the picture was not unsatisfactory. The slow progress of production, however, and the still high level of unemployment once more gave rise to demands for more expansionary policies. In support it was pointed out that the uptrend was no longer being sustained by internal forces but

TABLE 13: *Economic*

Month	Industrial production 1936 = 100	Employment (millions)	Unemployment (% of labor force)	Basic materials prices 1950 = 100	Factory prices 1950 = 100	Cost of living 1950 = 100	Gross hourly wages 1950 = 100
1951							
July	131			119	118	108	
August	130			121	119	108	
September	137	14.9	7.7	121	119	109	118.0
October	144			123	120	111	
November	153			126	123	112	
December	140	14.6	10.2	127	123	112	
1952							
January	135			127	122	112	
February	135			125	122	111	120.5
March	138	14.6	9.8	125	121	111	
April	141			125	122	110	
May	142			127	121	109	122.3
June	145	15.2	7.6	127	121	109	

Sources: Bank deutscher Länder, *Monthly Reports; Wirtschaft und Statistik,*

seemed to depend mainly upon the active balance of payments. Any subsidence of world demand might lead to a depression.

Some observers held that to meet this danger and to exploit the growth possibilities inherent in the supply of idle labor an aggressive policy of expansion was urgently required. Any unfavorable repercussions upon the balance of payments were to be blocked through tight import controls, the direct channeling of resources into exports, raw-materials allocation, and the like. Internally, nonessential investment was to be prohibited and investment in bottleneck industries to be promoted by similarly direct measures.

These suggestions, which ran counter to the government's economic philosophy all along the line, found few followers. A more moderate expansionary approach, which had some backing with the government, dwelt mainly on the alleged

Indicators, July 1951–June 1952

Currency and demand deposits (billions of DM)	Time and savings deposits (billions of DM)	Bank loans (short and long term) (billions of DM)	Rediscounts (monthly average) (billions of DM)	Discount rate	Exports (millions of $)	Imports		Net foreign exchange reserves (millions of $)
						Total (millions of $)	Commercial (millions of $)	
19.7	9.6	21.9	4.3	6	321.3	283.4	243.6	158
20.4	9.8	22.5	4.2		314.6	287.5	251.8	253
20.6	9.9	23.3	4.6		324.9	375.2	336.8	307
21.1	10.2	25.0	4.3		301.3	281.6	264.2	346
21.9	10.3	24.7	4.2		278.9	301.9	291.3	365
22.5	10.7	25.6	4.8		377.6	327.6	315.9	363
21.6	11.4	25.5	4.8		313.5	333.0	324.0	408
21.7	11.8	27.1	4.4		304.3	347.7	339.2	458
21.9	12.1	27.6	4.5		329.0	347.0	341.1	509
21.9	12.4	27.7	3.9		312.1	304.4	297.8	575
22.1	12.8	28.1	3.4	5	336.0	279.0	275.7	669
22.6	12.8	28.2	3.5		329.0	266.4	257.0	802

various issues.

need to lift the restrictive monetary measures that had been carried over from the inflationary phase. Attention was drawn to the slowing of the price and wage rise, to the gradual removal of bottlenecks, the impressive recovery of savings, and the great improvement in the balance of payments. These factors, it was suggested, warranted a rapid lifting of the existing monetary restraints.

On the opposite side it was argued that balance of payments equilibrium was not yet firmly established; that until early 1952, at any rate, it rested upon deliberalization of imports; and that the closing of the import safety valve meant greater inflationary pressure at home. The view that the natural dynamics of the economy had spent themselves was rejected by these observers, particularly in view of the steady reduction in inventories, which suggested a resumption of activity in the near future. The sustained rise in bank credit and the money supply was also cited as evidence that continued caution was advisable. Finally, attention was drawn to the need for maintaining a reserve of productive capacity. The event most likely to make a call on this reserve appeared to be the creation of the European Defense Community, but for a vulnerable economy like Germany's a reserve would be advisable in any case.

The policies followed by the fiscal and monetary authorities hewed close to this latter line. On the fiscal side the tax brakes were applied through increases in the corporation and turnover tax and through removal of certain important income-tax deductions. On the side of monetary policy the brakes were kept firmly set for a while and then relaxed very slowly. The credit ceilings were the first to be eased, initially through flexible administration and then through complete lifting in October 1951. The 50 per cent deposit requirement for import applications was removed in September, mainly because the device had been found to distort the credit structure. Reserve requirements for the banks were first lowered in May 1952, and repeatedly thereafter. At the same time the discount rate was reduced from 6 per cent to 5 per cent, with further cuts following later on.

These measures to ease credit were compensated in part, however, by others that, in effect if not in purpose, tended to tighten it. One was the establishment of rediscount ceilings for individual banks (far above the prevailing level of rediscounts for most banks). A second was the extension in scope and hardening in content of the guiding rules issued sometime earlier. The immediate restrictive effect of these actions was probably minor; the limitations left most banks adequate scope for maneuver. Their main purpose was to create a weapon for future use. A strong restrictive effect, however, was exerted by the large-scale open market sales that the Bank deutscher Länder initiated in the fall of 1951. The Bank's chief purpose seems to have been to divest itself of various securities that it had acquired through the work-creation program and other expansionary operations of 1949–50 and that it considered unsuited to its portfolio. The open market impact of these operations seems to have been regarded as secondary. The effect, however, was to reduce bank reserves by approximately 1.1 billion DMark between July 1951 and June 1952. This offset, although only in part, the liquidity-generating influence of the balance of payments surplus. In consequence the fall in rediscounts from 4.3 billion in July 1951 to 3.5 billion in June 1952 was much smaller than it would otherwise have been.

The cautious policy of the authorities was vindicated by events, insofar as it rested upon an optimistic appraisal of the buoyancy of the German economy. Despite the absence of major stimulating measures, business turned up in the second half of 1952. Main reasons were the revival of consumer goods production after stocks had been worked off and the steady uptrend in exports. In other respects, however, the policy makers' luck did not quite hold. The European Defense Community was stalled, and the boost that arms production would have

supplied failed to materialize. Since nothing immediate occurred to make a call upon the capacity reserve, some productive factors remained idle. Meanwhile fears that the balance of
payments might turn against Germany, which had contributed
to the policy of caution, were proved superfluous by the
steadily increasing external surplus. One must conclude that
the insurance premium which Germany paid during this
period by not extracting a little more output from her economy turned out to be on the high side. At the time the policies
were formulated, however, this could hardly have been foreseen.

*Equilibrium and Export Boom (July 1952–December
1954)*

The upward trend that was resumed in the second half of
1952 carried through, with minor interruptions, to the end of
1954. Production continued to advance, often running as
much as 10 per cent ahead of year-ago levels. Unemployment
shrank with seasonal fluctuations until in the fall of 1954 a
low of 4.7 per cent of the labor force (excluding self-employed)
was reached. Exports continued to mount, and a strong balance of payments surplus was the rule. Reserves of gold and
foreign exchange advanced to reach 2,606.1 million dollars
at the end of 1954. Interest rates tended downward, thanks in
part to the liquidity generated by the balance of payments
surplus. Public budgets showed substantial surpluses despite
previous tax cuts. Toward the end of 1954 the upward movement was beginning to show many of the earmarks of a very
powerful boom and gave rise to fears of price increases. Wage
increases, however, remained small until the summer of 1954.

The renewed expansion could be traced to various factors,
but the most outstanding undoubtedly was the rise in exports.
Monthly exports averaged throughout most of the period 20
per cent above the levels of the preceding year. This performance was all the more remarkable because much of it oc-

curred in the face of an American recession. It was aided, no doubt, by relatively stable wages and growing productivity. A further stimulus to exports may have been the limitation of the domestic market, relative to growing productive capacity, a situation which traditionally has spurred German industry to intensify its efforts in foreign markets.

Since imports failed to keep up with exports, the balance of payments surplus was high most of the time. The sluggishness of imports was in part the result of declining raw-material prices (in constant prices imports advanced almost as much as exports), but other and more complex factors also played a role. Important among these was the budget surplus, unintended but seemingly unavoidable, which to some extent neutralized the effects of the active balance of payments. Without this, the rise in exports and the attendant gain in liquidity would probably have produced more of an expansion.

Though exports were dominant, investment also had a share in promoting activity. This was particularly true beginning with the second half of 1953, when gross investment rose 14 per cent above a year earlier. The greater ease of financing as well as the optimism generated in the export industries, which are among the leaders of industrial opinion, materially improved the investment climate.

In this generally bright situation enough soft spots nevertheless appeared from time to time to give some observers pause. Toward the end of 1953 such doubts led to a further round in the debate over the possible need for expansionary measures. At one extreme some labor circles propounded the doctrine of an expansionary wage policy. The unions were urged to strike for what they could get; this would give a fillip to purchasing power; the rise in costs would compel business to speed up modernization, and this in turn would prevent higher wages from being translated into higher prices. Less drastic was the middle-of-the-road suggestion for a boost to purchasing power through more consumer credit and tax re-

TABLE 14: *Economic Indicators,*

Month	Industrial production 1936=100	Employment (millions)	Unemployment (% of labor force)	Basic materials prices 1950=100	Factory prices 1950=100	Cost of living 1950=100	Gross hourly wages 1950=100
1952							
July	138			127	121	109	
August	141			129	121	109	123.0
September	154	15.5	6.4	129	122	109	
October	160			127	121	109	
November	168			125	121	110	125.0
December	154	15.0	10.1	125	121	110	
1953							
January	142			124	120	110	
February	143			124	120	109	200.6
March	153	15.2	8.4	123	120	109	
April	158			122	119	109	
May	158			122	119	108	126.0
June	159	15.8	6.4	122	118	108	
July	154			122	118	108	
August	156			120	117	108	128.6
September	169	16.0	5.5	120	117	107	
October	173			120	117	107	
November	180			120	116	107	129.4
December	170	15.6	8.9	120	116	107	
1954							
January	155			121	116	107	
February	159			121	116	108	129.0
March	165	15.8	8.3	121	116	108	
April	172			121	116	108	
May	178			121	116	108	129.7
June	178	16.5	5.8	123	116	108	
July	172			123	116	108	
August	173			122	116	108	131.0
September	188	16.8	4.7	122	116	108	
October	193			123	117	109	
November	202			123	117	110	n.a.
December	194	16.5	7.2	123	117	110	

Sources: Bank deutscher Länder, *Monthly Reports; Wirtschaft und Statistik,*

July 1952–December 1954

Currency and demand deposits (billions of DM)	Time and savings deposits (billions of DM)	Bank loans (short and long term) (billions of DM)	Redis-counts (monthly average) (billions of DM)	Discount rate	Exports (millions of $)	Imports		Net foreign exchange reserves (millions of $)
						Total (millions of $)	Commercial (millions of $)	
22.7	12.9	29.3	3.1	5	355.6	294.7	280.8	898.4
23.2	13.2	30.0	3.0		322.0	283.7	274.1	942.1
24.0	13.6	30.9	3.1	4½	340.4	301.3	286.5	1,013.2
24.0	14.0	31.9	2.7		348.9	355.9	343.6	1,056.1
24.3	14.4	32.5	2.8		327.9	335.6	326.6	1,062.3
25.2	14.9	33.7	3.9		418.3	403.2	393.6	1,094.9
24.5	15.9	33.9	3.1	4	301.7	322.1	317.1	1,143.8
24.8	16.3	34.6	3.0		294.1	279.8	276.1	1,207.5
24.9	16.6	34.6	2.8		352.7	304.1	300.7	1,236.7
25.1	17.2	35.0	2.4		364.5	297.9	292.0	1,299.6
25.4	17.7	35.7	2.3		340.9	294.2	289.7	1,367.1
25.8	18.0	36.4	2.5	3½	372.1	319.3	313.0	1,438.9
25.9	18.7	37.7	2.1		373.9	305.5	300.0	1,550.2
26.5	19.1	38.6	2.3		358.0	295.8	292.2	1,639.5
26.9	19.3	39.7	2.5		360.1	323.3	319.3	1,685.1
26.9	19.6	40.2	2.2		411.3	340.6	336.0	1,755.0
27.6	19.8	41.0	2.3		392.6	350.8	343.0	1,828.4
29.2	20.6	42.0	3.2		499.8	376.1	367.1	1,928.8
28.8	21.7	42.8	2.1		359.1	312.5	302.0	2,006.8
29.1	22.3	43.7	2.2		360.2	288.7	280.9	2,070.2
29.5	23.0	44.5	2.4		461.5	377.3	363.9	2,151.9
29.7	23.1	45.0	1.9		396.6	350.1	341.3	2,203.9
30.0	23.3	45.6	2.0		435.3	370.7	364.4	2,231.7
30.4	23.4	46.4	2.4	3	407.5	370.9	368.3	2,267.6
30.5	23.7	47.1	1.9		459.6	374.3	369.6	2,356.5
30.6	24.0	47.7	1.7		439.0	361.3	357.8	2,440.0
31.7	24.3	49.3	1.8		439.4	407.9	404.0	2,477.7
31.6	24.8	50.2	1.7		472.9	439.7	435.3	2,498.2
32.4	24.9	51.1	1.8		483.1	463.1	460.4	2,526.8
33.9	n.a.	53.3	3.2		549.3	484.5	481.9	2,606.1

various issues.

ductions. A major tax cut was being planned for the beginning of 1955. By advancing the date, it was argued, the reduction could be made to serve the purposes of a flexible fiscal
policy. A moderately expansionary policy along these lines
appeared to be favored by many in responsible positions.

In any event little was done, and little if anything turned
out to be needed. The Bank deutscher Länder, reacting to the
downward tendency of interest rates in the money market,
had for some time been helping to ease credit by bringing
down its discount rate. By small steps the rate was lowered
from 6 per cent in May 1952 to an almost unprecedented 3
per cent in May 1954. By this action the Bank contributed also
to the downward movement of long-term rates, which began
to make itself felt in 1954. At the same time, however, the
Bank continued its open market sales on a small scale, reducing
its securities portfolio to 116 million DMark on March 31,
1954. These sales, as pointed out before, were intended to
divest the Bank of securities that it regarded as unsuited to
its portfolio. They exerted a contractive effect upon the market, but because of the small amounts involved the effect was
very minor.

On the fiscal side a mild stimulus had been applied to the
economy late in 1952 through a salary increase for public
servants and raises for pensioners. Another boost was given
early in 1953 through the "little tax reform," which cut income-tax rates by as much as 15 per cent. Thereafter the influence of government finances was largely on the restrictive
side. During 1953 the federal and state governments accumulated a cash surplus of 2.3 billion DMark. Some 0.6 billion of
this was the result of loans floated in advance of need. Though
not technically a surplus, such accumulations in the presence
of a large unsatisfied demand on the part of other borrowers
were bound to have a restrictive effect almost as strong as a
surplus arising from taxation. The rest of the cash accumulation corresponded in amount, though not in all other respects,

to the unspent funds of the occupation authorities. Owing to delays in their investment program the occupation authorities had allowed their calls on occupation-cost funds to drop below the scheduled rate of 7.2 billion DMark per year. Since the difference was payable on demand, the Finance Ministry felt compelled to carry a corresponding balance. If the Allies had been able to foresee when they would need the money, or if the German fiscal machinery had been more flexible, the accumulation of these balances and the resulting deflationary effects might have been avoided. As it was, there seemed to be no other solution than to let the money remain idle in the Bank deutscher Länder. The consequent curtailment of expenditures and the reduction in money supply and bank reserves were the main deflationary factors of this period.

Meanwhile debate continued about the pending proposals for tax reform and reduction. Efforts to advance their effective date substantially for the purpose of stimulating economic activity diminished as the gathering momentum of the economy reduced the need for such a boost. It is quite conceivable that the prospect of tax relief alone had some of the desired effect. The reform finally became reality in December 1954.

It is perhaps an exaggeration to compare the debate over the need for expansionary measures in 1953–54 with the more intensive discussions of 1949–50 and 1951. This third round was distinctly muted and not accompanied by any great sense of urgency. But it is interesting because it falls so completely into the pattern set by its predecessors. As before, those responsible for policy rejected most of the expansionary advice. They remained confident that the economy would continue to advance without special action, and they were proved right as before. Toward the end of 1954, in fact, when the expectation of rearmament began to add fuel to the boom, it plainly proved fortunate that no strong expansionary measures had been taken earlier. The problem was once more becoming one of how to restrain a boom. But with the situation of a year

before in mind, there remained perhaps a trace of doubt—
not altogether absent in the earlier cases either—whether the
renewal of momentum was due to the inherent qualities of the
German economy or whether it was a stroke of luck that had
once more kept the boom from slowing down.

Evaluation

The preceding sections have presented the record of German
monetary and fiscal policy. The time has now come for an
attempt at evaluation.

Achievements. The West German recovery from defeat, destruction, and chaos has been one of the most impressive performances of the postwar scene. To some it has seemed little
less than a miracle. What strikes the casual observer most
forcibly is probably the increase in activity and living standards, i.e., the internal improvement, particularly if he knew
Germany before the currency reform. Great as this improvement has been, it is not the outstanding part of the German
performance. Compared with the productive gains achieved
by other European countries, German income and production
do not rank particularly high, although the annual growth
rate has been exceptional. On a per capita basis income is only
slightly ahead of 1938. This performance is very satisfactory,
considering the burden of partition, destruction, dismantling,
forced coal exports, and refugees. For a country that lost one
of the most destructive wars in history, merely a return to prewar levels would be a remarkable feat. But the German production achievement, during the recovery phase at least, could
be explained by the fact that despite all that had happened
the German economy was still a very powerful machine. Its
postwar capacity, after relatively minor repairs, was still approximately that of 1938. When food, fuel, and raw materials
were fed into the machine it started up and began to produce
again.

What does seem almost miraculous is the balance of payments recovery. For most European countries the experience has been that it is easy to increase production but hard to increase exports. This is why the dollar gap, open or concealed, has been so hard to overcome. For Germany the road to external viability seemed virtually blocked by the consequences of partition, loss of eastern markets, complete stoppage of overseas trade for nearly a decade, and the competitive head start enjoyed by other European countries. Today, nevertheless, Germany can look back upon four years of balance of payments surpluses; she owns in the middle of 1955 nearly 3 billion dollars of exchange reserves, is servicing her foreign debt, and is closer to convertibility than any other country in Europe except Switzerland and Belgium. If there has been a German miracle, this surely is it.

Monetary policies. The superior balance of payments achievement reflects the basic principle of German monetary policy during recent years: priority of external considerations over domestic, of the balance of payments over income and employment. This policy was imposed by the near desperate problem facing a country living on foreign aid, with a greatly increased population and practically no exports. The rebuilding of foreign trade was without doubt priority number one. Balance of payments priority was in accord also with two basic convictions: faith in a free economy and in the importance of a stable currency. These convictions implied a rejection of policies designed to push output and employment at the cost of rising prices or controls. We shall presently revert to the experiences and the philosophy that helped to form these convictions.

The description of the goals and principles of German monetary policy suggests a severely restrictive policy. Indeed this characterization has often been applied, both by critics and by the policy makers themselves. The facts presented above bear out the contention only in part. If we go back to

the two inflationary periods (the postcurrency-reform boom
and the Korea boom), we find that monetary restraint was
fairly moderate in intention as well as in outcome. In intention moderation was shown through flexible handling of
credit ceilings and related measures, and through the exemption of various types of credit from the restrictions. In outcome policy was moderate because, even where it was meant
to hurt, its tools did not bite very deep. This was particularly
true during the currency-reform boom.

It will be recalled that even at the times of maximum restraint the expansion of short-term credit was never reversed.
It was halted only once, for a brief period during the Korea
boom. The volume of money expanded uninterruptedly,
through thick and thin, during restraint and through ease.
If we did not know from other facts that monetary policy had
been orthodox, the rise in the money supply from 12.3 billion
in September 1948 to 25.9 billion in July 1953 would scarcely
lead us to believe it. Monetary policy contributed importantly
to halting the price increases and the external deficits of these
boom periods. The main factors that produced the turn in
each case, however, as our detailed analysis has shown, were
others.

During slack periods the monetary authorities were slow
to take off restrictions put on during the preceding boom.
They were also slow (or refused altogether) to accede to demands for positive expansionary financing. In this sense their
policy was restrictive, and it was over this issue that debate
was liveliest. They banked on the strength of the production
incentives in the German economy and allowed them to become effective by making credit available with moderation.
But the state of the economy at which they aimed was always
one of buyers' not sellers' markets.

It is tempting to speculate what would have been the results if the Bank deutscher Länder had accepted the recommendations of its critics and had conducted an expansionary

policy during the two slack periods. Very probably Germany
would not have gone as far internationally as she did. Whether
domestically she would be further along seems an open question. In the short run, given idle resources, it is normally possible to increase output somewhat by pumping money into
the economy. Very probably this would have been true also of
Germany. In the long run it may be a question of technique,
of national temperament, and of luck whether the familiar
evils of an overfull-employment economy can be overcome
through the forced draft generated by such a system. Many
observers who might believe in the technical possibilities of a
forced draft economy in Germany would nevertheless object to
it on political grounds.

Fiscal policy. Throughout the present chapter the discussion
of fiscal affairs has been confined to certain limited aspects.
We have not dealt with public expenditures, whose high
investment content will later be seen to have greatly aided
the revival (Chapter 6). Neither have we been concerned with
the tax structure and its powerful effects in building incentives
and channeling private investment (Chapter 5). Our interest
has focused on the management of the budget as an instrument of economic and financial stabilization.

In this respect fiscal policy has played a very basic but not a
very flexible role. Strong finances have provided the foundation for a sound currency. The fiscal authorities have fully
shared the belief of the central bank that the goal of sound
money must have top priority. They have solidly backed up
the Bank deutscher Länder against pressures and temptations.
Balanced budgets have been a pillar of strength for the DMark.

Relatively little attention was paid by the authorities, in
formulating the fiscal policies discussed in this chapter, to
the potentialities of fiscal policy for controlling economic
fluctuations. Any fiscal policy action—changes in tax rates or
in expenditures leading to a budget surplus or deficit—has its

effect upon the level of business, whether the finance minister intends it or not. Several of the tax measures taken since 1948 had, as we have seen, quite pronounced cyclical effects. In several cases the effect was unfortunate—the tax cut of 1950 aggravated the Korea boom, the increase of 1951 contributed to the subsequent lull.

To some extent this was due to the difficulty of proper timing inherent in all fiscal policy. Tax rates have to be set ahead of time and cannot be adjusted flexibly to conditions as they develop. More importantly, however, it reflected the philosophy of the Finance Ministry, whose views on tax changes and the resulting deficit or surplus differ significantly from those prevailing in the United States. According to the Finance Ministry's view the important effect of a deficit-creating tax cut is not the increase in purchasing power of consumers, as one would say in the United States. It is the greater incentive given to producers who now can keep a larger fraction of their income. The deficit is viewed more as an unfortunate by-product, a temporary violation of the principle of a balanced budget, soon to be made good through rising revenues from a higher national income. The repeated cuts in personal and corporate income taxes have been intended in this sense. The apparent lack of interest in the expansionary effect of the deficit as such, so hard to understand for American economists, has in practice been in some measure justified by the rapidity with which rising revenues did wipe out occasional deficits.

The reasons for this rejection of a flexible fiscal policy are several. First, there is the genuine dislike of deficits, based upon fear of the inflationary dangers of large-scale deficit financing and coupled with a firm belief, bolstered by experience, in the incentive effects of lower taxation. Second, there has been until quite recently the real difficulty of financing a substantial deficit. Third, there are the constitutional and statutory provisions that confine deficit financing to "productive" purposes. The meaning of this term seems to be sufficiently broad so as not to interfere seriously with financial flexibility when it is really desired. Some restraint on the public discussion of deficit possibilities seems to be imposed by these provisions, however. This also serves the purpose of keeping in bounds the sometimes alarming spending propensities of the legislature.

In summary, fiscal policy has supported the major goals of monetary policy by pursuing a generally conservative line. It has not operated on an anticyclical basis, however, and in that sense has sometimes been at cross-purposes with the short-run aims of monetary policy.

Background of experience. The evaluation of German monetary and fiscal policy has made clear that they rest upon firmly held convictions. A full appreciation of the policies requires some understanding of how these convictions came to be formed. Germany has experienced what is probably the greatest variety of economic misfortunes among Western countries. Like the United States it has the memory of the great depression and its mass unemployment. In addition it has twice gone through a total collapse of the currency attended by destruction of savings and social upheaval. Finally, it has had a full-dress experience in peacetime of an overexpanded economy with planning and thoroughgoing controls.

Germany has been burned so often that it has cause to be shy many times over. The unemployment during the great depression left its scars mainly upon labor, making it relatively receptive to full-employment policies. The fear of inflation, however, is universal, although it naturally touches the middle class most acutely. An allergy to controls affects all classes of society—controls are tainted with the memory of dictatorship on the one side and of postwar chaos, corruption, and starvation on the other.

The ultimate lesson drawn from all this by those responsible for making fiscal and monetary policy is a rejection of full-employment policies. They carry the threat of inflation and controls and thus touch the two most sensitive spots in German economic experience. It is only fair to say that this conclusion is not shared by the leadership of the Social Democratic party. They continue to adhere to full-employment policies like those of the British Labor party, but they would probably pursue them much more moderately. Their statements, however, sound academic and uncertain. At the time of the 1953 elections it was clear that a great majority of the population was backing the government's policies.

The intensity of German monetary experience has produced not opinions but uncompromising convictions. Principles rule and are not easily dented by short-run expediency. There has been little inclination to sacrifice the long run to the short, or to buy an increase in the production index with a rise in the price index. The currency has not been treated as though it were capable of taking indefinite punishment; stable money, like democracy, has been accorded its price of eternal vigilance. Putting currency stability ahead of full employment has sometimes been regarded as a harsh policy. It is harsh in the sense that all German policy since the war has been harsh. Germany has experienced—as well as caused—a great deal of suffering. The policy makers have been willing to accept hardships for the sake of long-run progress. The harshness has been softened, however, by the broad social security system and by the effort to inject an element of social consciousness into the market economy—the Soziale Marktwirtschaft to which we now turn.

CHAPTER 5

The Free Market Policy

GERMANY'S ADOPTION of a policy of free markets and free enterprise is probably the most widely discussed of her postwar measures. It does not imply an economy altogether free from government intervention or monopoly; on the contrary there still exists a good deal of state control and market restriction in Germany. But it does represent a sharp change of direction, and there is ample justification for regarding freedom as the keynote of German economic policy. That Germany with an experience of full-scale peacetime planning unique among Western nations should have chosen this road is not without wider significance.

The free market policy has a variety of aspects: the theory upon which it rests, its application in the lifting of controls and the creation of incentives, the still unresolved struggle over cartels, and the seeming incongruity of the government's continuing large role in the nation's economic life. Their review will bring us face to face with some of the most controversial topics of contemporary Germany.

The Doctrine

When a country has been through the tremendous experience that Germany underwent, one would not be surprised to find her people engaged in some fairly basic stock-taking. When that country has to rebuild its existence virtually from scratch a variety of new and radical suggestions has to be expected. One of the curious and to some extent discouraging facts about postwar Germany is how little of this basic think-

ing seems to have been going on. The theory here discussed
is an all too rare effort to come to grips with the causes of
Germany's terrible career of the last twenty years and to point
the road to a different future.

In the grim climate of the Nazi period and throughout the
war a small group of thinkers developed the doctrine of what
later was known as the Soziale Marktwirtschaft, the socially
conscious free market economy, that has had considerable influence upon Germany since 1948. The movement centered
upon the University of Freiburg but received support from
other scholars inside and outside Germany. Its chief figure
was Walter Eucken, whose untimely death in 1950 unfortunately deprived the school of much of its vigor. Some important aspects of the doctrine thus remained unresolved and
exposed to easy criticism.[1]

During the Nazi period the school represented a kind of
intellectual resistance movement, requiring great personal
courage as well as independence of mind. The free market
doctrine protested against the dominant conditions of the
times. It sought to construct an ideal system that would em-
body the opposites of these conditions and guard against re-
lapses. The most oppressive condition was totalitarianism.
Freedom therefore is the prime tenet of the doctrine, and its
program is designed to safeguard freedom. Planning and controls were a second major aspect of the contemporary scene.
The free market doctrine rejects all planning and controls except those needed to insure competition. A third important
fact of German economic life was thorough cartelization of
industry. The free market doctrine opposes all restraints upon
competition.

The instrument with which the Freiburg school seeks to
overcome dictatorship, state controls, and private monopoly
is the free competitive market. In an economy built on free
markets there is no occasion for excessive public or private
power. The prevention of public and private concentration of

power, through avoidance of government planning and private monopoly, is the best insurance against loss of political freedom. Planning and monopoly are evil also because they are the enemies of economic efficiency. Planning is inefficient because correct planning is a technical impossibility, and because it runs counter to ordinary human incentives. Monopoly is inefficient because it distorts the structure of prices and the allocation of resources. Thus the free, competitive market becomes the main answer to all our problems. Any compromise with this principle, in the form of government intervention or monopoly, is bound to become cumulative and to lead ultimately to a totally planned dictatorship.

One cannot help feeling that the free market doctrine in its more extreme formulations draws a comparison between an abstract system on one side and harsh reality on the other, in which the abstract system is bound to come off a little too well. The free market doctrine thereby reverses the process which gave rise to socialist utopias a century ago. Faced with a reality very close to socialism, it creates for itself, in the good sense of the word, a capitalist utopia.

The world that the Freiburg school painted was not the world of old-fashioned liberalism with its ideal of laissez faire. The school specifically rejects the optimistic assumption that freedom of enterprise assures competition and stability. History has shown that laissez faire is likely to lead to monopolistic practices and that a free system is exposed to cyclical fluctuations. The government must therefore take measures to prevent the formation of monopolies and to insure competition, and must moreover create a framework of anticyclical measures to maintain stability. These stabilizing measures must be as automatic as possible to avoid arbitrary intervention. Major inequalities of income, if they arise despite competition, should be moderated by means of a progressive income tax, which, however, must be mild enough not to interfere with incentives.

There is an obvious resemblance between the free market doctrine and the views of a group of writers in the United States sometimes described as the Chicago school.[2] The writers of the Chicago school, too, have sought to show that the best economic system would be one of universal free competition and nonintervention, operating within a framework of "built-in stabilizers." There is a considerable difference between the two schools, however, in the degree to which the various parts of the doctrine are elaborated. The Germans have spent a great deal of effort in proving that competition leads to an orderly price system and to a desirable allocation of resources. This was necessary because in the prevailing climate of German opinion a considerable section of economic theorists and practitioners alike tended to regard competition as something leading to chaos and bankruptcy and generally as a lower form of economic life. The task of translating the doctrine into a concrete program has lagged in Germany.

The question of how to enforce competition, for instance, is treated only briefly in the free market literature. An interesting argument is put forward to refute the widely held view that competition tends to decline as the economy grows older. The familiar difficulties of unregulated competition in declining-cost industries, however—railroads, utilities, and probably others—receive little attention. The delicate question whether labor unions have a place in a free market economy is not raised. In the United States problems like these have led to the conclusion that universal competition is virtually impossible.

The built-in stabilizers whose automatic functioning would forestall depressions likewise have not been considered realistically. It is merely asserted that it must be possible to construct them. In the United States the Chicago school and others have put much thought and effort into this task. The results have shown, to my mind, that a system that would work satisfactorily under realistic conditions is not likely to be found.

The prospects for economic growth in a free market economy have also received only scant consideration. Intensive competition, one may assume, would aid growth through cost-cutting inventions and the efficient use of savings. The volume of such savings, however, would probably be affected adversely if a socially fair distribution of income could really be attained. Capital formation by the government would of course be ruled out, except for roads and other nonrevenue-producing investments. It is quite likely, therefore, that an economy in which the government forms capital by taxing the people heavily and investing the proceeds might show a higher rate of growth. Even though capital formation by government might be less efficient than capital formation by private enterprise, the sheer bulk of this investment might allow the less efficient economy to grow faster than the other. For Germany, where living standards are below the rest of Western Europe, this would be a serious matter. Adherence to a system that is slow in accumulating new equipment, however efficient it might be in its use, would mean to freeze the country at a low level. In practice Gemany has disregarded the advice of the Freiburg school in this respect.

Finally, there remains the question of how much social justice a free and competitive economy would really produce. This problem is considered in great detail by the Freiburg school but not, it would seem, very conclusively. It may be taken for granted that in a competitive economy the distribution of income will be more even than under monopoly. One might take the view that this competitive distribution is "socially just," in the sense that everyone gets as much as his contribution is worth. But most adherents of the German school do not argue that. They seem to feel that a "just" distribution might differ considerably from what the market dictates. To correct this they suggest redistribution of income via a progressive tax system. At the same time, however, they tend to argue that the rate of progression must not be so steep as to hamper initiative and distort markets. There is little reason to believe that a tax moderate enough not to be harmful would be sufficiently productive to allow a major correction in the distribution of income.

There is no need to dwell longer on the details of the free market doctrine. When one is in basic agreement about the direction in which to move, it is awkward to find oneself engaged in argument as to the road to be traveled or how far to proceed along it. The questions I have felt compelled to raise about the doctrine relate not to the basic belief in a free competitive society but to the rather extreme conclusions and demands which emanate from the doctrine. This liberal radicalism seems to derive from the assumption that there are only two lasting possibilities: freedom under universal competition and totalitarian planning. Any compromise solution that admits some degree of government intervention is regarded as unstable and in danger of sliding into full planning. The doctrine thus seems to reject moderate adherents.

There seems to be no need to pursue the principles of freedom to such extreme conclusions. The contention that limited government intervention is bound to become unlimited fails to distinguish two quite separate situations. One of them is the case of steadily growing inflationary pressure characteristic of a war economy. It is from this experience that the contention largely derives. Here indeed history and logic suggest that controls, at first moderate and limited, will be pushed further and further unless the inflationary pressure abates. Quite distinct from this short-run situation is the long-run emergence of various kinds of government intervention, from protective tariffs and child labor legislation to agricultural price supports and foreign exchange restrictions. Whether this is a trend toward more and more government control is a matter of opinion. Certainly it is a slow-motion process that can be, and at present is being, reversed. Along the wide scale running from less to more government control, any point represents a compromise between freedom and control. None of these positions need be unstable and in greater danger of sliding into total planning than any other.

Compromise positions, therefore, seem perfectly acceptable. The members of the Freiburg school, in rejecting the middle way, pass a judgment on the common sense and political aptitude of their compatriots that is less than complimentary. For policy purposes the possibility of compromise is the essential point. In practice we are not likely to get universal competition nor complete freedom from government intervention. If nothing short of that could do, the outlook would be black. There is no reason to take this view.

Germany has in effect carried out the teachings of the free market doctrine only in limited respects. Its experience shows that the compromise solution so far adopted can be highly effective. This experience in the practice of Soziale Marktwirtschaft we shall now consider.

The Freeing of Markets

Controlled chaos. The West German economy from the end of the war to the currency reform was a caricature of a planned economy. Controls were universal and so was evasion. To live on legally procured food was almost impossible for city dwellers. To do business without going into gray or black markets would have meant a quick end for most enterprises. The result was the chaotic situation described in the preceding chapter.

The controls were only in part fashioned by the occupying powers. To a large extent it had been necessary to take over those previously existing in order to cope with the immensity of the job. Thus the price ceiling (*Preisstop*) of 1936 and the trading ordinance (*Warenverkehrsordnung*) of 1942, amplified by a series of state laws, remained the source of most administrative wisdom.[3] Only at the beginning of 1948 was some order brought into the situation by means of a unifying ordinance which, however, left the old underlying legislation temporarily in force. It is not surprising that this array of controls, and particularly the price ceiling of 1936 which had been preserved more rigidly than wartime price ceilings in the United States, was frequently out of touch with reality. To administrate such a system efficiently under the conditions of the times would have taxed the powers of a host of angels, let alone those of army officers and temporary government employees.

The debate over decontrol. No major changes in the controls system were practicable prior to the currency reform. A removal of price ceilings would no doubt have brought the German economy back to life very rapidly. Prices would have shot up, probably anything from five to ten times or more, black markets would have disappeared, and the economy would have begun to function again. A currency reform would have become superfluous. But this experiment found few supporters because of its uncertain impact on wages and prices and on the distribution of income and wealth, and because of the danger of a continuing inflationary spiral.

With the approach of the currency reform, however, a decision had to be made whether or not to continue the controls beyond the reform. A continuation of tight controls was strongly demanded by labor and hence by the Social Democratic opposition in the Bizonal Economic Council. Their view was supported by the British and also by what was probably a majority of the American occupation authorities. Professional opinion among economists, it is probably fair to say, leaned very predominantly in the same direction. Decontrol, it was felt by these observers, would endanger the success of the currency reform by permitting unforeseeable price movements at a psychologically critical moment. A price-wage spiral might result and might lead to open inflation. The net effect of decontrol would be to increase the inequality of incomes. Although many agreed that decontrol should be accomplished as soon as possible, further progress toward recovery was thought necessary before ceilings and rationing could safely be removed. There were others who regarded permanent control as desirable, because they questioned the capacity of the market mechanism to achieve the long-run adjustments that the German economy would have to make.

A rapid loosening of controls was urged, of course, by the industries whose interests were affected. The consuming public hated rationing but was fearful of price increases. Among technicians and politicians decontrol seems to have been favored only by a small group, whose center was Director (later Minister) of Economics Erhard. While Erhard's views seem to have found little sympathy among his administrative staff, they were vigorously supported by his Advisory Council of academic economists. This group, on which the Freiburg school was strongly represented, rendered a report in April 1948, two months before the currency reform, in which it recommended far-reaching decontrol after the reform.[4] A minority of the council submitted a dissenting report. It required great courage on the part of Erhard to shoulder the responsibility for decontrol in the face of so much opposition and skepticism.

The case made for decontrol reflected partly a lack of confidence in the technical feasibility of effective control and partly a positive belief in the superiority of free markets. The existing price ceiling, based on 1936, was obviously untenable given the cost situation created by wartime destruction, partition, dismantling, the rise in world market prices, and generally low labor productivity. While provisions had been made prior to currency reform for the adjustment of price ceilings, the execution of such adjustments was bound to be immensely

difficult. The association of controls with the Hitler regime
and with the postwar period of utter prostration had made
all such devices extremely unpopular. The spread of gray and
black markets, finally, had visibly so undermined the morale
of business, consumers, and even of the German bureaucracy
that effective administration of controls became doubtful. On
the positive side there was the belief—held with utter conviction by Erhard but probably shared only in part by most of
his colleagues—that decontrol would bring an outpouring
of productive energies which would accomplish infinitely
more than could the best designed and administered controls.

The currency reform and other events accompanying the
freeing of prices, and the extraordinary transformation which
these actions brought to the German economy, have been
described in the preceding chapter. The success of decontrol
may fairly be regarded as a major piece of evidence in favor
of the Marktwirtschaft doctrine. Nevertheless, some restraint
is needed in appraising the achievement. The impression has
sometimes been conveyed that the German policy consisted
of the uniform application of a simple principle. This was by
no means the case. The lifting of controls was a bold step but
not a blind one. It was limited to sectors of the economy where
incentives were likely to have the greatest effect, where instability of prices could do relatively little damage, and where
controls would have been hardest to administrate. It centered
therefore upon manufactured consumer goods. Clothing and
shoes, though they remained rationed, were freed from price
control, and the rationing was desultory. Most other manufactured goods of daily use were completely free. Wages were
freed three months after the currency reform. Subject to continued control were most basic foodstuffs and agricultural
products; basic materials like iron, steel, coal, and oil and some
nonferrous metals; utilities and transportation, rents and
many services. While a substantial part of the consumers'
"market basket" thus remained under controls, many of these

were administrated perfunctorily and soon allowed to die away, stimulating a general sense of derationing euphoria. In addition controls were retained over all international transactions, though many imported goods were freed from domestic price ceilings. The securities market also remained under administrative control. In other words a great step had been taken toward a free economy, but the ideals of a free market economy were still far from full realization.

It has been suggested that with more complete decontrol the recovery would have moved faster. From this point of view the selectiveness of the action was interpreted not as wise balance but simply as excessive caution and weak policy. It has also been suggested that the selection of areas to be decontrolled reflected not a rational weighing of the pros and cons but simply the range of power of Minister Erhard. As far as his influence reached, according to this view, he lifted controls; beyond it they stayed on.

Both views probably contain an element of truth, but only a limited one. It is probably true that a freeing of steel (Allied ceilings permitting), coal, and agricultural products, for instance, would have led to a more rapid rise in their production, and that a removal or easing of rent controls would have stimulated the construction of dwellings. In the light of subsequent developments, however, one may wonder whether in that case the upward pressure upon prices would not have become too great. As it was, prices rose, but basic stability was maintained because labor did not press strongly for wage increases. This restraint would have been almost impossible if food prices and rents had not been kept down. An all-round rise in living costs would probably have resulted in a price-wage spiral or in the reimposition of price controls. Either development would almost certainly have slowed down the recovery. All in all, therefore, the policy of selective decontrol seems to have achieved a fairly good balance between boldness and caution. The German experience demonstrates the effectiveness of free markets, but it does not speak against the use of controls where pressures are powerful.

The maintenance of controls in certain sectors, important though it was for stability, has of course exacted its price. The low ceilings for coal, iron, and steel have made it difficult for these industries to finance capital expenditures. Financing out of retained profits, the method practiced with such success by most of German industry, was not productive because low prices kept profits down. Access to the very limited capital market was handicapped by the same element of low profitability, apart from the uncertainties created by Allied deconcentration measures. Counterpart and Investment Assistance funds were made available with relative generosity but could not fill the tremendous needs. That coal and steel remained among the worst bottlenecks of the recovery was in part due to the maintenance of controls, although the slow-maturing character of investment in these industries was a contributing cause.

The tight control of rents has had the usual result of discouraging landlords from making repairs. More important, it has compelled the government to subsidize new housing heavily. The capital market had to be placed in a strait jacket in order to make mortgage money available at 5 per cent, the maximum that the rent level could stand. The volume of construction has been so high that it would be unfair to blame rent control for the failure of housing to catch up with demand. Nevertheless the very satisfactory performance of the building industry could probably still have been exceeded if rent ceilings had been relaxed.

The control of the capital market, through the fixing of a 5 per cent rate where 8 per cent would have been closer to equilibrium, also exacted its toll. It channeled funds away from the market and probably has increased the volume of self-financing. The market's function of selecting investment projects was further curtailed, and financially weak industries were handicapped. This is a particularly striking example of how controls in one sector tend to have repercussions in others.

Many of the controls discussed above have meanwhile been greatly eased or removed. All consumer goods at the retail level have long been free. Iron and steel are free, coal is virtually free. Rents are in the process of being raised. The capital market has been disencumbered of the 5 per cent interest ceiling, but until the end of 1954 it was still enmeshed in a complicated system of tax subsidies. International trade has been greatly liberalized. Agriculture is the main exception. It continues under a special system of price stabilization which through subsidies and taxes brings the price of imported commodities in line with German prices.

In summary one may say that while the ideal of an economy free from direct government control has not been fully realized a good approach to it has been made.

The Creation of Incentives

The freeing of markets together with the currency reform set the stage on which the strong latent impulses to produce and consume could work themselves out. These impulses had existed before, of course, but in the chaotic conditions prior to currency reform they had been working at cross-purposes. The policies pursued after the reform, on the contrary, created strong incentives, mainly on the side of production. Given the great consumption demand that existed, a certain balance of the production- and consumption-oriented elements in the economy resulted, which were already referred to in Chapter 2. In the present section we shall deal with the policies responsible for creating the incentives that have been characteristic of the German economy.

Lest the term "incentive" prove misleading I should add that it is being used in the sense of stimulus to effort, be it reward or penalty. Some of the incentives to be described also have had the effect of a subsidy, merely inducing a shift from one line of effort to another without increasing the total. This is not the primary connotation here. Subsidies of various kinds exist in the German economy, but they are generally in conflict with the free market doctrine. Characteristic of the doctrine are the incentives that tend to increase total effort.

The destruction left by the war provided the Germans with the strongest possible incentives to go to work and repair the damage. Plant and equipment that was bombed out or dismantled had to be rebuilt. Personal effects and homes had to be replaced. Social status—very important in Germany—had to be recovered where it had been jeopardized by war losses. The refugees, who had to start practically from scratch, were under particular pressure to exert themselves.

Prior to the currency reform much of the effort thus engendered was dissipated by the immense waste of the barter, compensation, and foraging system. With the reform and the associated decontrol and tax measures, existing incentives were once more able to express themselves effectively. These incentives were further intensified and guided by various policies: the free market policy, the tight monetary and fiscal management, and the tax system.

Free market incentives. For the businessman the free market policy has intensified both rewards and penalties. He has been up against fluctuating markets in which he could use his ingenuity to make large profits, but also stood to lose by wrong decisions. In a tightly controlled economy both opportunity and risk would have been smaller. The increase in competition, which has been the corollary of the free market policy, has put pressure upon the businessman to improve his performance.

For the consumer the free market policy has meant the ability to buy freely, without coupons or shortages. He has been rationed only by his purse, and this has been a strong incentive to bestir himself to earn more money. Opportunities have not been lacking, unemployment notwithstanding—overtime, double jobs, work by several members of the family. In this way despite high prices and low wages the average German has been able to feed himself fairly well, restock his wardrobe, refurnish a home, and replace some of the other personal effects that he had bartered away during the bad years when a typewriter went for five to ten pounds of butter.

Luxury consumption played a special role in this context. The free market policy raised no objections to luxuries, from whipped cream and candy to night clubs and limousines, though they were embarrassing to Erhard politically. Much of this type of consumption was indeed caused by the high level of taxes, which encouraged generous business entertainment and the like. Some of it was indulged in on a small scale by people who would have been better off buying a pair of shoes. For most people, however, according to a frequently heard observation, the main significance of luxuries was that they were there, that one could buy them if one wanted. By increasing the range of options they added to the consumer's sense of well-being. By acting as incentive goods they stimulated not only consumption but also effort.

Effects of tight monetary and fiscal policies. The tight monetary and fiscal policies served to maintain the incentives created by the free market policy and added some new ones. Had money been made easy the ensuing inflationary climate would probably have spelled the end of free markets. The tight policies made possible ever widening decontrol. They intensified competition and pushed the economy increasingly toward a buyers' market. They created penalties for insufficient effort: failure for the businessman, unemployment for the worker. Neither threat was very imminent—as witness the relative paucity of bankruptcies—but a mild sort of pressure undoubtedly existed that would not have been felt in an economy with excess liquidity.

The prevailing monetary and fiscal climate also provided strong incentives to seek export business. It was not easy for German firms to get back into world markets. Many of them would have much preferred to do their business at home had they encountered sufficiently receptive conditions there. The trend toward buyers' markets forced them outside.

Finally, tight money provided the essential incentive for a revival of consumer saving: confidence in the currency. Without this the numerous tax concessions offered to savers would not have been nearly so effective.

Incentive taxation. Tax incentives have been used in Germany for two main purposes. One was to reduce the marginal tax load (i.e., the top bracket tax) on the tax payer. It is generally believed that this tends to stimulate effort—in the sense that high marginal tax rates tend to kill off incentives. The second purpose has been to stimulate saving and investment. In this context tax incentives have had the character mainly of subsidies; investment has been subsidized at the expense of consumption. This investment stimulation has been very important, however, in aiding the German recovery.

The stimulation of effort through tax incentives has been accomplished in two ways. First, it has resulted from the basic structure of taxation, in which turnover and sales taxes play an important role.* As a result income-tax progression, although it has been sharp, has not had to be quite so pronounced as would have been necessary if an effort had been made to relieve the lower-income groups of a larger part of the burden. The presence of a strong nonprogressive, even regressive component in the tax structure thus has served to reduce a disincentive.

Second, there have been and in part still are tax concessions which have the effect of reducing marginal taxation and,

---

* In 1950–51 they accounted for 47 per cent of total revenues, as against 25 per cent in the United States.

usually, of stimulating saving and investment. Many of them originated in a difference of opinion between the Germans and the Allies as to the appropriate level of income taxation. The German side had maintained, when the 1948 tax law was being discussed, that the rate cuts proposed by the Allies were not sufficient to provide adequate incentives. The Allies refused to accept lower rates but agreed to a series of provisions, some already included in earlier legislation, giving relief in the form of special concessions for income saved and invested. These concessions were expanded in the income-tax laws of 1949 and 1950 but again considerably reduced in those of 1951 and 1953. Their details are given in Chapter 6.

In the aggregate these provisions added up to a very considerable reduction in the marginal tax burden and hence were very probably a major incentive to effort. Top bracket rates were, in effect, reduced for all those able to save. Independent businessmen were given special advantages, as compared with earners of high salaries, through the deductibility of what in many cases were living expenses and the possibility of building up capital in the business. The advantages were so pronounced that they must have exerted strong pressure upon anyone at all able to do so to go into business for himself. The incentive to entrepreneurship was undoubtedly of great value to the German economy. The tax obstacles to longer hours on the part of labor, so familiar in postwar experience elsewhere, were largely removed through virtual exemption from income tax of overtime earnings.

At the same time, the granting of most of these tax concessions in a form benefiting saving and investment had extraordinarily favorable implications for private capital formation. The government of course lost money through the concessions, which it could have devoted to planned investment. There is no way of proving that the concessions increased the total volume of savings, government plus private. Neither can one prove that private investment was directed more effectively than public investment might have been. What stands out is the great driving power generated by businessmen's realization that after years of destruction and stagnation they had been given a chance to build up something of their own that the tax collector could not touch; and a similar feeling on the part of labor that here was a chance to lay the foundations for a decent existence. Reports coming from that period indicate a kind of pioneer spirit that for a few years swept the economy and carried with it businessman and worker alike.

Beginning in 1950, when regular income-tax rates were cut for the first time since 1948, some of the tax concessions were also curtailed or altogether removed. This process continued with the laws of 1951, 1953, and 1954, compensated, however, by preferential tax treatment of corporate income paid out in dividends and of interest received from securities, and by a renewed cut in income-tax rates in 1953 and 1954.

The effect of incentives. The incentive elements in the German picture—free markets, tight financial policies, and pro-business taxation—created an economy with certain well-defined characteristics. The German system gave freedom to the strong. A great deal of pent-up vigor had accumulated from the precurrency-reform frustration. During that period of near-starvation and chaos, when survival was at stake, many people had become accustomed to use their elbows. For the weak only a minimum of consideration was shown. A floor was put under them through the comprehensive social security system. But the payments, though accounting in the aggregate for almost 40 per cent of the budget, were desperately small for many individuals. Beyond this bare minimum the strong were not weighed down by the burden of carrying the weak. The times were too hard to permit fairness to everybody. It was a question of giving the strong a chance of saving themselves in the hope that if they succeeded they would later pull the others along.

For the strong themselves the system provided no guarantee of success. A system relying on easy money and the stimulation of aggregate demand would provide such guarantee by giving businessmen a sellers' market in which to make sure profits. But such a system, if it is to avoid inflation and extreme inequalities of income, must also impose very high taxes and maintain price and other controls. This is the familiar system of the highly developed welfare state, which offers businessmen virtually guaranteed profits but allows them to keep only a small fraction.

Contrasting with this combination of sure but small profits was the German system. By seeking to create buyers' markets and competition it gave the businessman no more than a chance to make a profit. But if he made one and if he knew his tax law he could keep a good part of it. All parts of the system, moreover, were designed to encourage him to work for that profit—except that the system refused to provide him with sellers' markets if it could help it. There have been periods, of course, during the 1948 and 1950 booms, when sellers' markets prevailed despite monetary and fiscal action to keep the lid on. Then producers enjoyed the unwholesome combination of sure profits and a lenient tax law. But this has not been the rule.

The German system has emphasized qualitative factors. Free markets, competition, sound finances, incentive taxation are all such qualitative elements. Through them the system seeks to intensify the response of businessmen and workers to a given state of demand. It seeks to improve the working of the economic machine, without pouring more gas into it. By piecemeal progress, through work on each of many separate parts, the economic machine is being brought to a state where, one hopes, extra injections of fuel to step up aggregate demand will be necessary only on rare occasions.

Here also lies the danger of the approach: The sum total of all the qualitative improvements may fail to add up to stable high capacity operation. It would be unfortunate if intensive concern with the qualitative side should induce a belief that measures of this kind are adequate under all circumstances. The adoption of the work-creation program of early 1950 seems to indicate that the German government has not placed one-hundred per cent reliance upon them. It is in the nature of qualitative processes that their results cannot be estimated. In this they contrast with the quantitative approach emphasizing aggregate demand. Within reasonable limits the effects of a given amount of deficit spending upon demand and output can be calculated. Moreover, however rusty the machine and however out of balance its component parts, it can probably be pushed to full employment by sufficiently large injections of demand. That this is done at increasing risk to the machine and its users and with increasingly unpleasant secondary results is the other side of the story.

The features of German economic policy here described illustrate and confirm the view expressed in Chapter 2 that German policy has been oriented mainly toward production. Almost all of its leading aspects are characteristic of production orientation. For one, there is the emphasis upon the creation of incentives for businessmen and labor. For another, there is the general effort to improve the working of the economy instead of pushing the existing machinery harder through injections of purchasing power. For a third, there is the stimulation of savings and the accompanying encouragement of autonomous investment. Reflecting these various aspects there is the confidence that production can be trusted to create its own demand, and that increases in production can be relied upon to raise general welfare. Government action to increase demand or to interfere with free markets in order to aid welfare is kept to a minimum.

The harshnesses characteristic of the production-oriented policy are also present. Considerable inequality of income is tolerated. The strong are given free rein, the weak are barely protected by individually meager social security payments. The policies that have been pursued have greatly strengthened the production impulses that were inherent in the German postwar economy. In conjunction with the strong consumption impulses of the bombed-out, starved-out population a powerful driving force was brought into being that has helped to carry the German economy forward without a single year's let up.

The State of Competition

In the preceding sections we have dealt with the main achievements of the free market economy: decontrol and creation of incentives. Now we must turn to what many readers will probably regard with misgivings: the relatively feeble state of competition and the proliferating economic activities of the state.

What we shall find in the field of competition is probably not very surprising. Restraint of free competition through cartels and combinations has always been a German practice. If today there is more competition than formerly, it is due probably as much to the good times the German economy has enjoyed as to American efforts to spread the gospel of competition. Cartels have gone underground, but it would be surprising if they stayed there for good.

Cartel arrangements. The German tradition of legalized cartels is almost as old as the American antitrust legislation. Not only have combinations in restraint of trade never been effectively attacked by German law, but the law has even supported them by making such contracts enforcible. This interpretation of the freedom of contract was carried one step further under the Nazis, when cartel membership became compulsory for many industries. These organizations were used by the government as instruments of planning and control. During the war, when shortages removed the ordinary raison d'être of cartels, their instinct of self-preservation caused them to concentrate on production and distribution control. When the Allies took over, cartels, trade associations, and other institutions suspected of having served to restrain trade or to prepare military aggression were banned.[5]

This was, however, by no means the end of cartels or of other forms of monopoly. Allied action, it is true, accomplished a good deal toward their removal, particularly in the American Zone. Through the deconcentration procedure extreme concentrations of power in the coal and steel industry, the chemical industry, in banking, and less intensively in three or four other fields were broken up. This action, the purpose of which was of course not wholly economic, did serve to reduce somewhat the "degree of monopoly." Few observers believed, however, that very intense competition was established thereby, or even that the dispersion of power was likely to last. More details about these Allied measures will be given in Chapter 13, "Allied Aid and Occupation Policy."

Decartelization affected a much wider range of industries than did deconcentration, but it was implemented with less vigor. The more extreme types of cartels disappeared, such as sales syndicates and rigid market quotas. These could hardly exist without legally enforcible contracts and openly visible administration, which were outlawed by the Allies. The lesser types are reported to persist in many industries in one informal way or another. Information on the subject naturally depends on hearsay. The impression is conveyed, however, that there still are price maintenance arrangements for many homogeneous products and agreements on terms and conditions of sale for heterogeneous and hence less cartelizable merchandise.

The mechanics employed leave open to some extent the question whether the arrangements can be considered cartels in the technical sense of the word. In some cases the medium might be social get-togethers—the so-called luncheon cartels. Some arrangements are referred to as telephone cartels. In still other cases the trade associations, meanwhile revived because they proved to be an essential element in the German framework, might issue more or less confidential "recommendations" to their members. Methods and openness of procedure are said to vary from product to product and particularly from zone to zone. The continued underground existence of mild cartel activities in many industries, however, is generally conceded, side by side with bitter competition in others.

The effectiveness of such arrangements has undoubtedly been reduced by the impossibility of legal enforcement and by the aura of illegality surrounding them. A rule of thumb often quoted in Germany regards 8 to 10 firms as the practical maximum for an informal agreement in the absence of a dominant price leader. Even where numbers are small the impossibility of binding commitments probably prevents extreme deviations from competitive pricing. The expansionary climate of the times no doubt has also served to reduce the restrictive effect of the arrangements. The real problem may not have to be faced until and unless prolonged depression or serious excess capacity should make themselves felt.

Other restraints of trade. Apart from cartel-like arrangements, competition is limited by retail price-fixing on the part of manufacturers. This practice is almost universal where the nature of the product permits. In contrast to cartels it is perfectly legal, after the manner of fair trade laws in the United States.

Finally, certain restraints upon the freedom of economic activity are imposed by trade-licensing requirements. The Hitler regime had reintroduced a variety of these long forgotten guild practices which had been in disuse for many years. Under these rules anyone wishing to set up an artisan's shop had to be licensed by a board dominated, in effect, by his future competitors. For Western Germany, faced with the need to reorient its economy and to absorb 10 million refugees, such restraint on mobility would have been serious. Licensing practices were therefore banned in the American Zone, with exemptions where public health and safety were involved. No equivalent action was taken in the British and French zones. The United States occupation authorities had reason to believe that the *Gewerbefreiheit* established by them had increased greatly the number of healthy new businesses and artisans' shops established. Soon, however, under the pressure of powerful middle-class interests legislation was being proposed at the state as well as the federal level to reintroduce licensing. While the issue has not been fully settled, the United States authorities have been fighting a rear-guard action.[6]

German views on cartels. Of the various restraints on competition, cartels undoubtedly are the most important and carry the most critical implications for the future. This is recognized in Germany and explains the intensity of the debate over the pending cartel legislation. Once this legislation comes into force Allied anticartel laws will lapse, and Germany will be able to shape conditions in this field to her own taste. To understand the forces that are behind this legislative struggle it is necessary to look at the basic German attitudes on monopoly and cartels.

Germany has never known anything like the fear and resentment that monopoly used to arouse in the United States. The general tone for the German attitude was set by the historical school of economists and the academic socialists. They regarded competition as a rudimentary, even chaotic stage of capitalist development. Concentration and particularly cartelization appeared as an intermediate stage in the evolution toward socialism, which they regarded as historically inevitable. Only very recently, through the work of the neoliberals, has a hearing been gained for the usual Anglo-American view that competitive markets mean equilibrium, and that indeterminacy and disorder are characteristic of monopolistic, not of competitive, markets.

Of the various economic interests involved, none has ever taken much of a stand against monopolistic practices. Labor has in the main regarded cartels as promising better job security than competition could and, until very recently at least, as a desirable step in the direction of socialism. Its feeling of being exploited, very strong at least in the past, has been directed against capitalism in general, not against monopolies in the technical sense. The consumer has remained apathetic and unorganized. Business with few exceptions has endorsed the idea of limiting competition, although it is noteworthy that since the war the number of voices on the other side has been growing. Unrestricted competition is usually referred to as "destructive." Small business, particularly, has seen in cartels a protection against being competed down or swallowed up by larger firms. The governments of the past have generally gone along with these attitudes.

In some measure the predilection for cartel-type arrangements can perhaps be explained by certain habits of thought and personality traits that can frequently be observed in Germany. One familiar trait is the German love of order and organization. Many Germans find it difficult to believe that something growing up without order and control, like a competitive market, could not be improved by applying a little discipline.

A second trait is the relatively high importance attributed to wealth as against income. It is the reverse of the approach prevailing, for instance, in the American securities markets, where value is simply capitalized earning power and book value counts for very little. The German respect for substance tends to attribute value to an object because money has been invested in it, even though it may produce no corresponding income. This is very apparent in the behavior of corporate stocks paying no dividend. Hence, when a formerly income-producing asset ceases to be profitable the German reaction tends to be not that it has lost its value but that something ought to be done to restore its income. Cartelization is a logical means of protecting substance against secular erosion or shorter-run fluctuations.

Finally, there is the strong emphasis on preservation of status within the community. To lose this status is far worse a calamity in Germany than it would be in a mobile society like the American. To rise in the scale, on the other hand, is not as widespread a goal as it is in the United States. Hence it becomes relatively more urgent to defend one's position than to improve it. This contributes primarily to trade restraints of the trade-licensing type, but it also gives an impulse to cartelization.

Has Germany's predominantly positive attitude toward cartels a basis in any real benefits obtained for the economy? That special interests would favor them may be taken for granted; but if cartels had in practice been a great evil for Germany would one not expect a much stronger opposition than there actually appears to be? There is indeed some reason to think that the evils of cartelism have not been overwhelming and have not been altogether uncompensated by advantages.

The main evils generally charged up to cartels are the unjust enrichment of the participants through excessive prices, and the holding back of efficiency and progress through restriction of output and of new investment. On the other side there is the view that certain monopolistic practices, by creating larger profits, can also serve to stimulate investment and technological advancement. One may expect these bad and good aspects to appear with varying strength in different industries. Germany seems to be well represented in those industries whose present stage of development invites research and innovation, and where monopolistic conditions tend to help growth. The chemical and electrical industries, for instance, seem to be in this position. But Germany also has her share of industries where little technological progress is going on and where monopoly profits are unlikely to do very much for the efficiency of the industry. It is easy to point to numerous industries in which inefficient producers have been kept alive only through restrictive practices.

Yet in an economy as widely cartelized as the German it is difficult to believe that cartels are guilty of two sins at once which, in the aggregate, would conflict with each other: the extortion of excessive profits *and* the restraint of investment and expansion. For it is clear that if large producer groups make excessive profits, the distribution of the entire national income tends to be shifted in favor of profit receivers, who are also high savers. The result of successful monopoly, therefore, would be a tendency toward higher savings. Higher savings mean higher investment unless the savings are hoarded, which would become evident through chronic unemployment. Looking at the German economy over the long period during which cartels have been in existence one does not get the impression of such chronic unemployment, although there has been much cyclical idleness. The period since the currency reform, with its strong structural unemployment, is not characteristic in this respect. The rapid growth of the German economy over long periods does stand out, however. While there are more convincing explanations for this than the existence of cartels, the record at least does not show any obviously disastrous influence of those organizations.

A few generalizations suggest themselves as to why cartelization, even in its clearly negative aspects, may have done relatively little harm in Germany. In most cases cartelization probably has not permitted an industry to deviate very far from what it would do under competitive conditions. Germany has a large foreign trade. Cartels are exposed, therefore, to foreign competition. This is stronger today than it has been since the early 1930's because of far-reaching import liberalization. It is true that customs duties are high and facilitate restrictive practices. There is also competition in third markets, however. For many German industries export business is vital, and they cannot afford to fall behind technologically. On the other hand, where a strong domestic position can be achieved thanks to restraint of competition, aggressive sallies into foreign markets may be facilitated.

At home, too, there are limits to what a cartel can do. Prices fixed too far above the competitive level invite outsiders to enter the industry. They also encourage cheating by cartel members—shooting under water, in the picturesque language of cartel managers. Efforts on the part of the weaker members to restrain new investment or aggressive salesmanship have a habit of causing the cartel to blow up. Through such upheavals, or through peaceful renegotiation of quotas and prices, the more hard-driving members of the group are likely to have things their way eventually, although more slowly than otherwise. Given the compulsive work habits of many German businessmen, a cartel in which no one disturbs the peace by hard work is likely to be the exception rather than the rule. Over a long period of years this picture may change; the retarding forces may gain the upper hand and general ossification may set in. Up to the present, however, perhaps because of Germany's turbulent economic history, such a trend cannot be proved. All in all, and granting that there probably are specific cases of severe overpricing and of extreme laggardness, one may suspect that cartels in Germany have not made a really decisive difference.

There remains the political side of the matter. The view that German cartels have been a major threat to peace, so prevalent during and shortly after the war, seems to have subsided on the whole. The German opponents of cartels argue, however, that on political as well as economic grounds cartels have no place in a socially conscious free market economy. If producers have been given freedom from controls under the banner of Soziale Marktwirtschaft, it is up to the government to keep its promise to the public by removing private restraints upon free markets. They further argue that cartels are a threat to democracy, because they create concentrations of private power which in turn invite and facilitate government domination and ultimately socialism.

These possible political consequences are hard to evaluate. All one can say is that at the moment there seems to be no great public outcry demanding the full implementation of the Erhard program—although it is noteworthy, for Germany, that the program is getting as much support as it does. That the destruction of cartels would greatly diminish the trend toward the formation of pressure groups, so universal in all countries, or would greatly alter the prospects for socialization, whatever they may be, likewise requires a great deal of proof.

Statism

Paternalistic and authoritarian government intervention in economic affairs is a German tradition that goes far back into history. During the Hitler period intervention was carried to its ultimate extremes. The present trend toward a liberal economy has been a remarkable break with tradition and is probably to be explained in part as a reaction to the extremes of state control. One may hope—its sponsors firmly believe— that it is not just a swing of the pendulum but the lasting application of a painfully learned lesson. Nevertheless, the free market policy has not succeeded in changing some of the more basic manifestations of statism. The public budgets still absorb a very large part of the national income, many economic functions continue to be exercised by the state, and a high degree of administrative authority continues to be wielded by government departments.

The big budgets. The combined federal, state, and local budgets absorb approximately 35 per cent of the gross national product of Germany. Precise comparisons with other countries are difficult, but it seems clear that the German tax burden, including the very heavy social security levies, is above that of almost all other Western European countries and also of the United States, and is about equal to the British burden excluding subsidies.[7] These figures give the measure of the tax pressure resting upon the German economy and emphasize the importance of the tax incentives described earlier. Of the total taxes, not quite 40 per cent are accounted for by social security payments of all kinds,[8] nearly 20 per cent are investment expenditures, and about 15 per cent are occupation costs. The rest goes for general purposes. The real burden of the fiscal levy is mitigated, therefore, by the high proportion of transfer payments, i.e., social security expenditures. A relative advantage may further be seen in the fact that of the exhaustive expenditures so large an amount goes for investment. The same can be said of the indirect influence of the tax system upon saving and investment, which has on balance been stimulating. But this only emphasizes the fact that the influence of government finances has been extraordinarily great.

Another though perhaps temporary aspect of the tremendous financial importance of government are the cash balances accumulated by federal, state, and local bodies and by the Allied authorities. Early in 1954 they amounted to about 11 billion DMark. They accounted for about one-third of total bank deposits, excluding interbank deposits.[9] Some 20 per cent of this was held by or for the benefit of the Allied authorities; 20 to 25 per cent were investment funds of the social security institutions; much of the remainder was explainable as accumulations of state and local authorities in preparation for public-works expenditures. But whatever the reasons for the piling up of this enormous total, it documents both the financial weight of government operations and the lack of flexibility with which they are handled.

Strong government penetration of financial affairs is not

something to be welcomed in a liberal economy. Damage can
be minimized, however, and some compensating advantages
extracted if the government deploys its finances with a view
to minimizing friction, unsettlement, and disincentive and
uses them to aid stability and growth. The German authorities
have put much effort into minimizing the disincentives of a
heavy tax burden, and with great success. They have paid
relatively little attention, however, to the unsettling and
sometimes deflationary effects of the movement and disposition
of large sums of money. They likewise have made only limited
use of the potentialities of fiscal policy to influence cyclical
conditions. The disinclination to use fiscal policy as a positive
tool is deliberate; its reasons have been discussed in an earlier
chapter. The relative unconcern over the accidental disturbances created by the movement of public funds on the other
hand, seems to reflect a belief that such disturbances are not
significant. But when the operations of the public accounts
involve one-third of the country's income and bank deposits,
this expectation is almost sure to be disappointed.

Nationalized sectors. Quite a number of functions that in
other countries are carried out by private enterprise or have
been nationalized only since the last war have long been
publicly owned and operated in Germany. The list is long
and varied; it includes the railroads and most local transportation, a large part of the utilities, telegraph, telephone, and
radio, the savings banks, and quite a few industrial enterprises,
including Germany's star performer of recent years, the Volkswagen Works.* The number of workers employed by the
industrial enterprises alone exceeds 200,000. In addition social
insurance is comprehensive and to some extent displaces private life insurance; public health insurance is compulsory
for the lower income groups. How compatible is the existence
of large nationalized sectors with a market economy?

* The precise legal status of this enterprise is still subject to litigation.

Two main dangers seem to exist. One is that the publicly owned sectors may be less efficient than the privately owned ones and may fail to be guided by market influences, thus slowing down growth and misallocating resources. The other danger is that the rest of industry, under the constant fear of further encroachment, may itself become stagnant. In Germany, however, these dangers seem on the whole to have been avoided, although there have been minor instances. A conclusive judgment would require detailed examination; we shall have to limit ourselves to a survey of the highlights.

Of the German Federal Railways it must be said that they are in a bad way and since 1953 have been running a mounting deficit. Part of their plight is no doubt due to their character as a public enterprise: They must carry excess labor and must grant "socially necessary" fare reductions to a large part of their passengers and even to some freight. Perhaps their methods of operation would be modernized more quickly if they were privately owned. But the basic difficulties seem to reside in traffic structure and in truck and automobile competition, troubles that are common to railways all over the world. Some legislation limiting the growth of truck transportation seems to be in the making, which would probably not be the ideal solution from a market point of view. But that is after all in the German cartel tradition. A privately owned railway system would probably be allowed to reach a similar solution. As for the quality of service it is generally considered excellent.

The utilities are frequently of mixed ownership, municipalities participating with private enterprise. The arrangement has had certain financial advantages, since the municipalities were able to provide financial support. Electric power has repeatedly been a bottleneck in the German recovery and threatens to become one again. Rates are high and modernization urgent. In the main this has been due to lack of capital, in some measure perhaps to lack of foresight. One rarely hears the view expressed, however, that private or public ownership is responsible. If anything, the publicly owned concerns have better access to capital than the others.

Nor are any very striking economic consequences of public ownership to be reported of most of the other sectors. Telephone and telegraph function excellently and at reasonable cost. Publicly owned radio has meant a loss of advertising potential, but advertising is underdeveloped in all its media by American standards. Programs are different in content but not in degree of appeal to intelligent listeners from those elsewhere. Municipal savings banks, the largest single sector of the German banking system, seem under no particular temptation to divert funds to politicians or wild municipal schemes; they are as vocal as any private group in promoting their interests.

Of the innumerable large and small industrial concerns that the old Reich government collected, it is generally said that they are run in a businesslike way—the government just happens to be the shareholder. Even if this report should be on the idyllic side, it is fair to say that the many demands that are constantly being voiced for the disposal of such holdings to private hands rarely if ever take present mismanagement as their major premise.

In the insurance and health sector public old-age pensions have maintained full payment after the currency reform, while private life insurance was scaled down 10:1 although later partially revalued. The social security institutions are free to invest their reserves in any security on the "legal" list and thus do a much broader financing job for the economy than the social security trust funds in the United States. Nationalized medicine is reportedly being abused to some extent and is subject to criticism from liberal sources, but most people seem to regard it as a blessing, except perhaps for the doctors.

This bird's-eye view of the nationalized sectors of the German economy leaves one impression: In the view of most Germans inefficient or noneconomic behavior on the part of publicly owned enterprises is not a major issue. In the absence of striking evidence to the contrary one may perhaps conclude that public ownership, widespread though it is, has made no great difference to the operation of the economy. It is just something to be borne in mind whenever one feels tempted to claim too much for the extent of private Marktwirtschaft in Germany.

The same conclusion obtrudes itself when one asks whether German entrepreneurs fear the encroachment of further nationalization. It seems clear that since the war, at any rate, this factor has played no role. In the coal and steel industries investors have shown pronounced hesitancy; this, however, has been due mainly to the uncertainties of deconcentration and only serves to underline the unconcern prevailing everywhere else. The fact is that public ownership in Germany is of very old standing. Nationalization of the railways, for instance, occurred under Bismarck. Over the years the public sector has been expanded here and there, but since the war there has been no further trend in this direction. That seems to have been the important factor.

The paternalistic government. Beside what it does through the budget and through public ownership and operation, the German government at its various levels can engage in a good deal of intervention through simple administrative action. That there are fairly important sectors of the economy still subject to controls has already been said. But quite apart from this, German public agencies possess a degree of authority unspecified by law that is surprising to outside observers. An example of this is the action of the Bank deutscher Länder in imposing ceilings upon the credit volume of individual banks. Although the Bank had no statutory power to enforce its request, compliance was universal. The action, it is true, was backed by the concealed threat to cut off rediscount facilities to offenders. But either the action or the sanction if imposed could have been challenged in the courts. They never were.

This respect for the authority of a government agency is probably a widespread characteristic of German industry. Industry as a whole no doubt wields a great deal of influence over the government. But the government dealing with individual firms can make its wishes felt in a way not common in the United States.

Conclusion

The socially conscious free market economy, as we have observed it, has perhaps not been altogether free nor especially outstanding for its social consciousness. Its chief characteristic, one might say, is the scope and incentive it has given to individual initiative. But, such as it is, it has done a great job.

Its accomplishment was not, it may be repeated, in the absolute level to which German production was raised. That is still below the level of some other European countries. It was the restoration of life and viability to a country that seemed too *kaputt* to rise again for many years. In helping to accomplish this, the free market economy proved to a world in which only a minority of disinterested observers had any real faith in a system based on individual initiative that the system still works. And this proof is the more impressive because it was supplied by a country that has had a rich experience of the opposite type of economy.

The evidence of the contribution made by the free market policy cannot, in the nature of things, be final and conclusive. It must remain a matter of opinion. There are critics who believe that Germany recovered not because but in spite of her policies. These critics agree that the recovery has been magnificent, but they argue that with proper planning more could probably have been accomplished, and that in any case greater

equality in the distribution of income could have been preserved.

In support of this thesis the critics point to unused resources
and misdirected investments of various sorts. Such can always
be found in a market economy, and the planner can generally
prove that he could have avoided this particular waste and thus
bettered the performance. What he cannot prove is that he
could have done as well as the free economy.

In the case of Germany we have records of planning goals
and estimates that show how well their authors thought they
could do. A comparison of these goals with the actual performance of the lamentably unplanned economy should allow
some judgments as to the relative effectiveness of the two
approaches. One such set of planning estimates is contained in
the Long Term Program submitted to the Economic Cooperation Administration in 1948.[10] It was developed largely by
German experts but reportedly revised upward under the
persuasion of the American occupation authorities. Thus it
was estimated in 1948 that after the end of the European Recovery Program in 1952-53 the index of production would
have reached 110 per cent of 1936 (the original German estimate reportedly had been below 100). Agriculture according
to the program would have returned to prewar levels. Foreign
trade would be in approximate balance, but only on the assumption that East-West trade could be resumed on a large
scale and that Germany would somehow earn 300 million
dollars a year from other dollar-short countries to meet a
Western hemisphere deficit. The effective implementation of
a given investment program was regarded as essential for the
attainment of these goals.

Reality has not dealt kindly with these estimates and programs, which of course were never carried out except in narrow sectors. Industrial production in 1952-53 averaged about
150 instead of 110. Net agricultural output was 111 per cent
of prewar instead of 100. The over-all balance of payments

was highly favorable and even the dollar sector was approaching balance.

There is another set of estimates, prepared in 1950 by a group of four of the major German economic research institutes.[11] These estimates were made at a time when the production index was already around 100. The authors concluded that the attainment of full employment, of balance of payments equilibrium, and of the industrial and agricultural output required for viability would require, as a minimum, five more years, i.e., until 1955, and might well take longer. To accomplish the necessary readjustments in the two years still allowed by the European Recovery Program they regarded as impossible. They assumed moreover that over the five-year period in question an investment of 60 to 80 billion DMark would be required and that 1 to 1.5 billion dollars of United States aid would be needed after the end of the Marshall Plan. The authors seemed to favor, at least implicity, a high degree of planning in the use of these investment funds. As we know, all of the goals mentioned with the exception of full employment were attained or bettered in 1952 or 1953.

It is perhaps not quite fair to put so much stress upon the miscarriage of these prognostications. They were made by competent people, working with inadequate information, and were perhaps not uninfluenced by the fact that they were being made in support of requests for American aid. They were made in ignorance of the tremendous upset about to be produced by the Korea boom. But insufficient information and ignorance of the future are no excuse for poor planning, for they are part and parcel of the problem. Plans drawn on the basis of forecasts such as these would, if adhered to, almost certainly have slowed down the recovery. The view that private initiative was a more effective agent of reconstruction than planning now seems to be accepted, to some extent, even in certain labor circles which in principle lean toward planning.

It remains to pull together the evidence regarding the free-

dom and the social consciousness of the Soziale Marktwirtschaft. We have found that both have fallen short of the
postulates of theory in a number of respects. Large sectors
of the economy are still kept, or were kept for a long time,
under controls. The government has continued to play a preponderant role through its large budget, through the indirect
control exercised over investment by means of the tax system,
through ownership and operation of important industries,
and through its somewhat paternalistic habits. A not incon-
siderable volume of investment has been centrally planned.
From the side of private enterprise, too, freedom of the market
remains restricted. Cartels and other restrictive trade practices
have been eliminated only in part. In many cases they have
merely been driven underground at a time when, because of
favorable economic conditions, they would not have been very
active in any case. These are things to give one pause when
one thinks of Germany as the test case of a "free" economy.
Its freedom has been only relative, by comparison with the
preceding period of monolithic control. It is only by virtue of
a major shift in emphasis that Gemany may be regarded as a
protagonist of a free economy.

The shortfall from doctrinal purity, however, has not meant
an equivalent shortfall from maximum performance. On the
contrary, there are reasons for believing that, in some respects
at least, these compromises with principle have been beneficial,
even essential. There may be reasonable doubts as to whether
some controls could not have been removed more rapidly. But
on the whole it seems clear that the prolonged maintenance
of controls over basic foodstuffs, rents, and some other key
items was an essential part of the decontrol scheme. Removal
of all controls would have generated pressures that would
almost certainly have wrecked the free market policy.

Likewise, the preponderant economic role of the government, though obviously no advantage, was seen to be more
innocuous than might be expected. The breaking of bottle-

necks through centrally guided investment has been a valuable contribution. Privately imposed restraints of trade likewise seem to have done no extreme damage. Their loosening through Allied legislation has undoubtedly done much good; more competition and greater freedom to start a business have aided the adjustment to partition and the absorption of refugees. But we also noted that most cartels in Germany probably were less harmful than they might be in the United States, and that some of them were distinctly beneficial. On the whole, one may say that by design or by accident a balance of freedom and control has been achieved that has worked well.

The last question: How well has the Soziale Marktwirtschaft kept its social promises? It has been noted repeatedly that the German system was a harsh one. In the desperate situation in which the country found itself the watch word was not "fair shares" or "women and children first." The strong were given a free hand and relieved of the burden of carrying the weak, except for the bare subsistence minimum awarded to practically everyone. According to the doctrine, social justice should have been achieved through elimination of monopoly and some redistribution of income after the market had rendered its verdict. This remained theory. High profits were not seriously curbed by competition, and effective taxation was probably less sharply progressive than in the United States or England.

But in a broader sense the Soziale Marktwirtschaft produced great social results. By rapidly lifting total income, however ill distributed, it eventually raised everybody's income. This was what had been intended when private enterprise was given a free hand. It worked, even though under the protests of those who looked more at the distribution than at the rapidly rising total. A few years' per capita gain at an annual rate of 3 to 5 per cent are worth more to the lower income groups than the redistribution of a stagnant total within the narrow range that is open to such maneuvers. Through the rapidity of its advance the Soziale Marktwirtschaft has largely fulfilled its promise. The gradual move toward a more even income distribution that has been taking place since 1951 has made a further contribution. That a great majority of Germans are satisfied with the performance they showed in the election of September 6, 1953.

CHAPTER 6
Investment and Its Financing

AMONG THE FACTORS responsible for the rapid build-up of
Western Germany, the high rate of saving and investment oc-
cupies a foremost position. Gross investment of approximately 24.4 per cent of the gross national product, as was
achieved in 1953–54 (Table 4), is an impressive figure and
well above that of most Western European countries. To
which parts of the economy did these resources go? How were
they channeled there? How was their flow financed?

The Record

A detailed analysis of the distribution of investment, if one
could be made, would no doubt throw some very interesting
light upon the factors that made possible the rapid German
advance. Unfortunately such an analysis is not possible with
the data at hand. In discussing the distribution of investment
we are entering into statistically uncharted territory. All that
the Federal Statistical Office is willing to commit itself to—
even this is a bold commitment—is a breakdown into durable
equipment, construction, and inventories.

Significant conclusions are not easily wrested from these
meager figures. It is interesting, however, to note the great
thirst for stocks the German economy seems to have felt,
which carried inventory increases to 21.6 per cent of total investment in 1951 and 18.8 per cent in 1952. A more detailed
breakdown of investment was shown in Table 6, but its reliability is subject to even greater doubt than that of the aggregate data. An unusually high proportion of resources appears

to have gone into industry in the two years immediately following the currency reform, while little went into mining (mainly coal) and utilities. This disproportion seems to reflect the financing difficulties experienced by these last industries and may help to explain the bottlenecks that developed there. A larger volume of investment in these areas would probably have accelerated the general advance.

TABLE 15: *Gross Investment, 1949–53*
(in current prices in millions of DMark)

	1949	1950	1951	1952	1953
Machinery and equipment	9,130	10,335	13,345	15,489	14,565
Construction	6,524	8,400	10,775	12,065	13,170
Inventories	1,247	1,974	6,211	5,863	4,518
Total	16,901	20,709	30,331	33,417	32,253
Minus investment of occupation authorities	600	467	1,180	2,126	1,565
Gross investment, excluding occupation investment	16,301	20,242	29,151	31,291	30,688

Source: Wirtschaft und Statistik, various issues.

The most impressive fact, if we may trust the data, is the sheer volume of investment that has been poured into the German economy. This brings us to the question of its financing. How did the German economy, in its depleted postwar state and despite the freedom that it permitted to the goods-hungry consumer, manage to squeeze out savings larger, in relation to national income, than the United States?

The sources from which the funds came are shown in Table 16. A study of the data reveals that, the freedom of the consumer not withstanding, the bulk of the savings was not altogether voluntary on his part. About 70 per cent or more of total investment funds, in all years but 1953, was derived from exceptionally high profits and amortization charges of business, plus some short-term bank credit. Budget funds from tax revenues accounted for about 15 per cent. If counterpart funds are added the percentage rises by about 3 per cent on the average. The capita market, including long-term funds supplied by banks, provided no more than 10 per cent of total funds up to 1953. It is in this latter category that consumer savings are mainly registered. It is clear that not a great deal would have been accomplished had decisions regarding the formation of savings been left to the free choice of consumers. It was business saving that very largely carried the burden of financing.

A good deal will have to be said about the various sources of investment financing and the role they have played in building up the German economy. We shall study them in detail, but before doing so we must devote some attention to the role of government in the channeling and financing of investment. The question obtrudes itself: How far was German investment "planned"?

Investment Planning

"It is surprising that there does not appear to be a really up-to-date German investment program; at the levels where economic policy is decided, there appears to be a quite insufficient appreciation of the importance of the issues involved in it." [1] This was the conclusion of Professor Cairncross, whose penetrating and generally favorable report on Germany, rendered jointly with Dr. Per Jacobsson, had played a role some months earlier in connection with the European Payments Union's emergency credit to Germany. In this day and age of development programming the Cairncross statement is of special interest. If the German revival was indeed accomplished without benefit of planning it would seem to constitute evidence of the effectiveness of a no-planning, laissez-faire approach to investment. In fact, the conclusion that will emerge from the present chapter is that Germany probably did well in keeping herself free of the manifold controls that a thoroughgoing investment plan implies. It would

TABLE 16: *Sources of Investment Funds*
(in millions of DMark)

	June 21, 1948– June 30, 1949	second half 1949	1950	1951	1952	1953
1. Capital market	*830*	*840*	*2,327*	*2,478*	*3,552*	*6,639*
a. Longer-term bank credits *	220	429	1,214	1,224	1,604	3,345
b. Insurance companies	274	242	414	562	713	917
c. Building and loan assoc.	76	86	475	368	406	657
d. Securities purchased by banks, businesses, and individuals †	260	83	224	324	829	1,720
2. Budget funds ‡	*2,110*	*1,620*	*3,305*	*5,320*	*6,245*	*7,350*
a. Federal, state, and local authorities	—	—	2,550	3,615	4,695	5,535
b. Immediate Assistance	1,950	1,370	—	—	—	—
c. Equalization of War Burdens Fund	—	—	445	1,020	790	1,035
d. Social security funds	160	250	310	685	760	780
3. Special public programs	*179*	*270*	*2,357*	*1,044*	*864*	*835*
a. Counterpart funds	179	199	1,771	820	548	335
b. Investment Assistance	—	—	—	80	316	500
c. Prefinancing by central banking system	—	71	586	144	—	—
4. Self-financing and short-term bank credit	*15,817*	*6,086*	*11,470*	*19,488*	*18,996*	*17,429* §
a. Ordinary depreciation and amortization	6,600	3,050	6,364	8,070	9,543	10,189
b. Profits, accelerated amortization, short-term bank credit, and all other	9,217	3,036	5,106	11,418	9,453	7,240 §
Gross investment	18,936	8,816	19,459	28,330	29,657	32,253

* Excluding public funds and prefinancing by central banking system channeled through banks, to avoid double counting.

† Excluding purchases of securities by public authorities and insurance companies.

‡ Excluding funds obtained through borrowing, to avoid double counting.

§ Figure probably considerably understated, since a good part of the funds be wrong to assume, however—and the Cairncross statement presumably did not mean this—that no part of investment was centrally guided. A good deal of planning took place, and there is evidence, confirmed by the policies of Economics Minister Erhard himself, that this planning was valuable and might profitably have been expanded by a small margin.

The extent of planning. The question of investment planning is part and parcel, of course, of the general issue of free markets versus controls. The German government, and particularly Minister Erhard, had little sympathy for planning. To be made effective it would have required intricate controls over materials and sources of financing. It would have thrown heavy administrative burdens upon the government and have paralyzed private initiative, upon which Erhard's policy rested. It would have antagonized the German public, made allergic to controls by past experience, and particularly also the businessmen, who were the strongest political supporters of the Adenauer government.

On the other side of the debate stood the social democratic opposition, whose general conception of a firmly controlled economy—subsequently somewhat watered down—called for thorough planning of investment. They could argue, moreover, on the neoliberals' own premises that so long as several important industries were not allowed to raise prices, so long as the interest rate remained fixed at an unrealistically low level and the capital market was dormant, the uncontrolled distribution of capital funds was bound to produce distortions. Similar views were expressed by American officials in Germany. Particularly the ECA representatives, concerned

---

raised through sales of securities, which in the table are assumed to have been employed for investment financing, have been withheld temporarily from such use. The gap to be filled by self-financing is correspondingly larger.
Source: Bank deutscher Länder, *Report for the Year 1952* and *1953;* and *Wirtschaft und Statistik.*

with the most effective use of American aid, laid stress on the
need for investment planning.

Under the influence of ECA demands for the presentation
of short- and long-term programs, various investment projec-
tions were actually undertaken. An example is the "Lang-
fristiges Programm (1952–53) für die amerikanischen und bri-
tischen Besatzungsgebiete in Deutschland" drawn up with
Allied collaboration in 1948. It is not quite clear, however,
how far these "plans" were expressions of serious government
intent to bring about certain results and how far they were
merely estimates of what it hoped would happen. They had
probably best be regarded as a mixture of both, with the true
planning being limited to those fields where the government's
powers were strongest.

In the absence of administrative powers to curtail private
investment or to force it into specific channels, the planners'
main tool was control over finances. To get an idea of the
scope of government influence over investment, therefore, we
must survey the financial resources and devices at its disposal.
Two approaches were employed. One was the use of govern-
mentally owned or controlled funds to finance certain investments. This also included various devices of only moderate
potency that the government employed to influence the capital market. The other approach was the use of the tax mechanism to encourage savings and channel them into certain
fields. Both deserve our attention.

Planning of public investment expenditures. Government
revenues (excluding loans) available for investment averaged
15 per cent of gross investment. Only the smaller part of this,
however, was amenable to central control. Under the system
of decentralized public finance established by the Allies most
of the money was spent by state and local authorities. Coordination of their investment activities proved virtually impossible. Nevertheless, since in practice these funds could go only

into housing and public works, both of which had high planning priority, the general direction of state and local investment activities was in fact both foreseeable and desirable. The regional distribution, however, and the details of project selection escaped the control of the planners.

Counterpart funds and the very small volume of central bank investment financing were the chief objects of planning. They accounted for slightly over 4 per cent of gross investment from 1948 to 1952, though in 1950 the proportion rose to about 12 per cent. Very detailed plans were put forward and thrashed out at length between the Germans and the Allies. The use of counterpart funds in key areas was undoubtedly of prime importance in breaking bottlenecks and achieving balance in the pattern of investment. The experience also revealed, however, some of the inherent difficulties of planning in Germany. Bureaucratic decision-making proved a time-consuming process. Political considerations inevitably entered, particularly into the distribution of the funds obtained from the Bank deutscher Länder. Many projects, therefore, materialized rather slowly and often in not quite the form that the planners had intended.

The funds that were directly subject to central planning probably did not go beyond 15 per cent of gross investment. Efforts were made to give them leverage by requiring private funds to be matched against them, particularly in the case of counterpart investment. In addition, efforts were made to reach agreements with banks, insurance companies, and the social security funds for the investment of certain sums in specific fields. These arrangements were voluntary, however, and probably did not greatly alter the direction in which those funds would otherwise have flowed. It is difficult to give an estimate of the total sums thus brought under some degree of control. By participants in the planning operations it has been said that of bulky investment projects—excluding reinvestment of amortization allowances, inventories, and minor repairs of war damage—perhaps as much as 50 per cent could be regarded as more or less closely "planned" during the first two years after the currency reform.

Capital issues control. For the sake of completeness more than because of its quantitative influence in controlling investment, the Capital Issues Committee must be mentioned at this point.[2] The committee, which functioned from 1948 to 1953, was primarily concerned with the operation of the capital market and only indirectly with investment priorities. For the latter purpose the small capacity of the capital market during most of these years offered little scope. Insofar as the committee did, however, exert an influence over the pattern of financing it also influenced the pattern of investment. It may thus be counted among the instruments of investment planning.

Planning through the tax mechanism. The second and quantitatively perhaps more important approach to planning was via the tax mechanism. A great variety of tax privileges were available to firms and individuals willing to save and invest. Some of these privileges sought to channel savings into specific industries, while others merely aimed at stimulating capital formation in general.

The famous housing loans (section 7c of the Income Tax Law), shipbuilding loans (section 7d), and more recently loans to the Fund for Equalization of War Damage (section 7f) constituted the main instances of specific channeling. Under these provisions firms and individuals could, within generous limits, make interest-free loans to third parties for the purposes indicated and deduct them from their taxable income. If and when the loans were recalled they became fully taxable as income. For individuals in the lower-income brackets, where tax deductions meant little, the government offered matching grants of 25 per cent of the savings devoted to residential construction.[3]

These privileges were attractive in two respects. First, they allowed firms to provide urgently needed housing for their own labor force. In such cases they did not expect to recover the money in the near future, but housing often essential to the firms' operation was provided at low real cost. For the small but important number of firms interested in shipping, analogous considerations applied. Second, the privileges offered a means of creating reserves against lean years to come and of taking advantage of future tax cuts. The lender could eventually call back his loans and, because of a lower tax liability, pay a lower or perhaps no tax. In this way important resources could be set aside though it meant the amounts were not thereafter available to the lender for current operations.

It is estimated that the volume of housing loans (7c) ranged as high as 1.2 billion in 1951. The funds so channeled into housing accounted for approximately 15 to 20 per cent of total investment in that sector. In the shipbuilding field the proportion must have been much higher.

Tax privileges of the other type, which did not aim to push funds into any particular industry, probably generated an even larger volume of savings. Accelerated depreciation was permitted for capital expenditures incurred in repairing war-damaged equipment (section 7a), for new residential property (7b), for new industrial, commercial, and agricultural plants (7e), and for investments financed through the Investment Assistance operation (section 36). Small capital expenditures of up to 600 DMark, such as for office equipment, could be charged off immediately. Finally, businesses were allowed to revalue their assets arbitrarily at the time they converted their accounts from the former Reichsmark to the new DMark. This created enormous possibilities for high annual write-offs, excessive valuations being discouraged in the main only by the rather substantial taxes on the stated value of assets. In the aggregate, these accelerated depreciation provisions were largely responsible for the tremendous volume of internal financing of business. They allowed business to keep and plough back a good part of the big profits made during the early years after the currency reform. They also created a certain pressure, perhaps not completely rational but very understandable, to keep investing in order to have something to write off.

Additional privileges reduced the tax rate on a moderate part of the earnings retained in the business (section 10*a*); others permitted the deduction of life insurance premiums as well as of various other forms of personal savings provided they were held for three years, fully for modest amounts and partially for higher limits (section 10, 1–2). For people who were able to save or to make their existing capital appear as current savings (or could use credit for the same purpose, although technically this was illegal), these privileges meant a substantial easing of high income-tax rates.

Some of the privileges available to business firms were discontinued after 1951 or limited to the financially not very important group of expellees and persecutees (7*a*, 7*e*, 10*a*). It was apparently felt that self-financing had been pushed far enough and that more emphasis should from then on be placed on stimulating the flow of savings to the open capital market. In the rather loose sense in which these privileges can be regarded as a form of central planning they greatly expanded the scope of such planning.

The effect of tax privileges upon investment. In an earlier chapter we discussed the role of the tax privileges as a stimulus to effort. Now we shall have to deal with them as aids to saving and as a mild form of planning. In these respects, in fact, the tax privileges were at the center of the debate over how much or how little central planning was desirable. Their appropriateness was challenged with a multitude of searching questions. How effective were the privileges in accomplishing their purposes? Were the savings they produced really greater than the taxes the government was giving up? If they cost more in taxes than they produced in savings, was not the government better advised to eliminate the privileges, collect taxes in full, and use them for centrally planned investment? If, on the other hand, the tax loss was less than the additional savings generated, and the privileges worth while in this sense, was it not better to channel all savings arising under them into a central pool, such as the Reconstruction Loan Corporation (Kreditanstalt für Wiederaufbau)? Thus ran the line of argument pursued by the political opposition and by some German and American technicians.

It is probably true that the privileges did not increase and quite possibly reduced the volume of investment capital available in the aggregate, if one takes into account the loss of investible public revenue.* Criticism on this score leaves out of account, however, one of the major purposes of the concessions. Their legislative history makes quite clear that they were intended not to maximize savings but to lower the effective rate of taxation. The German administration would have favored a flat cut in rates, but Allied opposition forced the adoption of this compromise. Given the fact that the government did not want to collect taxes at the full rates, the method of reducing them by means of special concessions for savings undoubtedly produced more such savings than a flat rate cut would have.

As for channeling these funds through a central pool, there was perhaps a good deal to be said for it. The fact that the Investment Assistance operation was undertaken shows that the government felt the need for a larger volume of centrally planned funds. But there were also fears, probably not unjus-

---

* That is to say, the beneficiaries probably reduced the savings that they would have made in the absence of the privileges by as much as or more than the amount of the "gift" that the government handed to them. To believe otherwise would be to assume that an increase in the taxpayer's income (through the privileges) caused him to reduce his consumption. An analysis of the amounts saved in the various privileged categories confirms this impression.

tified in the light of many savers' experience with the "iron savings" schemes of the Nazi period, that an attempt by the government to commandeer savings would cause them to dry up. This seemed particularly plausible with respect to any attempt to take over the large amount of "purposive savings," funds set aside to accomplish some particular goal; these would largely vanish if the government frustrated the purpose by its action.[4] A further consideration was the reluctance of business to accept a very large part of its financing from the government, with the inevitable increase in governmental influence and the ultimate risk, perhaps, of nationalization. These considerations seem to have strengthened the authorities' natural preference for giving free rein to the private disposal of savings.

As for this private use, in the absence of an over-all investment program, many minor but no really major instances of misallocation are in evidence. Some low priority consumer goods industries obtained funds while temporary bottlenecks developed in coal, steel, and power. But there seem to be few or no cases of permanent misallocation of capital such as would manifest themselves today in large-scale excess capacity. Initially the need for investment was so intense all around that practically all investment was fruitful. The economy grew sufficiently fast to absorb temporary overinvestment in particular lines except in rare cases. The fact that the tax collector shared rather heavily in the cost seems to have induced a certain amount of unnecessarily conspicuous investment. More marble, chromium, choice woods, and fabrics seem to have gone into office buildings and factories than were strictly called for. That these things, though eye-catching, were quantitatively important may be doubted. On the whole, however, no serious permanent misdirection of capital seems to have occurred.

In other respects, admittedly, the tax privileges had serious defects. They abetted the emergence of a severe inequality in the distribution of wealth by promoting the self-financing of business. They pushed to an extreme the principle of favoring the independent businessman as against the fixed income receiver. They introduced fantastic complications into the tax structure and frequently made the search for loopholes the most interesting and profitable form of business activity. This warping of business motivations naturally brought the familiar warping of business decisions. The root of these evils, however, was not so much the system of tax privileges as the high level of taxation itself from which the privileges were intended to give relief.

Conclusion. We have found substantiated the verdict of Professor Cairncross that Germany lacked an effective over-all investment program. Nevertheless we have noted fairly extensive elements of planning. A certain amount of investment has been centrally guided through budget funds, counterpart funds, Investment Assistance, and other programs. Larger amounts, very likely, have been channeled into investment through the tax concessions. Part of these funds were guided into specific fields, mainly housing and shipbuilding, part of them were allowed to find their own way.

Very little money, however, moved into those basic industries, like coal, steel, power, and transportation, where prices were controlled, profits low, and the opportunities for self-financing through rapid write-offs small. The resulting bias could not at first be altogether offset by the channeling of counterpart and other public funds into these sectors. One might wish, therefore, that the central planners had had a little more money at their disposal than they did. They diagnosed correctly the places where bottlenecks threatened. Given added funds they might have been able to break the bottlenecks earlier than was done eventually with the aid of the Investment Assistance scheme. That this scheme was adopted by a government to whose philosophy it was basically alien sup-

ports the contention that a little more central planning and
financing would have been to the good. This, however, is no
argument in favor of a full-dress investment program centrally implemented. Whether or not such a program is regarded as desirable will always depend, to some extent, upon
an individual's broader social viewpoint. In the German experience those favoring thoroughly planned investment have
against them the record already analyzed of the extraordinary
underestimate of potentialities by the early planners.

Self-financing

Self-financing of business out of profits and amortization
allowances was the main method of securing investment funds
during the early years of the recovery. While the securities
market was still almost dead and bank credit tight and expensive, German business pulled itself up by its tax-exempt boot-
straps. Statistically very little can be said about the process.
Estimates are shown in Table 16 indicating that about two-
thirds of gross financing and half of net financing (exclusive
of amortization) fell under this heading. The estimates, however, are arrived at as residuals. They also contain some short-
term bank credit, which in the aggregate was growing at an
average rate of 3 to 4 billion DMark a year, as well as direct
loans and participations by private investors and all other
financing not accounted for elsewhere. All one can say is that
most businesses relied chiefly on self-financing for their supply of funds.

That this kind of financing could become so important was
the result of the omnipotent tax privileges combined with
the high level of profits. The process was a kind of forced saving that business imposed upon the consumer. Perhaps it is
more accurate to say that the consumer imposed it upon himself. This at least is the impression gained from looking into
the origin of the profits. Immediately after the currency reform the broad mass of consumers poured into the consumer

goods market their full incomes, to say nothing of their initial allowances of 60 DMark. The result was inevitable: When the totality of incomes seeks to buy what is only a part of total output, though a very large part, prices must go up. Since wages almost miraculously remained constant, an inflationary spiral did not develop and wide profit margins became established at high and fairly stable prices. These margins wilted somewhat in 1949 and early 1950 but blossomed out once more under the impact of Korea. Thereafter until the middle of 1953 they were gradually squeezed by falling prices and rising wages.

In German discussions of this phenomenon, which are numerous, the impression is often conveyed that industry deliberately raised its prices because it needed extra profits for self-financing. From this the conclusion is drawn that now, when the need for self-financing is in good measure past, prices should be lowered. This argument seems to be in conflict with the normal assumption that business seeks to make what profits it can regardless of whether it plans to accumulate them or pay out. Yet the idea is probably not without foundation. For one thing, the accelerated write-off provisions themselves encourage higher prices, since they can be regarded—by a sufficiently broad-minded accountant—as added costs. In this way the tax concessions probably help to create the profits that they protect. For another, it is not difficult to imagine that a firm depending upon this year's profits for next year's investment will be relatively disinclined to reduce prices to get larger volume. Once the need for cash abates there may be a greater willingness to seek larger turnover through lower prices. The prolonged downward movement of industrial prices lends some plausibility to this view.

The heavy reliance on self-financing had a variety of advantages. First and foremost it was in large measure an addition and not an alternative to outside financing. In the second place, self-financing was to some extent a condition of future

outside financing. Owing to the war and currency reform the
net worth of most firms was low in relation to their volume of
business. Slim equities made it hard to get money from banks
and other lenders. The building up of equities helped to
make business creditworthy.

Finally, self-financing created strong incentives. Businessmen would not have worked so hard to build up their firms if
in the end these were to be owned mainly by the banker. Nor
would they have worked and saved as they did had the savings
been drained off into a central pool instead of going into their
own firms. Internal financing meant encouragement and less
risk. Broadly speaking one might say that it stimulated the
autonomous investment which, as pointed out earlier, played
an important role in the growth of the German economy.

A variety of disadvantages, however, also accompanied this
kind of financing, and as time went on they began to weigh
more heavily, while the advantages diminished. The most frequently mentioned and potentially the most serious was the
unequal distribution of income and wealth. If business had
been compelled to raise all or most of its funds in the capital
market—not a realistic alternative—a wider circle of savers
would have participated in the rebuilding of business capital.
As it was, the perhaps 40 to 50 billion DMark of new business
equity formed from 1948 to 1953, plus all that was invested
before the currency reform, accrued to a rather limited group.
It must be observed, however, that this charge depends in
some measure on the assumption that self-financing really was
the *cause* of high prices and profits. If business had paid out
its profits instead of retaining them, but had nevertheless
charged the same prices, the recipients of this income would
still have been the main group from which business would
have had to seek its outside financing. The concentration of
ownership and wealth might not have been very much different in that case.

Self-financing also carried with it the steadily mounting

danger of misdirection of investment. Self-financing eliminated the capital market and the interest rate as selectors of
investment outlets. Initially, when there was great need for
capital in all lines, this did not matter too much. In fact, the
level of profits in an industry acted as a selector, although less
so than a good capital market could have done. High profits
implied a high demand for that industry's product and hence
a need for expansion. But the very ease of new investment, the
absence of the test of the market and of the advice of the
banker, together with the urge to invest in order to avoid
taxes, became increasingly dangerous as the limits of demand
were being approached. Another objection to self-financing
was that the relative ease with which it could be accomplished
threatened to become a block to the recovery of the capital
market.

Because of considerations like these steps were taken in
1951 toward the removal of some of the tax privileges upon
which much self-financing depended. The action seems to
have reduced the relative importance of that source of funds,
although the apparent decline shown in Table 16 for 1953 no
doubt greatly exaggerates the trend.

Public Investment

Public investment financed from all sources accounts for
close to one-quarter of total gross investment in recent
years. The bulk of this comes from the tax revenues of federal, state, and local authorities, and from the revenues of the
Compensation Fund and the social security agencies (Table
16). A further amount is financed by the same investors with
borrowed funds. (Table 17 gives the totals for this group, unfortunately not available for comparable periods.) A steadily
diminishing fraction derives from special public investment
programs, including counterpart funds, Investment Assistance (the resources of which remain privately owned), and
central bank "prefinancing" (Table 16). It should be noted

that in Table 16 public investment financed with borrowed funds is included under the respective source of funds, i.e., securities purchases and bank loans.

TABLE 17: *Public Investment 1950–53* *
(in millions of DMark)

	Housing	Aid to private business	Govern- ment enter- prises	Trans- porta- tion	Schools	Other	Total
Federal †	1,567	399	—	791	—	551	3,308
State †	2,687	1,089	350	740	713	1,397	6,976
Local †	970	—	360	930	770	2,135	5,165
Immediate Assistance and Equalization of War Burdens Fund	1,562	951	—	—	—	34	2,547
Subtotal	6,786	2,439	710	2,461	1,483	4,117	17,996
Social security funds							1,883
Total							19,879

* Excluding special public programs (see Table 16). Fiscal years beginning April 1.
† Segregation according to *source* of funds. Share of local authorities in *expenditures* is higher owing to transfers from federal and state budgets.
Source: Computed from Federal Ministry of Finance, *Finanzstatistik.*

Its bulk alone makes public investment a major factor in German capital formation. We have also observed its strategic importance in connection with investment planning, but have had to note that by no means all of it was amenable to central direction. The difficulties of coordination can be guessed from Table 17, which shows how large a part of total investment funds originated with state and local authorities. The share actually *spent* by local authorities is larger still, since a good part of the funds originating from federal and state sources are disbursed by local authorities.

We must now concern ourselves with the uses to which these public funds were put. It is important to note right away that about half of public investment outside the special programs took the form of financing of private or semiprivate enterprise, and that the special programs were directed toward private business almost exclusively. In particular, apart from the item "Aid to private business" (Table 17), the expenditures under "Housing" very largely went to finance either private builders or the building cooperatives, which are semiprivate if somewhat bureaucratic in character. To this must be added, no doubt, a large part of the social security agencies' investment, though details are not known. The important role played by private business in connection with public investment reduces somewhat the rather ominous impression conveyed by the statistical total.

Housing. Housing represents the core of public investment. That government at its various levels became so heavily involved in the housing picture, liberal principles notwithstanding, is the result of three factors: the extremity of the shortage, the desire to keep rents down, and the particular methods chosen to subsidize the rent level.

The statistics about the housing shortage are inconclusive. As of early 1951 the deficit was variously estimated at from 2.5 million dwelling units (Sonne Report) [5] to 4.8 million (Federal Ministry for Housing), [6] as against an existing 9.5 million dwelling units. The difference arose mainly out of different assumptions as to the number of occupants per dwelling unit appropriate to an empoverished country with a high proportion of one-member households. The degree of subsidization of rents would also play a role in the effective demand for housing. By any count the shortage was extreme and was being compounded by an annual increment in demand of about 250,000 units through population growth.

The housing situation has remained the one striking difference in living standards between Germany and its European neighbors. In 1950 one-fourth of all families had no regular home and was either sharing quarters or living in emergency homes, camps, bunkers, or cellars. In 1954 nearly half a million people still were living in camps. Virtually all dwelling space remained strictly controlled, with a maximum allowance of one room for each family member. With negligible exceptions all families whose apartment or home exceeded this allowance, and many whose did not, had others quartered with them. To the foreign visitor this extreme crampedness is the most distinguishing characteristic of the life of his German acquaintances who are otherwise in "comfortable" circumstances.

Strong pressures thus converged upon the government to do something about housing. Various programs were initiated. The most comprehensive was the first Housing Law,[7] which sought to coordinate federal, state, and local programs and called for the construction of 1.8 million units in six years. Special programs for resettlement, housing for refugees, miners' housing, and the like were pushed.

The bulk of the new housing was low cost (*Sozialer Wohnungsbau*), for which the law laid down precise specifications. Space was limited in accordance with the size of the family. Rent per square meter was specified, and the return to the landlord allowable in the cost calculations was fixed. Private financing was to be sought as far as possible, but to the extent that its cost could not be covered public funds were made available. To keep down the cost of private financing steps were taken to limit to 5 per cent the rate on mortgage bonds, these bonds being the chief means by which mortgage banks obtain funds for their operations. The rate on public funds was usually around 1 per cent, with very long amortization.

Other forms of residential construction, where greater freedom was allowed as to space and rent, received no direct subsidies but were in most cases aided by tax privileges, including the availability of interest-free loans under section 7c of the Income Tax Law. In the aggregate public funds contributed about one-half of total construction costs, while the capital market and the internal funds of builders supplied the other half in roughly equal shares. In 1953 the share of public funds began to decline.

The volume of construction has increased each year (see Table 18). In 1953 it reached 515,000 dwelling units, it will

TABLE 18: *Financing of Housing Construction, 1950–53*
(*in millions of DMark*)

	1950	1951	1952	1953	1954
Institutional investors	1,411	1,209	1,525	2,600	3,802
Public funds *	1,849	2,408	2,412	2,500	1,958
Other, including private	540	1,083	1,574	1,700	1,390
Total	3,800	4,700	5,511	6,800	7,150
Number of new dwelling units	360,000	430,000	440,000	515,000	550,000 +

* Including counterpart funds, except in 1953, for which year they are included under "Institutional investors."
Source: Dr. Walter Fey, "Leistung und Investition im Wohnungsbau der Bundesrepublik 1952," *Bundeswohnungsblatt*, 1953, *4*, 153. Figures for 1953 are estimates. Figures for 1954 are estimates computed from the Bank deutscher Länder, *Wirtschaftsstatistik*, Table IV, 1.

probably have exceeded 550,000 in 1954, and has throughout exceeded the annual goal of 300,000 set by the Housing Law. The investment for the year 1953 totalled 6.8 million DMark, with an average cost per dwelling unit of about 13,200 DMark.

The volume of housing created represents a tremendous achievement and a marked success in the battle with the housing problem. The 1954 rate of construction was equivalent to better than one dwelling unit for every 100 inhabitants. This exceeded peak levels of building in the United States and was far above comparable figures for the rest of Western Europe. All critical comments on particular aspects of the housing performance must first and foremost acknowledge these facts.

Nevertheless when one considers the shortage of capital, particularly prior to 1952 and 1953, it is perhaps not unreasonable to ask whether it might not have been better if the government had done more for utilities and transportation, both of which were important bottlenecks, even if this meant doing less for housing. It is true that at that time to aid housing was to aid productivity. It can hardly, however, have contributed as much as some other forms of investment might have. It is a matter of social viewpoint, therefore, whether housing, however urgently needed, is regarded as worth the sacrifice of an equivalent amount of more directly productive investment. In the last few years, however, when the supply of capital became more ample, this alternative has not really presented itself in a serious form.

A question also deserves to be raised with regard to rent policy. The rent freeze has been a strong element in wage and monetary stability. It has also, however, had a number of adverse effects. There were the usual unpleasant repercussions in the housing field itself, but more important have been the indirect effects upon the capital market, where the interest ceiling imposed on mortgage bonds and later the tax exemption accorded them have led first to a state of near paralysis and then to all manner of distortions. The heavy burden upon public budgets has been another unhappy consequence.

In some cases financial support seems to have been somewhat generous and to have enabled the builders to pay bootleg rates for funds in the capital market. The fact that the subsidies were given as capital sums, rather than as interest subsidies that would have enabled builders to borrow more from private sources, is another point about which criticism is sometimes heard. But all this is relatively minor. The outstanding fact remains that the tremendous job of rebuilding Western Germany, which immediately after the war was thought to require "one or two generations," has already been better than half completed.

Not much of a general character can be said about the rest of public investment, apart from the special public programs which are discussed below. The categories distinguished in Table 17 comprise a broad range of expenditures. "Aid to private business" includes such things as loans and grants for the repair of damage from war and dismantling, consolidation of small agricultural holdings, rural resettlement, and soil improvement. "Government enterprises" covers a good deal of utilities investment. It does not include the extensive self-financing of successful government-owned businesses like the Volkswagen Works. "Transportation" includes roads and bridges as well as government aid to the ailing Federal Railways. The allocations for utilities and transportation certainly have not been large. In appraising these figures it must be remembered that in large part they do not reflect the execution of a preconceived investment plan but are the final adding up of a variety of activities at various government levels.

Counterpart investment. Counterpart funds have played a strategic role in German investment, although their purely quantitative importance must not be overrated. The total employed from the currency reform to the end of 1953 was 3,852 million DMark, out of a total of 7,298 collected from GARIOA (Government and Relief in Occupied Areas) and Marshall Plan sources.[8] The balance in part went for aid to Berlin, in part was spent earlier or for noninvestment purposes, while a small amount remained in the bank. In 1950, however, the year of peak expenditure, counterpart amounted to 8 per cent of gross investment and to a much higher proportion of funds from sources other than business self-financing.

Apart from the Investment Assistance funds, counterpart investment was probably the most carefully planned of all capital expenditures. In 1949 and 1950 the underlying principle was to spread the money widely, with a view toward making up the deficiencies of the capital market and aiding export-intensive industries. When the Korea crisis revealed serious bottlenecks in coal, steel, and power the program was shifted mainly to these sectors. Later the program was reoriented once more, this time to support the Western defense effort.[9] A summary of investments programmed from counterpart funds is shown in Table 19.

TABLE 19: *ECA-MSA Counterpart Investment Program*
(programmed to November 30, 1954)

	Millions of DMark	Per cent
Food and agriculture	451	12.4
Electric energy	736	20.2
Gas and water	107	2.9
Coal mining	442	12.2
Iron and steel	228	6.3
Other industries	552	15.2
Transport and communications	293	8.0
Housing	497	13.7
(Miners' housing)	(169)	(4.6)
Expellees and refugees	181	5.0
Tourism	24	.6
Research	31	.9
Pending	95	2.6
	3,637	100.00

Source: Office of the U.S. High Commissioner for Germany, *Handbook of Economic Statistics,* (Bonn, January 1, 1955).

The disbursement of the funds, including the choice of a specific borrower within the general field to which they were allotted, was handled by the Reconstruction Loan Corporation, an independent government-owned institution.[10] The corporation generally sought the cooperation of the borrower's own bank as well as governmental or other guarantees. By approaching its problem along banking lines, the corporation scored a remarkable success in the difficult task of lending money to borrowers whose position often was uncertain.

Investment Assistance. The Investment Assistance was an interesting operation through which funds from all industrial sectors were made available to two or three industries that were in particular need of financing.[11] Contributions were assessed upon all major industrial firms and collected like a tax. But to minimize the flavor of statism the creditors received not a government security but obligations of the particular concerns to whom they were compelled to lend their money.

The operation arose out of the realization that existing sources of financing were insufficient to meet the urgent needs of the bottleneck industries—coal, iron and steel, and utilities. It has the appearance of an admission, therefore, of a greater need for planning than the architects of the German system had originally envisaged. At the same time it must be pointed out that the financial plight of the coal, iron, and steel industries, if not of the utilities, was itself the result of a government policy which, through price ceilings, limited their ability both to finance themselves internally and to attract external funds.

The total amount aimed at was one billion DMark, which has since been exceeded by something over 100 million. It was collected in installments through the regular finance offices, allocated by a board of industry representatives, and distributed through the Industriekreditbank, an institution created for "industrial self-help." [12] The allocation of funds is shown in Table 20. Despite strong initial resistance on the

TABLE 20: *Allocation of Investment Assistance*
(as of June 30, 1953, in millions of DMark)

	Industry quotas	Disbursements
Coal	234	173
Iron and steel	278	219
Electric power	252	211
Gas	126	73
Water	60	57
Equipment for Federal Railways	50	50
Total	1,000	783

Source: Kuratorium für das Industriekreditbank-Sondervermögen Investitionshilfe, *Annual Report,* 1952–53.

part of industry the plan, once imposed by law, seems to have worked satisfactorily within the rather narrow limits of its resources.

Bank Credit

Bank credit has played a very great role in the financing of investment. Immediately after the currency reform many businesses used short-term bank loans to finance capital expansion. Later on the banks became the chief recipients of consumer savings and engaged in large-scale lending on medium and long term. The exact dimensions of these operations, however, are not easily defined.

The volume of bank-credit financing. Total loans of banks (including savings banks) in November 1954 amounted to 51.1 billion DMark, of which 26.9 billion were medium and long term. Securities holdings of 4.0 billion must be added. A very large part of the medium- and long-term bank credit went into investment including inventories. A good part of this was accounted for by operations in which the banks acted merely as intermediaries, without initiative or discretion, such as the distribution of funds from public budgets, counterpart, and central bank prefinancing. Medium- and long-term loans financed from sources other than those just mentioned and exclusive also of operations financed with mortgage bonds are shown in Table 16.

The contribution made by short-term credit cannot be specified even approximately. In Table 16 a certain amount of it is merged with self-financing, as a balancing item. A large part of short-term credit no doubt failed to lead to an equivalent volume of capital formation. A reconciliation of actual capital formation with the increase in net liquid assets of businesses and individuals is unfortunately not possible.

Some idea of the relative importance of different forms of saving in financing the expansion of bank credit can nevertheless be obtained from the following calculation. The combined gain from mid '48 to December 1954 in medium- and long-term loans (excluding those financed from special sources) and in long-term securities holdings, amounting to 26.4 billion DMark, is just slightly larger than the aggregate gain of time deposits, saving deposits, and bank capital of about 24.5 billion. One may say, therefore, that long-term bank credit expansion has been approximately compensated by new savings deposits and bank capital. This means very roughly that all short-term credit has been financed through money creation. Whatever contribution to investment financing was therefore made by short-term credit has been financed, in effect, by money creation. This is a very interesting conclusion. Ordinarily one would expect any rapid and substantial money creation for investment financing to produce inflationary pressure. One would further expect, in an economy with an orthodox and generally restrictive monetary policy, that such financing would have been kept low. Evidently Germany has been able to get away with a good deal of it without paying a penalty. How did this happen?

The answer that suggests itself is two-fold. First, the economy was so far stripped of its liquid resources by the currency reform that a large increase in money was needed to reconstitute normal liquidity. Second, the rapid increase in national income called for a commensurate increase in cash balances. A very considerable amount of investment financing through money creation could therefore be absorbed because of the great need to accumulate cash balances. This accumulation represented as genuine an act of saving as any savings deposits or securities purchases.

It would in my view be erroneous to argue, as has sometimes been done, that the noninflationary character of this financing was due to the fact that the credits were short rather than long term. Even in those limited cases where short-term credits were technically self-liquidating they have financed an expansion of inventories and productive activity that is an integral part of the economic structure. Credits which may be self-liquidating from a private financial point of view are in effect permanent for the economy as a whole. They could not be liquidated in the aggregate without bringing business to a halt. What made these credits noninflationary was therefore not their short-term character but the capacity of the economy to absorb the resulting increase in the volume of money.

With the slowing down of growth and the reconstitution of cash balances the possibilities for investment financing through money creation have diminished, if not disappeared altogether. The banking system seems to have made the necessary adjustment to this situation automatically, for in 1953 the creation of money through bank credit came practically to an end.

Banking structure and practices. The pattern of financing has been largely determined by the structure and practices of the German banking system. The largest single component of the system is represented by the commercial banks (consisting of the successor institutions of the former *Grossbanken,* the state, regional, and local banks, and private bankers). These account for about 30 per cent of total bank resources (excluding the central banking system). They hold better than 60 per cent of the total short-term credits and of sight and time deposits. Their role in the long-term credit field is relatively modest. Large business firms deal predominantly with banks in this group.

The second largest group consists of the savings banks, with about one-quarter of total bank resources. Nearly half of their deposits, however, are sight and time deposits, and short-term credits account for over one-third of their loans. These short-term credit relations are predominantly with smaller firms. The savings banks are municipally owned and politically powerful. Their operations, especially in the promotion of saving and in credit assistance to small business, reflect a strong public service spirit.

Among the remaining institutions are the mortgage banks, with 10 per cent of total bank resources; the central institutions of the savings banks (*Girozentralen*), with 13 per cent; the credit cooperatives, with 7 per cent; and the latters' own central institutions (*Zentralkassen*), with 2 per cent. Of these groups the first two are important in long-term real estate credit.

Because of the magnitude of their operations chief interest attaches to the problems and policies of the commercial and savings banks. From the day of the currency reform they as well as the rest of the banking system found themselves under terrific pressure to rebuild their loan volume. The reform had cut total bank resources by 90 per cent or more. For a while it seemed almost impossible for the banks to cover even their operating expenses. Eager lenders, however, found eager borrowers. Both were aided by a central banking system that for the time did not inquire too closely into the quality of the material that it was asked to rediscount. The rapid expansion and high profits of the period prevented these loans from going bad. Many of them, however, having been used for equipment purchases, proved slow.

The problems arising out of the use of short-term credits for investment purposes affected particularly the commercial banks. In times gone by they would have been quite prepared to prefinance capital investment in this form. Such credits would eventually have been consolidated through issues of securities with which the banks would have liquidated their engagements. This was the practice—not considered entirely orthodox in Anglo-Saxon countries—by which the banks had helped to speed up German development before the first World War.

Although the practice had fallen into some disrepute during

the great depression, it would nevertheless have been logical
for the banks to resume it under the circumstances, had the
securities market been able to absorb an adequate volume
of issues. This was conspicuously not the case. At first almost
dormant, the securities market recovered very slowly and in
no way sufficiently to permit large-scale consolidation of the
banks' short- and medium-term investment credits. The banks
obtained some relief through the rapid rise in time and savings
deposits. This represented a kind of internal consolidation of
their position. The question remains, however, whether on the
basis of these resources they can afford to grant further investment credits with medium- to long-term maturities.

Rising savings deposits call for a compensating increase in
bank credit. The expansion of bank lending that is required
to prevent the increase in savings deposits from contracting
both the active money supply and the flow of expenditures
can equally well take the form of short- or long-term credit.
Either type will serve to maintain the money supply and the
expenditure stream. The needs of the market, however, have
run much more toward long- than toward short-term credit.
The rise in savings deposits suggests that long-term credit
ought to be available. But the channeling of long-term credit
through the banking system, particularly through the commercial banks, presents certain difficulties.

The capital needs of large industrial enterprises run into
enormous sums. Even if the banks are willing to make longer-
term loans the ability of any bank to lend to a single customer
is limited by the risk factor. The capacity of German banks to
grant large loans has been further reduced through the Allied
action of splitting the former Grossbanken into smaller units.

The banks might be able to make their time and savings
deposits available to long-term borrowers through the purchase of securities. Yet this is also no ideal solution. Given the
present narrowness of the market, securities do not offer a
high degree of liquidity. Securities investment, therefore,

solves only the problem of risk diversification, not that arising out of possible withdrawals of deposits. How great is this latter danger?

The rate of turnover of savings deposits has been high, about 0.7 times a year. A rather pronounced volatility appears to be indicated. Smaller banks are therefore exposed to a fairly high risk of deposit withdrawals directed specifically against them, as well as to the possibility of a universal shrinkage in deposits resulting from a passive balance of payments or from some other cause of monetary contraction. For the larger banks with their far-flung branch system only the second danger seems real, since they can count on retaining their usual share of total deposits. One may assume that a universal liquidity crisis resulting from an all-round drop in deposits would be countered by the central banking system. But this is something on which the banks cannot rely with certainty. The reluctance of the commercial banks to push their long-term credits or buy securities aggressively is understandable therefore.

It is true that the law partially or wholly exempting most fixed interest securities from income tax has created a strong incentive for commercial banks to buy securities.[13] The gradual trend toward lower interest rates, which has lifted the present 7½ to 8 per cent industrial bonds to a premium, has enhanced the attraction of such investment. Yet the banks' total securities holdings in November 1954 had not gone beyond 4.0 billion DMark, equal to only 5 per cent of their total resources. Of this the commercial banks held 1.7 billion, equal to 7 per cent of their resources.

The accelerating growth of savings deposits is likely to intensify the problem. Even if the banks should respond by expanding their long-term credits or by purchasing more securities, the situation would not be completely satisfactory. One cannot contemplate the prospect of a rapidly growing mass of highly liquid savings without a certain uneasiness, even though there is no reason to believe that they must inevitably become a source of instability. This emphasizes the critical importance attaching to the improvement of the securities market.

Securities Market

The narrowness of the securities market has not been as much of a handicap for the German recovery as had been expected. Through self-financing, through short-term borrowing, and in other ways business managed to obtain the funds that the open market was unable to supply. As time went on, however, the limits of this process were being approached. Qualitative factors such as the selection of projects, the length of commitments, and cost were becoming increasingly important. The financing of at least a part of total investment through the securities market was therefore becoming more and more urgent. We shall review first the various policies that were employed to regulate and revive this market. We shall then proceed to survey the various borrowers and lenders in it, and their respective needs and contributions.

Securities market policies. Official policies have been a curious mixture of stimulation and interference. Strongly stimulating was the income-tax provision that permitted savings invested in securities to be deducted from taxable income. However, this applied only to federal, state, and certain municipal bonds and to mortgage bonds for the financing of low-cost housing.* Industrial securities were excluded. Moreover, since life insurance, savings deposits, and other forms of savings were accorded the same privileges, the securities market still had to compete with these alternative forms of investment.

In this race the securities market was decisively handicapped by a ruling of the Capital Issues Committee limiting interest

---

* In all cases the securities had to be purchased from the issuer and held for three years.

on mortgage bonds to 5 per cent and on industrial bonds to 6½.[14] The purpose of this regulation was to keep the cost of mortgage money in line with the level of rents fixed for low-cost housing. Its effect was greatly to reduce the supply of investment funds for all users. Mortgage bonds at 5 per cent were bought only by certain public agencies, such as the social security funds, whose policy it was to aid low-cost housing. For other buyers a black market soon developed in which the bonds could be had at a discount of 10 to 12 per cent.[15] The entire securities market was thus stymied by the effort to harness it to the needs of some subsidized borrowers.

The deadlock was broken late in 1952 by the First Capital Market Law. Interest on low-cost housing mortgage bonds was fully exempted from income tax. Industrial bonds were subjected to a flat 30 per cent coupon tax in lieu of income tax. Interest rates were freed from controls in the expectation that tax-free bonds would sell easily at rates of 5 per cent or less. The purpose of the measure, very plainly, was to help borrowers get money, not to help tax payers reduce their burden. In effect, however, the second was accomplished along with the first to an unexpected degree.

Borrowers. The Capital Market Law had considerable effect in moving securities. In 1953 about 3 billion DMark were sold against 1.6 billion in 1952. A detailed picture of the volume and kind of securities coming to the market since the currency reform is given in Table 21.

Remarkable particularly has been the large volume of borrowing by public authorities. Most of this has been at 5 per cent or slightly higher and for relatively short periods. Industrial borrowers subject to the 30 per cent coupon tax have been forced to pay 7½ to 8 per cent in order to compete. It is widely argued in Germany that the public authorities have offered needlessly favorable terms and have borrowed far ahead of their current expenditure needs. In this way, it is said, they have made credit unnecessarily scarce and expensive for other borrowers.

TABLE 21 : *Security Issues 1948–53*
(in millions of DMark)

	Mortgage bonds	Munici-pals	Obligations of special credit insti-tutions and others	Indus-trial bonds	Federal, state, and other public bodies	Shares	Total
1948–49 *	217.4	35.3	19.9	105.7	170.4	41.8	580.5
1950	210.7	99.2	36.3	53.2	57.1	51.2	507.7
1951	468.0	158.9	1.9	61.7	56.9	164.7	912.1
1952	628.1	161.3	19.8	130.3	418.2	259.3	1,617.0
1953	1,043.4	429.4	258.4	396.2	486.5	268.7	3,182.6
Total	2,567.6	884.1	336.3	747.1	1,189.1	785.7	6,799.9

* Since the currency reform.
Source: Bank deutscher Länder, *Monthly Report,* March 1954.

Share flotations have been small. Moreover, even those appearing in Table 21 reflect in the main not issues sold to the public but private placements with existing large share-holders. The reason is the very high level of taxes on corporate income. Until 1955 corporate income tax of 60 per cent plus various minor taxes added up to an average burden of 70 per cent, except for income paid out in dividends, for which the income tax was cut to 30 per cent. This made common-stock financing extremely expensive to the corporation. On the side of the investor, stock purchases do not enjoy the tax exemption on income saved, while dividends are subject to the full income tax. These circumstances have long weighed down the price of shares and have further discouraged stock financing. Since the middle of 1953, however, stock prices have been rising continually despite these handicaps. During the latter part of 1954 the movement assumed boom proportions. The average yield on stocks, fully taxable, declined to 2.63 per cent as contrasted with *tax-free* yields of 5 per cent on bonds.

At these levels stock financing should prove considerably more attractive to corporations.

Buyers of securities. The principal buyers of securities appear in Table 22. The data are in some respects tentative, but the main characteristics stand out. It is evident that the market is highly institutionalized; individuals seem to account for little more than 10 per cent. The true amount under this heading may be somewhat larger since the table does not include securities purchased by the banks for investment that may later have been resold to customers, but the share of individuals is small in any case.

TABLE 22: *Buyers of Securities, 1953*
(*in millions of DMark*)

Banks	1,100
Nonfinancial businesses	325
Individuals	325
Insurance	275
Government and other	1,157
Total	3,182

Source: Estimated from data in Bank deutscher Länder, *Monthly Report,* March 1954.

The predominance of the public purse is even more pronounced here than on the side of the borrowers. A good part of these purchases is accounted for by the social security agencies, who along with other public bodies often employ low-cost housing mortgage bonds as a vehicle for financing specific housing projects. In such cases, where the mortgage bank acts purely as intermediary and without discretion of its own, a real capital market transaction can hardly be said to occur.

The banks are the second largest investor group. This is plainly a result of the income-tax privileges that bonds enjoy. Bank profits, like all business profits, have been subject to a tax burden averaging 70 per cent—somewhat lower if dividends are paid. The ideal position for a bank, taxwise, is to have its resources invested in high yielding loans up to the point where the returns cover costs, and to put the remainder, which brings in the profits, into securities with a yield of about 5 per cent net of taxes. The banks have not gone quite so far, in particular they do not seem to have cut down proportionately on loans. Instead they seem to have increased their securities portfolio by investing funds that might otherwise have gone to reduce indebtedness to the central banking system. It is via this unanticipated mechanism, which involves additional money creation, that the tax exemption of securities mainly appears to have increased the volume of securities bought. It may be added, however, that savings banks have played only a small role in the securities picture. They enjoy a special tax status with regard to earnings from loans, which approximately balances the advantages of tax exempt securities.

In the case of nonfinancial businesses, which at a rough guess may have accounted for a little over 10 per cent of total purchases, something similar has taken place. Five per cent net of taxes has been better in Germany than 15 per cent before taxes. This makes the temptation to put spare funds into tax exempt securities almost overwhelming. Some firms reportedly have even borrowed for the purpose; since the 6 to 8 per cent interest that they may have to pay is tax deductible, there is still a profit. These things are minor, of course, but they show how seriously the tax situation has distorted the market.

Insurance companies—life, health, and fire and accident companies—have placed only about one-quarter of their additions to reserves in securities. Since they pay only a nominal income tax, the tax exemption and coupon tax feature positively militates against putting money into securities. This has been an awkward result of the Capital Market Law and underlines once more the artificial character of the situation.

Under ordinary conditions insurance companies would be natural candidates for large securities purchases, though they will probably always do some of their investing through the present practice of direct placements.

Individuals are estimated to have bought about the same volume of securities as nonfinancial businesses. It is they whom the tax privileges were probably designed to attract. They have responded only moderately, however, and have no doubt done so more by shifting away from other forms of investment than by increasing their total savings.

The small participation of individuals reflects a situation familiar all over the world. The high income person, who used to be the mainstay of the securities market, has almost been taxed out of existence. In Germany special conditions prevail that further reduce his interest in securities: recollection of the bad treatment of bonds in the currency reform; the need to rebuild a home; in the case of independent businessmen, who are best placed taxwise, the usually urgent needs of their own businesses. It is likely that in the course of time lower taxes and a slower rate of business expansion may again increase the wealthy or highly paid man's interest in securities purchases. That he will again resume his dominant position in the securities market seems unlikely, however. This does not mean that the securities market itself is doomed to play a diminishing role in investment financing. It does mean that the growing institutionalization of the market must be accepted, and that the institutions in question must become aware of their responsibility.

For the German economy the advantages of securities financing over other forms of business financing are manifold. A better selection of investment projects is likely as compared with self-financing; longer maturities, greater flexibility, and greater independence are the advantages as contrasted with bank credit. Securities purchases by savers reduce the potential instability that would emanate from steadily rising bank deposits. Better regional distribution of investment could be achieved as contrasted with politically influenced public financing. A good securities market would probably bring down rates; the future volume of investment in Germany may well depend upon getting away from recent coupon rates of 7½ to 8 per cent. Monetary and fiscal policy also stand to gain from a broad market.

That the securities market, however, should completely displace internal financing seems neither probable nor desirable. Internal financing, as pointed out before, has the advantage of favoring anticipatory investment in which greater risks can be taken. A substantial amount of such investment has been one of the strong points of the German economy and is desirable for the future.

The German securities market has had to make a difficult transition. The Capital Market Law that finally expired at the end of 1954 had broken it up into many small compartments. Enormously complicated and often quite artificial considerations, differing from buyer to buyer and often giving quite unwarranted tax advantages, were created by that law. These things were remnants of a form of interventionism that the German economy had sloughed off more rapidly in other fields. The market probably will be the better for their elimination, although the temporary advantages of the law were considerable.

Conclusion

During the last six years Germany has invested very large amounts and brought about a tremendous increase in national income. Yet Germany is generally regarded as a capital-poor country. This seeming contradiction throws an interesting light upon several aspects of German investment and its financing.

Germany is undoubtedly capital-poor, in terms of past accumulations of capital, in comparison with the man-made resources stored up by some of her western neighbors. Comparative data are lacking, but the conclusion follows, inescapably from the relatively low productivity of German industry.

Germany also is capital-poor in terms of current savings flowing through normal channels. Long-term credit from banks or in the securities market is still scarce. Much of the industrial expansion has had to be financed from slightly abnormal sources: extraordinary profits and short-term bank credit, the latter reflected in money creation.

Germany has not been capital-poor in the sense that its physical resources have been strained by the high level of investment. The limitation upon capital formation has been not productive capacity but a monetary policy that limited credit expansion in order to safeguard the balance of payments and the currency. Investment could have been increased, at least in the short run, by drawing upon idle labor, though only at the cost of external imbalance. The capital shortage in this sense was the result of equilibrium policy not of physical limitations.

With the investment that took place Germany achieved a large increase in income. She was able to do this because at first investment was in good part reconstruction. Small amounts of capital, strategically applied, brought large additions to output. Germany was further aided by the concentration, natural in a free market when capital is scarce, of investment in fields with low capital intensity, i.e., with a low ratio of capital to output and with quick returns.

As a consequence, however, she has built up a backlog of investment needs of a different type, which will have to be met eventually if the economy is to enjoy balanced growth. These are the capital intensive investments that yield relatively low increases in output. Among these are investments in roads and other forms of transportation and in public utilities. There is also housing, which is already absorbing large amounts of capital. Finally, there is modernization of industry, which will call for larger amounts of capital per worker.

Investments of these types not only require very large amounts of capital but usually also offer only moderate rates of return. They will therefore confront the financing mechanism with new tasks. A good part of these investments is of the type that is best financed through the open capital market. A larger flow of funds than is now forthcoming will be required. Interest rates will have to come down from their present high levels, and terms may have to lengthen beyond what is presently customary. Germany needs much investment, but its realization will probably depend on easier financing conditions.

CHAPTER 7

Industrial Structure, Import Needs, and Export Capacity

THE MAIN CHARACTERISTICS of Germany's economic structure before and after the war are well known. Germany has for many years been a strongly industrialized country, with a preponderance in the heavy industries and a pronounced weakness in food and raw materials. Strong dependence on export markets and imported supplies have always made Germany's position precarious. After war and partition this position appeared to have become precarious in the extreme. Yet, remarkably, the fears widely harbored on this score have proved unwarranted, at least so far. Despite its seeming imbalance the present industrial structure of Western Germany has shown itself no obstacle to growth and a strong international position. On the contrary, it appears to have favored them in many respects.

The structure of the economy on the one hand has aided domestic investment and exports through its accent on capital goods. On the other hand it has helped to keep down the need for imported foodstuffs and raw materials to a remarkable degree. The origins of this favorable constellation are to be analyzed in the present chapter. We shall deal with (1) the evolution of the present industrial and agricultural structure through partition, war damage, and new investment; (2) the productivity of industry; (3) the factors that have kept down dependence on imports; and (4) the special ability of German industry to meet the present pattern of world demand.

Evolution of Present Industrial and Agricultural Structure

The industrial and agricultural structure of Western Germany has shown itself extraordinarily successful in meeting the demands made upon it, except for its inability for a number of years to provide full employment, a failure largely explainable by special circumstances. In the light of these accomplishments it would be hard to argue that the German economy does not constitute a well-rounded, integrated whole. How did this come about?

The present structure is the result of several conflicting influences. On the negative side there are partition, wartime destruction, and postwar dismantling and output limitations imposed by the Allies. On the positive side are the transfer or rebuilding of industries lost in the East and the repair and tremendous expansion of most existing industries.

Partition. When in the course of the early postwar years partition came to be understood as a definitive reality, it was widely regarded as a major catastrophe. This could hardly have been otherwise. A closely knit economy—even though since the war it had not functioned as such—was being torn apart into seemingly meaningless fragments. Prospects for revival had always been thought to rest upon the implementation of the Potsdam decision to treat Germany as an economic whole. The definitive loss of East German markets and sources of supply looked like a devastating blow to these prospects. "Without a return to the *status quo* in the East, only death or emigration of 20 million Germans can effectively ease the food situation," was the verdict of a major German survey at the end of 1947.[1]

An analysis of the data shows that the catastrophe was not nearly so great as feared. This is particularly true as far as industrial production was concerned. In agriculture it was graver, but even here countervailing forces arose to soften the impact. These conclusions are of course purely economic. They do not refer to the political problem created, nor to the suffering of millions of people under Russian rule, nor to the unhappiness of refugees deprived of their homes.

Industrially, Western Germany lost two highly important areas: Silesia, with its concentration in coal and heavy industry, and Saxony, which was strong in textiles and machinery. The industrial capacity of Berlin, dominated by the electrical industry, was also largely lost through the initial Russian occupation of the city. But even so the net result was that Western Germany, which before the war had accounted for 56 per cent of the population, found itself with 61 per cent of prewar industrial capacity.* [2]

For a surprisingly large number of industries the division ran close to this average. Only a few lost substantially more capacity than markets, with consequent undercapacity, or more markets than capacity, with consequent excess capacity. The broad picture appears in Table 23. The data show that in basic materials production Western Germany retained 66 per cent of prewar capacity. In capital goods it kept 61 per cent, and in consumer goods only 54 per cent.

These broad groupings tend to obscure, of course, the more severe disequilibrium produced in particular industries. Extreme cases of undercapacity were the electrical equipment industry, retaining only 38 per cent of prewar capacity, clothing 39 per cent, precision instruments and optical equipment 50 per cent, glass and ceramics 48 per cent. Substantial excess capacity occurred in the leather industry and in the

---

* Data regarding the division of industrial capacity are uncertain, even if we disregard changes brought about by post-1936 investment and wartime destruction. The figures above are based upon sales, not value added or actual plant capacity, and exclude food processing and stimulants, electric power, construction, oils and fats, and some minor items.

TABLE 23: *Effect of Partition and Rebuilding upon Industry*

| | Share of West Germany in 1936 Industrial Output * | Composition of Industrial Output * | | | Index of Production ‡ 1953 (1936 = 100) |
| | | 1936 | | West Germany | |
		Reich	West Germany	1952 †	
All industry §	61%				157
Basic materials industries	66	38.6	41.8	39.3	140‡||
Mining	65	8.1	8.7	5.7	129
Iron and steel foundries	77	7.4	9.3	9.1	100
Nonferrous metals	63	4.2	4.4	1.6§	141
Oil	65	1.9	2.0	2.9	300
Nonmetallic minerals	62	3.8	4.0	3.9	118
Chemicals and artificial fibers and plastics	65	7.8	8.4	11.6	182†
Rubber and asbestos	77	1.1	1.4	1.8	166
Paper	48	2.6	2.0	1.3	120
Wood processing	57	1.7	1.6	1.4	98‡
Capital goods industries	61	31.1	31.2	34.3	175||
Machinery	58	9.1	8.6	11.1	184
Vehicles	68	3.8	4.3	5.9	202
Iron, steel, and metal products	70	10.0	11.4	6.1	129

Column totals: 1936 Reich 100%, 1936 West Germany 100%, 1952 West Germany 100%.

Steel construction and shipbuilding	77	2.3	3.0	2.9	113
Electrical equipment	38	4.8	3.0	6.7	318
Instruments, including optical goods	50	1.1	0.9	1.6	196
Consumer goods industries	53	30.3	27.0	26.4	156‡ ||
Glass and ceramics	48	1.5	1.2	1.9	157‡
Wood products	60	2.9	2.9	3.1	
Paper products and printing	50	3.9	3.2	3.0	
Leather goods, including shoes, etc.	72	3.5	4.2	2.7	86
Textiles	55	14.9	13.2	11.2	146
Clothing	39	3.6	2.3	4.5	

* Data are based on sales, not value added. The table therefore shows not the absolute importance of different industries but only changes in their relative importance.

† In 1936 prices.

‡ Industrial average differs slightly from earlier columns.

§ Incomplete data, correct value higher.

|| The industries listed separately under this total do not comprise all the industries entering into the total.

Sources: Ifo-Institut für Wirtschaftsforschung, *Fünf Jahre Deutsche Mark* (München, 1953). Discrepancies, particularly in percentage data, are due to rounding.

iron- and steel-producing and -fabricating industries—where for other reasons, however, the problem generally did not become acute.

A few highly specialized industrial lines suffered complete disaster. Some forms of chemical production were lost entirely, likewise some stages of paper production, certain types of textile and office equipment machinery, the hosiery industry, the glove industry, and others. Agricultural machinery and shoe production had extreme excess capacity.

In addition there were certain losses that do not appear in a purely quantitative appraisal. Certain regions lost their natural hinterland and had difficulty developing new ties. Raw materials and output had to be shipped over long distances, and the resulting costs placed these regions at a permanent disadvantage. Along the iron curtain in eastern Bavaria and Lower Saxony distressed border areas have developed, while the center of activity has shifted increasingly toward North Rhine-Westphalia. These are regional losses to be set against the general ease with which the purely quantitative consequences of partition have been overcome. But painful as these things were in their spheres, they did not weigh heavily in the general picture. That picture is unquestionably one of a remarkably—and quite fortuitously—successful operation that left the patient with his vital organs in fair balance and working condition.

In agriculture Western Germany fared less well. The area of the Federal Republic, which in 1936 had 56 per cent of the population, retained only 51 per cent of the agricultural land and 54 per cent of the forest land. In the Oder-Neisse territories a food surplus sufficient to feed 7 million people was lost. Heaviest were the losses in bread grains—a surplus for the normal consumption of 13.5 million people. These losses, however, did not fall fully upon Western Germany, since middle Germany, which became the Russian Zone, had also relied on the eastern bread basket. In middle Germany, on the other hand, Western Germany lost part of its supplies of milk products and such special items as seed potatoes and seed grain.[3]

Yet, as we shall see, the seemingly desperate dependence upon imported food that these figures suggest did not materialize. Germany, perverse as this may sound, may even have benefited in some respects from the disappearance of some of her traditional sources of food. Grain from Eastern Germany had been expensive, kept above world market prices by a stiff tariff. West Germany had paid for it by shipping other goods to East Germany. Today she sells the same or similar goods in world markets and with the proceeds buys wheat at world market prices. One cannot say for sure that the new pattern provides better terms of trade, because West German goods may have brought better prices in East German markets than they do abroad, but the probability exists.*

There are certain other burdens that the economy of Eastern Germany formerly imposed upon Western Germany which have also been removed by partition. The relative economic weakness of the area had compelled the rest of the country to give it financial and economic aid. The great political strength of its ruling class tended to weight German economic policy in a direction favorable to these interests. The removal of such burdens means little in contrast to the general tragedy of partition, but their economic significance must be recognized.

War damage and dismantling. It is natural that after the great wartime effort made by the Allies to bomb German industry

---

* In actual practice much East German grain was sold not in Western Germany but to neighboring countries under an ingenious subsidy scheme. For each ton of grain so exported the exporter received a certificate authorizing the duty-free importation into Germany of an equivalent amount. This certificate represented a value equal to the amount of the duty and could be sold to German grain importers. The latter used it to import grain from the world market, and the producer received a subsidy equal to the tariff protection he enjoyed at home.

to a standstill the extent of war damage should at first have
been greatly overrated. As time went on initial estimates
were repeatedly revised downward. An early German estimate,
covering all four zones and taking into account the effects of
past dismantling, puts total capacity in 1947 at no more than
68 per cent of 1936.[4] The German long-term program for the
ECA, prepared a year or two later, estimates Western Germany's industrial capacity at 90 per cent of prewar. Later this
estimate was raised to 103 per cent. In addition to the overestimate of damage there was evidently an underestimate of
the German workman's ability and willingness to dig through
rubble and fit together the bits and pieces of his wrecked
machinery. The amount of repair work that could be handled
by a plant's own labor force—favored by its tax deductibility
—proved much greater than had been believed.

Dismantling and industrial limitations imposed by the
Allies likewise seem to have been less burdensome in the
aggregate than the discussion of them, particularly in German literature, tends to make them appear. The initial bark,
as expressed in JCS (Joint Chiefs of Staff) Directive 1067, was
a great deal worse than the eventual bite. Successive dismantling lists continually reduced the scope of the first sweep-
ing plan. Industrial controls, at first severe, were rapidly lifted
so that only a limited number of industries were effectively
restricted. In general ceilings on output were removed as
soon as production began to press against them.

Reshaping of industrial output. Having surveyed the damage
done by war, partition, and dismantling, we shall now take a
look at the new structure of industry and agriculture that has
emerged from the debris. For industry this is shown in Table
23. The table compares this new industrial structure with
that of 1936 as well as with that which emerged from partition.
The first comparison, with 1936, shows us the movement from
one integrated and balanced structure to another, using the

terms integrated and balanced to describe a pattern of production that meets the demands of its day. There is no reason to doubt that the economy of the 1936 Reich as well as that of Western Germany in 1952 were reasonably well integrated in this sense. The second comparison, of the new structure with that emerging from partition, shows us the distance that had to be traveled to correct the distortions produced by partition. It must be observed that the actual distortions resulted not only from partition but also from war and dismantling, compensated on the other hand by whatever new capacity was created during the years 1936–45. This second comparison, therefore, provides only a very rough measure of the reshaping of output that was necessary.

For lack of better data the structure of output is stated in terms of the volume of sales. Since some industries purchase the product of others, sales volume is very far from "value added." The data therefore indicate only changes in the relative importance of particular industries, which can be measured approximately by sales volume, and not the absolute contribution to national income. The *capacity* of an industry in 1936 probably may be taken as approximately proportional to its *output* for that year, since the German economy was then approaching capacity operation. When we compare 1952 output with that of 1936 the first important fact to be observed is that output, and hence probably capacity, in all major branches of industry has reached or surpassed the 1936 level.

Somewhat varied developments become apparent when we next look at the *structure* of output and compare the relative shares of the main industrial groups—basic materials, capital goods, and consumer goods—at different points of time. The capital goods industries, whose relative position was left practically unchanged by partition, increased their proportionate weight in 1952 by about 10 per cent above what it was in 1936. The consumer goods industries, which suffered badly from partition, failed to regain their old weight and dropped further to 14 per cent below 1936. (1952 was admittedly not a good year for consumer goods.) The basic materials group seems to have been the only one where an initial overweight due to partition was largely redressed subsequently. This impression, however, is due only to the performance of the mining industry, chiefly coal, which showed a severe loss in relative weight. If mining is excluded partition increased the share of basic materials industries by almost 10 per cent, a gain which was even slightly extended thereafter. Thus capital goods and basic materials in effect gained in relative importance, as contrasted with 1936, at the expense of consumer goods and mining.

The structural changes in industry have been of great importance for Germany's ability to carry out domestic reconstruction and expansion and to meet her balance of payments problem. The shift toward more capital goods and relatively less consumer goods reflects the high investment demand and the restraint of consumption. It has enabled Germany to take advantage of existing international demand and to push her exports. The increased weight of the basic materials industries (except coal) has probably helped to reduce the country's traditional dependence upon imported raw materials. We shall return to these aspects presently.

When we investigate how far the 1952 structure of output has overcome the distortions resulting from partition, further interesting facts appear. In many cases postwar development has reversed the effects of partition and has moved back toward the proportions of 1936. But these cases are by no means a majority. Often the effect of partition seems to have been accentuated by subsequent development, as in the case of many consumer goods industries. In some instances where the change has been reversed the reversal has been carried far beyond the 1936 proportion, e.g., in the electrical equipment industry.

Broadly speaking, the data suggest that any disproportionalities created by partition have been overcome and that the gaps in the structure of production have been filled. Where the present structure deviates from that of 1936 this seems to have resulted from adaptation to the needs of the day. German industry again appears to have an extremely well-rounded production program. Impressions gained from nonstatistical sources tend to confirm this view.

In purely quantitative terms the filling of the partition gaps, important as it was, represents no very surprising achievement. The gaps themselves turned out to be much smaller than had been feared. Given the fact of partition, the economy emerged about as well as one could have hoped. For a country of Germany's resources, therefore, it required no extraordinary effort to replace those few industries that were lost.

For some of the individuals and firms who performed the operation, however, it was a truly heroic feat. In many cases— some of the largest concerns—the reconstruction was done by refugees who had lost or given up their plants in the Russian Zone or eastern territories. Frequently the nucleus from which reconstruction started consisted only of the owner and perhaps a few employees with their know-how and the reputation of the product. Usually this group would be enlarged by the arrival of members of the old labor force, stealing across the zonal border or via Berlin. Often they would bring with them pieces of key equipment. Of some plants it is reported that they virtually came over the border—clandestinely—on the shoulders of their workers. Immense difficulties of financing and of finding temporary quarters among the rubble had to be solved. These achievements are very inadequately expressed by the bare figures.

Agricultural reconstruction. After a survey of the new industrial structure a word needs to be said about the reshaping of Western German agriculture. Achievements here, by the nature of things, have been less spectacular than in industry but nevertheless very gratifying. The small amount of agricultural land left after partition could not of course be increased. In fact, the land available for agriculture in Western Germany declined by about 3 per cent against prewar, the bulk of the reduction falling upon grain lands (Table 24). Nevertheless total agricultural output for 1952–53 was up 13 per cent above prewar, from 30.9 million tons of grain equivalent to 34.9 million tons.[5] Compared with the low of 19.1 million tons registered in the disastrous year 1947–48 the increase was 83 per cent.

Only moderate changes occurred in the structure of output. The share of vegetable products has been higher and that of animal products correspondingly lower. Vegetable products represented 26.6 per cent before the war (1935–36 to 1938–39), and 28.6 per cent in 1952–53. This mild shift reflects in part the fact that it is technologically easier to lift the output of vegetable products. In part, however, it also shows wartime and postwar deterioration in the German diet, which has so far not been fully made up. A second important shift was the increase of nearly 50 per cent in sugar beet output. This brought new strength to a branch of agriculture that had been particularly hard hit by partition.

The large gains in yield per acre, which were responsible for the rise in output except in the case of sugar beets, are the result of greater mechanization, more generous use of fertilizer, and improved agricultural techniques generally. Before the war the agriculture of Western Germany had not been noted for productive efficiency. Nearly two-thirds of the land under cultivation consisted and still consists of units of less than 50 hectares, and over 50 per cent of all units had and still have less than 5 hectares. Absence of international competition, insensitivity to economic incentives, and ingrained tradition had made many farmers resistant to new methods. Since the war, however, there seems to have been some change in attitude. Mechanization has progressed rapidly. Since 1950

TABLE 24: *Rebuilding of Agriculture*

| | Area | | | | Yield per Ha. in Tons | | Output | | | |
| | In 1,000 ha. | | Ha. per capita | | | | In 1,000 tons | | Kg. per capita | |
	1938	1953	1938	1953	1935–38	1953	1938	1953	1938	1953
Total agricultural area	14,584	14,195	.37	.29						
Arable land	8,492	8,089	.22	.17						
Bread grains	2,773	2,622	.07	.05	19.9	25.2	5,689	6,620	146	134
Feed grains	2,276	2,107	.06	.04	20.9	24.8	4,798	5,230	122	106
Pulses	94	55	.00	.00	18.5	17.8 *	168	105 *	00	00
Potatoes	1,174	1,163	.03	.02	168.2	208.0 *	19,538	23,854 *	502	485
Sugar beets	160	228	.01	.00	327.2	300.4 *	4,253	6,678 *	109	136

* Data for 1952.
Source: Statistisches Jahrbuch.

on the average over 50,000 tractors have been introduced each year. The use of fertilizer has increased by more than 20 per cent above prewar. Consequently Germany is now well ahead of France and Italy both in yield per acre and in output per agricultural worker, though still far behind Denmark and Holland.

Land reform has not been a significant factor in agricultural progress. Western Germany's problem in this respect is not the breaking up of the limited number of large holdings but the consolidation of the uneconomically small ones, including that of small dispersed plots owned by a single farmer. Although this *Flurbereinigung* has proved a great aid to productivity and stands in the foreground of agricultural reform, it has advanced painfully slowly. German agriculture has been shielded against competition and the play of market forces by a variety of protective devices. These are probably responsible, at least in part, for the magnitude of agricultural output in the aggregate as well as for the relatively low efficiency per unit of output. Support for agriculture has taken the form of tariff protection and import quotas as well as of domestic price stabilization. Aid has been particularly generous for grains, less so for milk products and eggs. Through flexible tariffs or subsidies, as the case may be, the international price level is adjusted to the German market. For grains a narrow spread is fixed periodically by the legislature, within which the responsible agency must hold the market by means of import licensing and storage operations. It must be added that through 1952 the total of 658 million DMark paid in import subsidies to bring down foreign prices to the German level by far exceeded the 128 million DMark from duties collected when the opposite case arose.

It would probably be an exaggeration to say that there is a firm national policy to push agricultural output regardless of economic considerations in order to reduce dependence on imports. The strong support given to agriculture, which suggests the existence of such a policy, seems to be primarily the result of successful pressure from farmers and big landowners. These interests are very effectively organized and can rally support throughout the legislature from right to left. The present agricultural policy appears, however, to have the support of the public in general, which has learned through two wars and two inflations what dependence on imported food can mean. The policy seems to be at least tolerated even by those groups in the government who by virtue of their liberal persuasion might be expected to stand against it.

Productivity

So far we have studied the impressive production engine that is Western Germany with an eye to its structure and capacity. We still have to investigate its productivity.

There seems to be a general agreement among observers that, measured against the well-known German efficiency, German industrial productivity is curiously low.

Developments of recent years can be observed approximately through the productivity index (output per hour worked). In 1949, when productivity had reacquired meaning thanks to the currency reform, the index stood at 82.3 per cent of 1936. Since then it has risen, first at an annual rate of 10 per cent and later at 4 to 6 per cent, to reach 117.8 in 1954 (Table 25). Very probably, however, the index greatly understates the true level in 1949 and exaggerates the rate of advance. The repair of war damage, which went on until 1950 or even 1951, was frequently handled by a plant's regular labor force, which was statistically assumed to be producing shoes or the like while it was actually repairing the roof. This practice was a great tax saving, since the repairs could thus be charged off to current labor costs. Its incidental result, however, was to confound not only the tax collector but also the gatherer of statis-

TABLE 25: *Index of Industrial Productivity*
(output per man-hour worked, 1936 = 100)

Year	All industry*	Coal mining	Iron and steel	Non-ferrous metals	Chemicals	Glass	Machinery	Vehicles	Electrical equipment	Shoes	Textiles	Food processing
1949	82.3	61.9	15.8	86.7	92.2	120.7	87.2	59.4	83.9	72.2	90.0	119.6
1950	92.8	64.5	91.9	90.7	109.3	107.8	97.3	90.5	94.9	73.0	97.8	142.6
1951	102.6	68.0	96.6	105.7	122.1	113.6	109.6	107.3	112.6	78.0	103.9	142.0
1952	107.5	69.5	105.0	112.0	125.3	101.6	117.9	119.4	117.7	78.2	106.0	151.3
1953	113.3	69.7	100.1	123.1	145.0	106.2	115.8	119.9	121.4	80.3	114.6	175.7

* Excluding electric power output and construction.
Source: Wirtschaft und Statistik, April 1954.

tics. The 4 to 6 per cent advances of 1953–54, nevertheless probably reflect genuine productivity gains; they are impressive and internationally unusual.

The productivity of individual industries differs rather widely, as one might expect, from the general average. Food processing and chemicals are far above the average. Coal mining and iron and steel production have done poorly, the former extraordinarily so. The backwardness of these branches explains the concern with which German industrialists view their position in the Schuman Plan. The big export industries —machinery, vehicles, electrical equipment—are above average, but not enough to provide a ready-made explanation of the German export success.

Germany's lagging productivity is not exclusively an outcome of the war, for it goes far back into economic history. It is the result, no doubt, of a great variety of factors: the late date at which Germany began to accumulate industrial capital and to acquire industrial skills, her large and rapidly growing population, her mediocre resource endowment, and perhaps certain peculiarities of her productive techniques. How much weight attaches to each factor is far from clear, for there are examples of countries such as France that despite better resources and less population growth did not succeed much better, and of others such as the United States that were also latecomers and did very well.

As a possible further influence that may have kept German productivity down in recent years one feels tempted to mention the low degree of international division of labor which Germany has practiced—witness the small share of foreign trade in the national income dicussed in the following section. But the remarkable increases in productivity that were scored during the last few years raise questions regarding the importance of this factor.

Some insight, however, into at least one of the determinants of Germany's present and future productivity can be gained from an analysis of the volume of capital already available and currently being added. Money is not everything in matters of productivity, but its importance is not to be underrated. At a bold estimate the total of productive capital outside agriculture in 1953 amounted to 215 billion DMark at the prices of that year.* In the same year about 18.4 million were productively employed outside agriculture, including those who were self-employed. This gives us in round figures 12,000 DMark per worker. While obviously a very rough average, it is in line with an estimate of the Federal Ministry of Labor of 5–8,000 DMark per worker invested in labor intensive industries, with another estimate by the machine-building industry of 10,000 DMark per worker in average plants and 15,000 DMark in advanced plants, and with an estimate of the Opel-General Motors concern of 20,000 DMark per worker in a new automobile plant. It should be observed that the 12,000 DMark average includes social capital like roads and schools (but not land), while the other figures do not. At the purchasing power parity exchange rate for investment of DM 2.58 = $1.00, the 12,000 DMark per worker would amount to 4,500 dollars.† [6]

---

* Derived, with substantial modifications, from O. Schörry, "Das deutsche Volksvermögen," *Finanzarchiv*, N.S., *11/49*, 386 ff., as follows:

		Billions of DMark
National wealth (Reich) 1939		450
National wealth (Western Germany) 1939		260
After discount for war damage		170
Revalued at 1948 prices		270
Including new investment through 1953		
and revalued at 1953 prices		420
Deduct:		
Land	80	
Dwellings	100	
Agricultural capital	25	205
Nonagricultural productive capital		215

† At European weights; at U.S. weights, equivalent would be 3,500 dollars.

From what we know of these things, through the work of Colin Clark and others, the German figure is internationally low.[7] It would go some way to explain the relatively low current level of German productivity.

More reliable and significant than guesses of existing capital per worker are estimates of the annual increase in recent years. The results are shown in the following calculation:

		Billions of DMark at 1952 prices
Gross investment 1949–53, including inventories		138.1
Deduct: Depreciation	43.8	
Housing	25.8	
Agriculture	8.2	77.8
Net productive investment outside agriculture		60.3
Deduct:		
Amount needed to equip increase in non-agricultural workers, at DM 12,000 per worker		30.0
Available to increase equipment of existing workers		30.3

Available per worker per year: DM 350.0
Increase per year: 3%

Sources: Statistisches Jahrbuch; Germany's Contribution to OEEC (Bonn, 1953).

The computation, obviously highly tentative, points up several interesting facts. First, the high rate of saving and investment has not been quite so effective in raising capital per worker as one might have hoped, because half of it, after necessary deductions for other uses, was required merely to equip the newly employed. The rest, however, was still enough to allow a 3 per cent annual increase in capital per worker. If one may assume that returns to capital do not diminish very rapidly in the short run, the 3 per cent increment in capital should permit an equivalent increase in productivity per worker. Actually, the annual gain in productivity was nearly twice as large.

Another observation suggested by these figures, though

somewhat outside the realm of productivity, relates to the ease with which savings are converted into investment. So long as the size of the labor force is rising rapidly this absorption may be expected to take place without much friction. The widening of existing processes of production is relatively easy. It does not involve diminishing returns or new techniques. The growing labor supply, moreover, keeps wage increases in bounds. Once the growth of the labor force tapers off, however, the matter becomes more difficult. New techniques are now required if more capital is to be accommodated; labor shortages force up wages, while the easiest outlet for new capital—equipment of the new labor force—closes up. More powerful incentives or lower financing costs will be needed under such conditions than were required earlier to absorb a high rate of savings. The rise in productivity, on the other hand, will continue all the faster if the economy does succeed in fully absorbing its savings, since a larger part of the savings would then go to increase capital per worker.

It is somewhat ominous, therefore, that the vegetative increase in the population of working age (15–65), which will reach its peak rate in 1954–55 with a gain of 350,000 persons, is expected to drop to minus 150,000 in 1959–60. That is the year in which the thinnest of the wartime age groups will enter the labor force. Fortunately the recent flow into industrial employment has been fed only to the extent of about 50 per cent from vegetative growth. The rest has come from newly arrived refugees and prisoners of war, from agriculture, and from the ranks of the unemployed. Some of these sources may be expected to continue to flow, although in diminished volume.

From these speculations with large quantities we must descend into the more realistic sphere of the businessman who makes the decisions that increase productivity. The high gains in the last few years document beyond doubt that the German businessman in general has been doing a good job in raising the productivity of his plant. Yet those whose duty it is to advise and prod him in the process sometimes seem to feel that he could do more. They report numerous cases where they have noted resistance to modernization of equipment and techniques. No doubt these things are common, in greater or lesser degree, to all countries. Yet it seems clear that if their occurrence could be minimized in Germany productivity would advance much more rapidly. Obstacles of this sort call for our attention, although they must not be exaggerated.

To begin with we must remember that the process of "rationalization," as it is referred to in Germany, is no new experience for the German businessman. After the first World War a wave of modernization swept German industry, its financing aided by inflation. After World War II, however, conditions were not favorable to such a development. The energies and resources of industry were absorbed first by repairs and then by expansion to meet the hunger for goods. Prices were high and selling was easy. This was not a situation that compelled modernization.

Upward wage pressure, which has been such a powerful force for technological progress in the United States, has been largely lacking in Germany. To some extent a similar function has been performed by the long downward trend of prices that began in 1951 and lasted through part of 1953. This trend, however, has been really intensive only in the consumer goods industries, where it seems to have been a reaction to a sharp spurt following the Korea invasion. Profits have been high although also in a decline from 1951 through the middle of 1953. Thus modernization was propelled not by an urgent sense of encroaching costs and a serious threat to profits but only by the possibility of further raising already satisfactory profits. This motive, in turn, was weakened by the high rate of taxation, which made it more interesting to pad costs with personal expenses than to cut them through modernization.

As regards the attitude of the individual German businessman, it is generally said that he takes special pride in the
smooth and efficient operation of his plant. In some cases
tradition-mindedness, fear of exhausting the market, reluctance to scrap old equipment, and unwillingness to make
major expenditures seem to stand in the way of modernization. The high cost and sometimes the absolute lack of credit
is of course a major factor. It is also said that German business suffers from weakness at the foreman and middle-man-
agement level. Many German foremen reportedly supervise
as many as 80 to 100 workers, far more than is customary in
the United States. The training at some engineering schools,
it is said, encourages a mechanical approach that does not
lead to continuing observation of new developments through
trade journals and the like.

The German worker seems to be less inclined than the
American to make suggestions for improvements and receives
only limited encouragement to do so. The suggestion-box
technique is reported to have had little success. From the side
of the unions few strong impulses seem to come that would
aid modernization. The unions are slow to push for higher
wages if they foresee job losses as a result of higher prices or
increasing mechanization. And somewhere in the back of
labor's mind there is still the old class-struggle idea that increases in output benefit only the owner.

There is one subject to which discussions of productivity
invariably return: standardization. The number of models
in most lines of production is extraordinarily high in Germany. Production runs are correspondingly short and hence
difficult to mechanize economically. It is estimated, for instance, that there are some 7,000 types of second hands for
watches, 5,000 types of shovels, and 20,000 sizes of piston
rings.[8] In one year the production of 17.3 million women's
shoes comprised some 76,000 models. This microbelike multiplicity is partly the product of postwar conditions—resump-

tion of production after total disorganization, appearance of new firms, the initial zonal division. In part, however, it also reflects ingrained habits and preferences of producers, dealers, and consumers.

Standardization would do a great deal for productivity and often with relatively little new investment. It offers many, though by no means all, of the benefits of a widening of the market, and it offers them to a much higher degree. An increase in the number of buyers by 100 per cent raises the length of production runs by just that much. A cut in the number of models by 90 per cent, as is believed possible in many cases, increases runs for the remaining types by 1,000 per cent.

Germany's present-day lag in standardization and other aspects of advanced technology implies a large reserve of potential increases in productivity. The possibility of adapting, within a relatively short time, methods and techniques which it took other countries many years to perfect seems to offer Germany a chance to cut down the productivity gap. A continuation of the recent 4 to 6 per cent annual gains would in fact allow Germany to catch up with other European countries fairly rapidly.

A catching up with the United States, on the other hand, is a different matter. The adaptation of American techniques on a full scale is not possible without proportionate investment. In that respect the prospects for a substantial narrowing of the distance that separates the per capita incomes of Germany and the United States are not encouraging. It is true that Germany's rate of saving, in relation to gross national product, is running well above that of the United States. The absolute amounts of capital per capita, however, that are becoming available annually are much lower. In 1952 gross investment per capita in the United States was almost twice that of Germany, even after adjusting for purchasing power difference. It is hard to see how, in the absence of quite novel developments, this handicap can be overcome. It might be argued that a cessation of the growth of the German labor force, such as seems to be in prospect for the end of the present decade, might double the amount of savings becoming available annually for each worker. But apart from the fact that this stagnation of the labor force would probably be a temporary phenomenon, the hypothesis of a country with a stable population and high savings and investment does not carry much conviction.

Export Capacity

The rebuilding and expansion of industry and agriculture have been decisive not only for the pace and direction of the domestic economy but also for the recovery of Germany's balance of payments. To begin with let us look at the export side.

"Export capacity" is a misnomer, barely excusable on grounds of common usage, for the conditions that determine a country's ability to export. For an industrial country like Germany there is no physical limit to what it can sell abroad. Its ability to export depends upon a variety of factors, some very important ones among which are clearly subject to its own control. Postwar experience has proved again and again that a country's export volume, in the face of any given state of world demand, is decisively influenced by its own policies. Monetary and fiscal policies, for instance, influence exports by determining the magnitude of domestic demand and the trend of domestic prices. Exchange rate policy, by altering the price level in international terms, can produce the same effect. We have touched in an earlier chapter upon the importance of Germany's tight monetary and fiscal policies for the recovery of her exports and shall have something to say about the exchange rate of the DMark in a later one.

Among the factors influencing export capacity that are not subject to a country's control there are three that have been particularly favorable to Germany and that will engage our attention. One has been the fact that Germany started out after the war with only a very small share of world trade and hence found it relatively easy to push her exports without bringing down prices. For a small supplier the elasticity of market demand is always bigger than for a large one. This accounts for part of the much greater difficulty that Great Britain has encountered in expanding her trade. German exports would have been aided by this factor even if world demand had been less buoyant than it was. The great expansion of world trade has of course been another decisive influence.

The absence of an arms burden has also materially aided Germany's ability to export. Other countries have had to devote scarce materials and industrial capacity to rearmament and have found their exports further hampered by the consequent price increases. Germany not only was free from such burdens but was able to take advantage of the increased international demand and reduced foreign competition.

But the core of the matter, and where the term "export capacity" does acquire a somewhat more literal meaning, lies in a country's industrial structure. Given all her other advantages Germany would not have done so spectacularly well if she had lacked her heavy industry, if what she had to offer to the world had been mainly textiles or luxury goods. It was her concentration on capital goods industries, her ability to supply machinery and equipment that floated her exports off, at ever improving terms of trade, upon the rising tide of world demand. This traditional characteristic of Germany's industrial structure, intensified, as we have seen, since the war, has greatly aided her capacity to export.

These facts are clearly shown in Table 26. Of total exports in 1952, 50 per cent consisted of capital goods. Another 17.8 per cent were represented by iron, steel, and chemicals, which are also heavy industry products. Consumer goods, with 10 per cent, played a quite subordinate role. At the same time,

the capital goods industries were placed under no great strain
by the need to supply 50 per cent of exports, thanks to the
fact that they account for so important a share of total industrial capacity. Only 21.8 per cent of their sales were ab-

TABLE 26: *Exports by Industrial Categories, 1952 and 1953*
(in per cent)

	Share of industry in industrial exports	Share of output exported *	
	1952	1952	1953
All industry	100.0	11.6	12.1
Mining	11.3	23.2	22.7
(Coal)	(10.3)	24.4	24.3
Basic materials	27.8	10.5	11.6
(Iron and steel)	(8.3)	13.0	13.1
(Chemical)	(9.5)	14.4	17.2
Capital goods	50.0	21.8	21.9
(Machinery)	(22.2)	30.7	31.8
(Vehicles, excluding railway equipment)	(7.1)	17.8	19.2
(Shipbuilding)	(3.0)	39.4	35.5
(Electrical equipment)	(6.1)	14.7	14.6
(Optical and other instruments)	(3.1)	34.7	36.6
(Light steel and metal products)	(5.0)	10.6	13.8
Consumer goods	10.0	5.5	5.7
(Textiles)	(5.3)	6.6	7.0
Food industries	0.9	0.7	1.3

* Based on total domestic and foreign *sales*, including interindustry sales.
Source: *Wirtschaft und Statistik*, May 1953, pp. 197–203, and Bank deutscher
Länder's *Wirtschaftsstatistik*.

sorbed by these exports. The consumer goods industries, on
the other hand, being relatively less developed, have not been
compelled by pressure of excess capacity to push their products
in world markets, where resistance to consumer goods imports has increased. In this respect Germany's industrial structure probably is better adjusted to present world market

conditions than, for instance, that of the United Kingdom, which is also strong in engineering products but has in addition a powerful textile sector that cannot use its full export potential.

Germany's export capacity, like that of other countries, is partly conditioned by the extent to which she can grant export credits. For the sale of capital goods credit facilities are especially important. In this respect, contrary to a widespread belief, Germany has not been well situated in recent years, but her lending capacity has been growing. Export credit has been limited by the shortage of longer-term bank credit and by the difficulty of raising funds in the capital market. The high cost of such credit, which over a few years can easily add 25 per cent to the price of the goods, has put Germany at a competitive disadvantage. This has been compensated only in part by governmental credit facilities and by what seems a remarkable willingness on the part of individual exporters to assume the risks involved in such credits.

Another form of export credit, however, has been forthcoming rather plentifully: that extended by the Bank deutscher Länder via the EPU and through the swing-margins of numerous bilateral agreements. The Bank has financed these credits through money creation at home. Germany's physical resources have been quite sufficient to support the drain, so that there have been no inflationary results. Details on export credits will be found in Chapter 8.

It remains to be observed that Germany has so far exploited her export capacity only to a rather limited extent. Her ratio of exports to gross national product, about 14 per cent in 1953, is quite low among western European countries. It compares with 20.6 per cent of national income for the United Kingdom, 12.7 per cent for France, and 41 per cent for Belgium (1952). Germany's share in world exports in 1952 was still about 22 per cent below 1938 (for the area now occupied by the Federal Republic), while that of the United Kingdom had remained approximately constant and that of France had risen over 40 per cent.[9] If Germany's import needs were materially higher the consequent passive balance of payments would very probably create conditions—lower prices and more unemployment, for instance, or a lower exchange rate—that would lead to greater exports. The structure of industry certainly would permit them without much difficulty. Since import needs in fact amount to only a modest proportion of the German gross national product, relative stability of exports seems to have been reached at a similarly modest level. One might express this by saying that Germany has taken advantage of her strong export capacity not in the form of high exports but in the apparent ease and speed with which the actual level was attained, and in relatively favorable terms of trade.

Import Needs

Germany's extraordinarily low import needs have been one of the most important and at the same time most puzzling features in her foreign trade picture. From 1950 to 1953 annual imports varied between 10 and 12 per cent of gross national product (at 1950 prices). This low import ratio is the main reason why Germany's foreign trade came into balance so quickly and then went into persistent surplus. It compares with 23 to 25 per cent for the United Kingdom and 11 to 14 per cent for France. It has worried Germany's EPU partners and has been the subject of much study by the Organization for European Economic Cooperation.

After the war it was widely felt that Germany's import dependence, aggravated by partition, would be one of her greatest difficulties. Yet here is a country, deprived of its former bread-basket provinces, with a 25 per cent population increase —"a new Belgium"—with its trade very substantially liberalized, and an import ratio nevertheless as low as that of self-sufficient France. Without strong conviction that the phenomenon can be fully explained by the facts at hand, or even that it will prove permanent, we must proceed with the attempt to understand it.

One major reason for the low money value of Germany's imports is of course the decline in raw material prices from their post-Korea peak. In terms of volume Germany's imports have shown quite considerable annual increases during the last few years: 13 per cent in 1953 and 25 per cent in 1954. The import ratio has been increasing in constant prices, although in current prices it has hardly changed since 1951. Compared with 1936, year of autarchy, imports have increased only very mildly, if at all, in relation to gross national product, taking both at constant prices.

A second factor is the well-rounded structure of German manufacturing industry. The acute foreign exchange shortage of the thirties, coupled with Dr. Schacht's autarchy policy, has left its traces here. Germany does import a wide range of manufactured goods, and their share in total imports, thanks to liberalization, is nearly twice what it was in 1936 (Table 27). But they are marginal to domestic supplies of the same

TABLE 27: *Commodity Structure of Imports*
(*in per cent*)

	1936	1950	1951	1952	1953
Foodstuffs	28.0	40.5	36.2	33.1	31.1
Stimulants	6.5	3.6	3.7	4.3	5.5
Raw materials	39.6	29.6	35.8	34.8	32.6
Semimanufactured goods	17.4	13.7	13.6	14.5	15.2
Manufactured goods	8.5	12.6	10.7	13.3	15.6
	100.0	100.0	100.0	100.0	100.0

Source: Bank deutscher Länder, *Report for the Year 1953*. Discrepancies are due to rounding.

kinds, for after the replacement of industries lost in the East it is hard to point to any major manufacturing line not represented in Germany (Table 27).

A third factor is Germany's broadened raw materials base.

Germany has always been regarded as poor in natural resources, apart from coal, and hence as heavily dependent upon
supplies from abroad. Yet Germany's raw material imports in
1953 and 1954 were only 125 and 164 per cent of 1936, in
terms of volume, while industrial production reached 158 and
176, respectively. The share of raw materials in total imports,
although still larger than any other single category of imports,
amounted to only 32.6 per cent of total imports in 1953 against
39.6 per cent in 1936 (Table 27). Here again the Hitler-
Schacht policies, together with the world-wide progress of
technology, have shown a belated effectiveness. The autarchy
program of the thirties centered—but not exclusively—on
four major commodity groups: (1) synthetic fibers and plas-
tics, (2) low grade iron ore, (3) synthetic rubber, and (4) oil
and gasoline from liquefied coal and from wells drilled in
northwestern Germany. Some of this production has vanished
through dismantling and for other reasons. Low-grade iron-
ore production may have to be closed down. But the rest of
the program, including oil production from domestic wells,
has stood the country in good stead. The general strengthening of Germany's raw materials bases can be seen in the rising
share of basic materials (excluding coal) in total industrial
output (Table 23).

A fourth point is the increasing share in total industrial
production of capital goods and the sharp decline in the share
of consumer goods (Table 23). It has been shown that the import content of consumer goods is a great deal higher than
that of capital goods or manufactured products in general.
For the leather industry, for instance, the import content is
31.0 per cent, for the textile industry 18.3. For industry as a
whole it is only 6.7 per cent.[10]

In the consumption sector, moreover, there have been
changes that have further tended to cut down imports. Among
them are the growing weight in consumer budgets of home
furnishings, travel, and entertainment, and the diminishing

role of textiles, reflecting the satisfaction of backlog needs and perhaps also the decimation of the old middle class with its high clothing standards. A sharp drop from prewar levels in the *volume* of stimulants consumed per capita—mainly imported coffee and tobacco—must also be noted, although in terms of *value*, including the heavy tax, their consumption has risen.

There remains the highly important food sector. Food imports have increased, both absolutely and as a proportion of total imports (Table 27), but nowhere near as sharply as partition and population increase would have led one to expect. In fact, the change that has taken place is quite astonishingly moderate. As a percentage of total imports food imports rose in 1953 to 31.1 per cent from 28.0 per cent in 1936. Part of the explanation is the rise in food production by 13 per cent above prewar. But why is it that this modest increase in the truncated area suffices to meet 65 to 70 per cent of the total food needs of a greatly swollen population, when the old Reich covered only 65 per cent of its needs in 1927 and 82 per cent at the height of autarchy in 1939? [11] The reason must be in the German diet. Daily caloric intake in 1952–53, per capita, stood at 2,838 calories compared with 3,072 in 1935–38. To some extent the declining amount consumed may be traceable to the big increase in the proportion of women in the population today. Looking at the food budget in detail we note that potatoes and rye bread still play a very large though diminishing role. In an average workman's household of four, where milk consumption is high because of children, potatoes nevertheless exceed milk in terms of weight, with bread a close third.[12] Meat consumption, which before the war was 52.5 kilograms per capita, in 1952–53 had reached only 41 kilograms. The quality of the German diet is improving, particularly with respect to fruits and vegetables. Nevertheless the diet still has far to go before it could be considered high grade. This is in good part the reason why German agriculture is

able to satisfy so large a share of the nation's food needs and
why food imports are so astonishingly low.

Of the many factors mentioned that have contributed to
reduce Germany's dependence on imports, some are very
probably permanent. Others may be temporary. Chief among
the latter is the level of import prices. If these should turn upward the money value of imports probably would rise, although hardly in direct proportion. A second potential cause
of higher imports would be a quick return of food consumption to prewar levels, accompanied by an improvement in the
diet. A rise in food consumption by a small percentage is
capable of increasing food imports by a much larger proportion because of the marginal character of its impact. But
though the present low level of imports may be the result of
an unusual combination of favorable circumstances and may
not last, it seems fair to assume that the high dependence on
imports that was prognosticated after the war will not materialize.

Conclusion

In the present chapter we have dealt with a number of
diverse but closely interrelated aspects of the German economy: its industrial structure as it has emerged from war, partition, dismantling, and rebuilding; its productivity; its capacity to export; and the degree to which its needs must be
covered by imports. Some of the findings suggest observations
of a broader nature.

One of these relates to the cyclical stability of the German
economy. We have seen that the capital goods sector, traditionally powerful, has further increased in weight. In the past
it has been customary to associate the capital goods industries
with instability—the prince or pauper industries. The wide
swings of the German business cycle have in part been a reflection of this. Does it follow that Germany now has become
even more vulnerable cyclically?

It is dangerous to approach such a question without a great many qualifications. I shall limit myself to putting forward certain points that ought to carry some weight in a more comprehensive analysis of the matter. It is quite obvious that since the war Germany's capital goods industries have been one of the more stable parts of her economy. There have been minor fluctuations in the general upward trend of output, but they have centered in the consumer goods industries. In the United States, incidentally, something similar seems to have happened, although perhaps to a lesser degree.

The present period of high-level demand for capital goods may of course come to an end. Yet as long as there are large parts of the world that are trying to industrialize rapidly, one should think that there will always be a demand for capital goods, though credit may have to be given to make it effective. The greater readiness of governments nowadays to engage in public works whenever depression threatens should work in the same directions. It may well be, therefore, that the vulnerability of the capital goods industries has substantially diminished. This would *ipso facto* reduce the vulnerability of the German economy itself.

Another matter enters into the picture. The ability of a country to steer clear of boom and bust is determined to some extent by its dependence upon foreign markets and supplies. A large export sector makes the economy vulnerable to depression abroad, and the heavy import dependence which normally goes with it hampers an aggressive countercyclical policy at home. The same applies to bursts of international inflation. For Germany we have noted the moderate role of exports and imports in the national income. Some German industries, especially capital goods producers, whose exports amount to over 30 per cent of their output would of course be hard hit by a depression abroad. For the economy as a whole, however, the impact of such a depression might be less severe than for most other European countries.

On the import side an analogous situation is to be observed. Germany's low import dependence and her strong exchange reserves would allow fairly large-scale antidepression measures to be taken before balance of payments considerations called a halt. One cannot help wondering whether Germany as a result of all that has happened may not have gained in strength to resist depressions. Other factors exist that might point in another direction—the high rate of savings, the eventual end of the housing boom, the diminishing rate of popula-strength to resist depressions. Other factors exist that might boomerang in a depression originating at home, since it would then deprive the economy of one of its potential props. It is impossible to weigh these divergent influences. But the elements of strength cannot be overlooked.

The second observation, which is perhaps even more speculative, deals with the significance of Germany's partition experience. We have seen that contrary to what one might have expected partition has dealt no devastating blow to the West German economy. An obvious question presents itself: If partition did Germany no great harm would European integration—the inverse process on a larger scale—do the participants much good? In fairness the question should be restricted to the beneficial effects, often quoted, of a wider European market. The broader impulses flowing from real integration would be of a different nature and may well prove tremendous in their effects. The emotional impact of unity, the creation of a new center of political power, these are forces of another order. They might bring a new outlook into the business world, a new approach to problems of production and marketing that might spark vast changes. But as far as the mere broadening of market outlets is concerned, with business psychology unchanged, what does the German example-in-reverse show?

There seems to be no evidence that the reduced market— it has meanwhile grown back to or beyond its prewar size

—has at any time been too small to permit the efficient operation of any plant or industry that operated previously. There have of course been industries, concentrated in the West, that lost more markets than capacity. This is not the problem here, however. The point to be made is that the German market, after partition as well as before, was so large that the attainment of an adequate scale of production was not seriously interfered with for any major industry. There may have been such cases, but they did not occur in the spectacular industries where large units are the rule, such as steel, automobiles, and chemicals. They may have appeared in the smaller and highly specialized industries that supply the giants with parts and subassemblies. It would be in these industries, therefore, that the expansion of the market, by permitting greater specialization, would be of particular value.

The German situation further reminds us that some of the advantages of a broader market can also be attained through a standardization of output. A European market is not likely to enable firms to increase their production runs by more than a moderate percentage. Standardization permits them to be lengthened by a multiple.

To avoid misunderstanding it must be repeated that the foregoing considerations in no way run counter to the principle of European integration, which remains a consummation devoutly to be wished. They raise questions only regarding the seemingly self-evident blessings of a broader market. Even on this score it remains to be observed that such broadening can, though it need not, bring advantages other than a larger scale of operation. Among them are greater competition, new products and ideas, and intensified standardization of output if specialties are supplied from abroad. Yet, the question posed by the experience of partition remains interesting.

Another and far less reputable doctrine finds itself placed in even stronger doubt: the old German idea of *Lebensraum,* living space. Its import was that economic expansion depended

upon geographic expansion. Germany meanwhile has undergone a drastic geographic shrinkage, but her economy has expanded as never before. It is true that this has happened in a
climate of world-wide expansion. The acid test of adversity
is still ahead. But as far as the evidence goes the refutation of
the Lebensraum doctrine could hardly have been more emphatic.

CHAPTER 8

Foreign Trade Policies

THE REBUILDING of Western Germany's foreign trade
duplicates in several respects the domestic performance. This
can be said, for instance, of the rapidity with which, after an
initial period of stagnation, German exports and imports regained a level adequate to the needs of the country. It is also
true with respect to the policies that guided the advance. As
in the domestic field, freedom of markets, achieved through
the progressive removal of restrictions, has been the basic principle. The principle, it is true, has by no means won a complete
victory. In some trade sectors controls have remained firmly
entrenched. Yet the general trend is clear. The rejection of
the Schachtian techniques of the prewar years by the country
that was their inventor and leading practitioner is an impressive demonstration in favor of liberal trade practices.

The influence of the occupation authorities was stronger
and longer lasting in the foreign sector than in domestic policies. Allied policy was responsible for the vacillations and ex-
periments of the earlier period. But Allied policy also deserves credit for the first steps that were taken along the road
to liberalization. Later, as Allied initiative was gradually sup-
planted by German, the drive for freer trade was even intensified.

The process of trade and payments liberalization is at the
center of German trade policy since the war. It will be the
first and main topic to engage our attention in this chapter.
Other policies to be discussed are export promotion, exchange

rate and tariff policies, and the settlement of Germany's foreign debts.

The Struggle for Liberalization and Convertibility

The revival of German trade started almost literally from scratch. After the surrender the Allies assumed complete control of relations between Germany and the outside world. Direct contact between Germans and foreigners was nonexistent. Trade transactions therefore were also exclusively in the hands of the occupation authorities.

It soon became obvious that disease and unrest could not be held in check without substantial imports. The Allies provided these imports and stepped up their volume as the emphasis of occupation shifted from holding Germany down to building her up. From 1945 to 1948 aid-financed imports increased steadily, accounting each year for the larger part of total imports (Table 28).

From bilateral restriction to multilateral liberalization. Exports revived with painful slowness. For the American and British zones they were in the hands of JEIA (Joint Export and Import Agency). That unhappy agency, whose efforts in

TABLE 28: *Foreign Trade 1945–49* *
(Federal Republic and West Berlin, in millions of dollars)

	Imports			Exports	Import Surplus
	Aid financed	Commercial	Total		
1945 Aug.–Dec.	64	32	96	52	44
1946	468	221	689	201	488
1947	606	243	843	315	528
1948	1,026	562	1,588	642	946
1949	956	1,281	2,237	1,123	1,114

* Data through 1947 incomplete.
Source: Bank deutscher Länder, *Report for the Years 1948–1949.*

the face of impossible odds deserve greater recognition than they have received, found itself cast in the role of an export monopoly for an economy that had neither the means nor the incentives to export. The low level and poor quality of industrial production severely restricted the scope for exports of manufactures. The difficulty of practicing in JEIA-controlled foreign trade any of the gray market tricks that kept business going before the currency reform diminished producers' interest in exports. The fabulous complications of licensing did their share to discourage export enthusiasts. Hence the curious phenomenon that prior to the currency reform the bulk of the exports of industrial Germany consisted of raw materials, mainly coal, wood, and steel scrap.

The currency reform brought great improvements in the export field as elsewhere. In December 1948, moreover, JEIA was finally able to withdraw from its role of intermediary and to free the channels of communication between German traders and their foreign customers. For the export of highly specialized merchandise like that of Germany the opening of personal sales contact was of course decisively important. Exports thereafter continued to rise rapidly.

The trade pattern that had established itself in Europe after the war was one of strict bilateralism. Countries were anxious enough to buy from each other, but only up to the level of their sales to each particular country, the trade being cleared via bilateral payments agreements. The main and surprising exception was Western Germany. The occupation authorities let it be known that they would pay dollars for what they bought from other European countries but would also demand dollars for all German exports. Their attitude was understandable. The resources they had available for imports into Germany were mostly dollars appropriated by the United States Congress. They had little money, but what they had was good. They intended to spend it on goods where they were cheapest, which meant mainly in the United States. They applied the same principle to the proceeds of the small volume of exports that they could squeeze out of the destitute economy under their control. One might call the system of dollar trading introduced by the Allied authorities a caricature of the kind of convertibility that has since become famous as "convertibility for nonresidents." Whatever obligations Germany incurred she paid in convertible currency, but at the same time trade restrictions remained so tight as to make this convertibility a mockery.

The eventual abandonment of this system in favor of a series of bilateral trade and payments agreements is an interesting demonstration of how a "hard" monetary system can be so far ahead of its day as to be self-defeating. The dollar trading policy of the Allies caused other countries to discriminate against German exports; they preferred to spend their scarce dollars on the more essential or lower priced goods offered by the United States. As long as most German exports could not stand up in competition with American goods they could be sold only against something softer than dollars: European currencies or equally uncompetitive European goods. The same applied to Germany's imports. There was little occasion for Germany to buy European goods so long as she was spending dollars, and European goods were thus placed in direct competition with dollar merchandise. Once the Allied authorities resigned themselves to bilateral operations Germany's purchases from Europe went up rapidly.

The adoption of the bilateral technique involved, of course, the familiar danger of pushing trade into uneconomic channels. This problem was used, as far as trade with OEEC countries and the sterling area was concerned, by the two Intra-European Payments Plans of 1948 and 1949. Beginning in 1950 it was resolved by the establishment of the European Payments Union. Thanks to its clearing mechanism, trade among the member countries could proceed multilaterally without regard to bilateral balances. With the creation of this important mechanism Germany, however, had relatively little to do, the initiative coming mainly from the U.S. government.

A second danger inherent in the trade agreements signed by Germany in 1949 and after was their use for protection rather than for maintaining balance of payments equilibrium. The import quotas that formed part of the agreements were far more powerful instruments of protection than tariffs could be. As balance of payments problems diminished, protectionist considerations inevitably gained the upper hand in the fixing of these quotas. The liberalization drive of the OEEC initiated in 1949 aimed at cutting down these quantitative restrictions. Germany, represented by JEIA, took a leading role in the liberalization movement.

The bilateral trade agreements with Holland and Switzerland that were signed in the summer and fall of 1949 provided for large-scale removal of quantitative restrictions on German imports from those countries. Further agreements followed, negotiated by the German government with the Scandinavian countries, Austria, and Belgium. Goods from these countries could enter Germany without quantitative limits, subject to a small "reserved list," and an over-all ceiling in the case of Switzerland and Belgium. In 1949–50 the degree of liberalization reached 47 per cent of imports from OEEC countries in the base year 1948–49, although this liberalization was still very predominantly bilateral. When the EPU was formally established in September 1950 liberalization was shifted to a multilateral basis. In accordance with the request of the OEEC Germany liberalized 60 per cent of her imports from OEEC countries (base year 1949). We shall presently have to go into the consequences that this bold action had for Germany's balance of payments, but first it will be advisable to inquire what prompted Germany to take it.

Motives for liberalization. A good part of the considerations involved seem to have related to Germany's domestic econ-

omy. One important point here was Economics Minister Erhard's desire to stimulate competition. Under the regime of
import quotas German industry, long cut off from all world
market contact, continued to be sheltered even against the
modest breezes of intra-European competition. Liberalization
of imports exposed it to this competition.

A second impulse originating in the domestic sphere was
the difficulty of administrating the quota regime. The allocation of the total import quotas to individual importers presented peculiar problems in Germany because of the lack of
an appropriate base year. The attempt to solve the problem
by letting importers enter bids led to fantastic padding and
grotesquely small percentages allotted. A "first come, first
served" procedure that was also tried put an undue premium
upon speed—it was referred to in Germany as the "greyhound
method." It favored firms able to keep their representatives
camping upon the doorsteps of the Bonn ministries. The lifting of quotas through liberalization did away with all this.
In addition it eliminated the monopolistic profits arising on
quota-protected imports.

A consideration of another order was Germany's desire to
cooperate fully with the OEEC and its member countries. For
a country in Germany's position it was obviously important
to prove its sincerity and good will. Every effort had to be
made, therefore, to comply with the liberalization requests of
the OEEC.

It is necessary to point up these corollary motivations, because in discussion they often tend to be overshadowed by the
major foreign trade objectives commonly thought of in connection with liberalization. It goes without saying, however,
that these major objectives weighed predominantly in the
German decisions. Germany was under overwhelming pressure to rebuild her foreign trade. Theoretically this might
have been done by means of the ingenious Schachtian devices
of the prewar period. In England at that time some observers

seemed to regard severe discrimination as essential to lift British trade to the required level. Yet in Germany the adherents of this view made little headway. It was widely felt that the best chances for German trade recovery lay in a world-wide re-establishment of free markets and that Germany had to do her share toward re-establishing them. In this way German conviction blended happily with the international climate, which in any case would have been hard to resist.

In a narrower sense liberalization could be regarded as a direct means of increasing German exports. So long as liberalization was bilateral the freeing of German imports could be employed as a bargaining instrument to obtain freer entry for German goods. It is true that Germany's partners in the early bilateral agreements did not reciprocate by immediately liberalizing on their part, but after a while the action usually bore fruit. In the multilateral liberalization program of the OEEC such bargaining was less easy. Nevertheless it was often said that despite the EPU clearing, which made bilateral surpluses and deficits irrelevant, the member countries continued to watch closely their bilateral positions. They were inclined to reciprocate, therefore, through appropiate selection of the products they liberalized, any increase in their exports resulting from liberalization by another country.

Progress of liberalization. We may now summarize in very brief form the progress of German trade and payments under liberalization and multilateralization from 1949 to 1954. From a balance of payments point of view liberalization constituted something of a gamble for Germany. There was no way of knowing how large an increase in imports might be ahead when quantitative controls were lifted from some important product. In the case of the 1949 liberalizations the gamble came off fairly well. Germany experienced a minor payments crisis, through which she lost 246 million dollars within six months in her clearing accounts, but thereafter things quickly

righted themselves. The experience seemed to show that the
initial rush of imports into empty pipelines tended to abate
after about four months. This rule of thumb was to prove
misleading, however, in the more serious crisis that followed
multilateral liberalization to 60 per cent in the fall of 1950.

To achieve this high percentage without exposing domestic
producers to severe competition, Germany had emphasized
raw materials in her liberalization list. In the scramble for
commodities that accompanied the Korean War and particularly the entry of China into the conflict, this intensified Germany's difficulties. The EPU had opened to Germany the
doors of many raw-material-producing overseas areas. German businessmen, more sensitive to anticipations of shortages than most others, jumped at their chance. From July to
October Germany's EPU quota was being used up so rapidly
that restraint upon the newly won freedom to import became
necessary almost immediately. Outstanding import licenses
under which contracts had not yet been signed, totaling 500
to 600 million dollars, were canceled in October. New licenses
were made harder to get, among other things by requiring a
deposit equal to 50 per cent of the imports applied for.

This time, however, the flood of imports did not abate after
four months, and the deposit requirements as well as the various credit restrictions of the Bank deutscher Länder proved
unavailing. At the very last moment before her funds ran out,
on February 22, 1951, Germany suspended liberalization. The
length to which Germany went to avoid this action may be
taken as an indication of the importance which was attached
to continued liberalization.

The shock left by the crisis was so severe that liberalization
was not resumed until January 1952, when 57 per cent of
imports (of the base year 1949) were returned to free status.
At that time Germany's cumulative balance with EPU, which
in February 1951 had reached a debit of 457 million dollars,
had already recovered to a credit of 43 million. Thereafter the

liberalized proportion advanced rapidly: 76 per cent in April 1952, 81 per cent in August 1952, 90 per cent in April 1953, and 91.4 per cent (basis year 1952) as of February 1954.

Invisible transactions on current account with EPU members were also substantially liberalized, although the transfer of investment income was delayed until September 1953. On capital account, too, the partial freeing in 1954 of existing blocked DMark balances for transfer, and thereafter the creation of "liberalized capital accounts," brought considerable relaxation. The effective solution in this manner of the blocked DMark problem that had so long overhung Germany's international financial position was an advance of the first magnitude, comparable in importance with the London Debt Agreement.

The progress of liberalization was accompanied by a rapid rise of Germany's cumulative position in EPU. At the end of 1953 its level had reached 821 million dollars, at the end of 1954, 1,239.6 million. This increase, which went far beyond Germany's quota with the organization, compelled the OEEC to bring continuing pressure upon Germany to expand liberalization. It is probably fair to say that without this pressure Germany would have found it hard to overcome the protectionist resistance at home that stood in the way of a high rate of liberalization.

Some qualifications must be noted along with these gratifying figures. The imports upon which the liberalization ratios are based did not comprise all of Germany's purchases from the OEEC countries. They excluded a considerable body of agricultural imports which, though conducted through private channels, were so tightly controlled as to be by definition incapable of liberalization. Perhaps 15 per cent of total imports from EPU countries fell into this category. In addition there were certain "switch imports" of dollar goods via EPU countries, by means of which Germany obtained goods from dollar countries against payment through EPU. These imports,

TABLE 29: *Balance of Payments*
(*Federal Republic and West Berlin, in millions of dollars*)

	Exports (f.o.b.)	Imports (f.o.b.)	Service receipts	Service expenditures	Balance on current account *	Balance of current capital receipts (+) and payments (−) †	Total balance (adjusted for errors and omissions)	Aid received (+) and rendered (−)	Gold and foreign exchange receipts (−) and payments (+)
All countries									
1949	1,136	2,247‡	150§	57§	−1,018	+ 8	−1,035	+861	+174
1950	1,985	2,543	234	283	− 607	+ 9	− 643	+491	+152‖
1951	3,480	3,112	462	644	+ 186	− 37	+ 51	+428	−479
1952	4,043	3,504	765	734	+ 570	−137	+ 466	+116	−582
1953	4,428	3,533	913	839	+ 969	− 47	+ 795	+ 63	−858
1954	5,271	4,278	1,057	1,217	+ 833	−248	+ 566	+ 69	−635
EPU countries									
1949	967	1,026‡	79§	52§	− 32	+ 8	− 71	− 63	+134
1950	1,504	1,845	127	181	− 394	+ 9	− 406	+ 12	+394‖
1951	2,621	2,039	268	349	+ 500	− 37	+ 396	0	−396
1952	3,011	2,419	389	527	+ 453	−106	+ 286	+ 2	−288
1953	3,258	2,558	459	615	+ 544	− 14	+ 482	0	−482
1954	3,877	3,000	543	814	+ 606	−108	+ 455	—	−455

Bilateral countries

1949	73	146†	11§	2§	− 64	0	− 16	0	+ 16
1950	252	187	15	25	+ 55	0	+ 35	0	− 35
1951	525	434	42	71	+ 63	0	− 35	0	+ 35
1952	647	480	62	84	+ 145	− 3	+ 203	0	− 203
1953	635	470	72	92	+ 145	− 9	+ 86	0	− 86
1954	664	619	95	123	+ 17	− 17	− 44	—	+ 44

Dollar countries

1949	96	1,075†	60§	3§	− 922	0	− 948	+924	+ 24
1950	229	511	92	78	− 268	0	− 273	+479	−206
1951	334	640	152	224	− 378	0	− 310	+428	−118
1952	385	604	315	124	− 28	− 28	− 23	+114	− 91
1953	535	506	382	133	+ 278	− 24	+ 227	+ 63	−290
1954	730	659	419	280	+ 210	− 123	+ 155	+ 69	−224

* Including balance of unrequited services.
† All nonaid capital transactions.
‡ Imports for 1949 are c.i.f.
§ For 1949, exclusive of receipts from and expenditures on freight on German imports.
‖ Including an increase in reserves that resulted from consolidation of clearing liabilities of 102 million dollars.
Source: Bank deutscher Länder, *Report for the Year,* 1948–49 to 1954.

which in 1953 amounted to about 7 per cent of total imports
from EPU countries, were likewise outside the liberalizable
range. Despite these qualifications, however, it is evident that
financial relations with the EPU countries, whose trade accounted for 71 per cent of German imports in 1953, had by
that time reached a very high degree of freedom.

Likewise highly liberalized was the bilateral sector of Germany's foreign trade, comprising a group of countries, mostly
overseas, which in 1954 accounted for 8.5 per cent of German imports. Except for the controls made necessary by agricultural protectionism, imports from these countries were virtually free by 1953.

Only the dollar sector, representing in 1954 about 21 per
cent of imports computed according to the country of origin,
remained very incompletely liberalized. The degree of liberalization was estimated at 42 to 45 per cent of 1953 imports.
Experience has shown that the first 50 per cent is by far the
easiest. Considerable uncertainty continued to prevail, therefore, as to the probable consequences of more generous liberalization of the dollar sector.

What has liberalization accomplished? Even though liberalization is considerably less than complete, it has certainly gone
far enough to permit us to ask how effective it has been. Its
main impact has been on the volume of trade. That Germany's
imports as well as exports increased so rapidly is unquestionably in good part the result of liberalization—Germany's as
well as that of other countries. That Germany came out ahead
in this game of mutual encouragement and has long been running a strong export surplus is due to a variety of special
factors, most of which have been analyzed in the preceding
chapter in the discussion of export capacity and import needs.

A second significant and on the whole beneficial influence
of liberalization has been that upon the geographic structure
of German trade. Since 1949 the share of imports from the

dollar area has diminished. This reduction, which has contributed importantly to the closing of Germany's dollar gap, is due at least in part to the rise in imports from EPU countries that was encouraged by liberalization. The virtual end of American aid and the better supply situation in the nondollar countries have worked in the same direction. As a result Germany's trade structure today is free from extreme triangular constellations. Substantial deficits are still the rule with the United Kingdom and the United States, but they cannot be said to dominate the structure of German foreign payments.

The remarkable balance that has been attained with most of the underdeveloped raw material countries cannot be attributed to liberalization. Before the war Germany had a structural deficit in this sector. Its closing, if it should prove lasting, would probably have to be attributed partly to the greater demand of those countries for capital goods imports, and for the rest to the improvement in Germany's terms of trade. All comments regarding the trade structure must be qualified, however, by the observation that the attainment of convertibility may produce further shifts.

A third field in which liberalization may have had an influence is in the terms of trade. It is the very essence of multilateral trade that it permits a country to buy in markets where goods are cheap and to sell where they are dear. Multilateral trade on a large scale has been made possible by the EPU payments mechanism and the associated drive for liberalization. Since virtually all EPU countries have liberalized in some measure, one may wonder, perhaps, how they would all have been able to improve their terms of trade with each other.*

* Such an event is not by definition impossible. Trade shifts that reduce or altogether eliminate a high-priced source of supply result in an improvement in the terms of trade for the country that now buys from a cheaper source. For the country that loses the business there is at least no deterioration. A group of countries performing this maneuver with each other could all improve their terms of trade. Their terms of trade indexes would show this, however, only if current weights are used, as is the practice of several European countries.

Nevertheless, the fact that Switzerland, Belgium, and Germany, all countries with especially high liberalization, have enjoyed particularly favorable terms of trade suggests that liberalization may have had some effect of this sort. The main causes that account for the great improvement in Germany's terms of trade since 1949 are of course of a different nature: the shift in German exports from price controlled basic materials to manufactured goods, the high world demand for capital goods, and after the upsurge of 1950–51 the decline in raw materials prices (Table 30).

TABLE 30: *Geographical Structure of German Trade*
(*in per cent*)

	1936	1949	1950	1951	1952	1953	1954
Imports *							
EPU countries	56.7	45.4	69.2	60.3	62.7	66.3	63.6
Dollar countries	17.2	41.5	19.5	25.0	23.1	19.8	21.1
Bilateral countries	25.8	11.3	11.2	14.7	14.2	13.8	15.2
Exports †							
EPU countries	60.4	84.6	75.5	72.9	72.1	71.5	71.6
Dollar countries	16.5	6.2	9.5	10.9	11.2	13.3	14.6
Bilateral countries	23.0	8.7	14.7	16.0	16.5	14.8	13.2

* According to country of origin, disregarding transshipments.
† According to country of ultimate destination, disregarding transshipments.
Source: Bank deutscher Länder, *Report for the Year,* 1948–49 to 1954. Discrepancies are due to rounding.

A fourth contribution that liberalization can make remains yet to be realized: the attainment of convertibility. The gradual progress of liberalization has brought this goal, at least in one of its more modest forms, almost within reach. Of course it has not been Germany's action alone but the combined efforts of the countries adhering to the OEEC program that have accomplished this. Germany is less immediately interested in convertibility than a country with a pronouncedly triangular trade structure would be, or one whose currency serves as an international means of payment. Nevertheless she stands to benefit considerably. As an exporter of producer goods Germany would be particularly interested in a freer international movement of capital, which should be the eventual result of solidly established convertibility.

When we consider the rapidity with which the policy of liberalization combined with multilateralization has produced many of its results, the verdict seems plain that it has been a remarkable success. This verdict, I believe, can be accepted with confidence. Nevertheless we should not forget that a contrary case could conceivably be argued. Germany, as well as other countries, has been able to reach a high level of liberalized trade because her conservative monetary and fiscal policies have kept imports in bounds and encouraged exports. The present state of near convertibility has been achieved, in other words, by foregoing the possibility of a more expansionary domestic policy. I am not referring now to the minor degree of expansion that would still have been possible and according to the OEEC even desirable in the light of Germany's persistent EPU surpluses. What is at issue is the type of aggressive expansion that would have necessitated continued import controls. On the whole it seems unlikely that, with a more expansionary policy but without the benefits of freer trade, Germany could have pushed her economy ahead faster. The growth of national income has been so rapid that little extra pressure could probably have been applied before inflation and dislocation began to set in. Yet the case can be argued, and while there are adequate reasons for rejecting it it should remind us that the domestic benefits which a rising external trade has bestowed might in some part at least have also been achieved by a policy of internal expansion.

It is not inconceivable that unhappy circumstances might supervene that some day would force us to make a different appraisal. If the laboriously rebuilt international economy should once more collapse into depression, as it did after 1929, we might be driven to the conclusion that the effort to establish a relatively free multilateral trade system had not been worth while. Schachtianism would then appear as the more dependable alternative in a disturbed world. It is a pessimistic speculation and I hope no more than that, but it cannot be altogether disregarded.

Export Promotion and Export Surplus

Exports are close to the heart of every German engaged in economic pursuits. A prominent journalist has called them the sacred cow of German economic policy. The salesman rolls up his sleeves, the businessman drops his competitive restraints, the worker postpones his wage demands, and the government official does violence to his liberal principles when exports are at stake. This is largely the result of a long tradition of uphill struggle in world markets, forced upon Germany by the fact that she was a latecomer. The postwar experience, with its need to rebuild export markets from scratch, has intensified the feeling.

A variety of export promotion schemes has been tried, though on the whole Germany's activities in this field probably did not go beyond what was done by other European countries. Among the devices to be surveyed here are: (1) export credit, (2) credit insurance, (3) tax subsidies, (4) foreign exchange retention, and (5) bilateral trade agreements. Import liberalization and conservative monetary-fiscal policies, while extremely potent as promoters of exports, deserve to be ranked outside this group and on a higher plane.

Export credit. There is a widespread belief among Germany's competitors that German exports are subsidized with plentiful credit, much of it on fairly long term. In Germany, on the other hand, the complaint is frequently heard that export credit is expensive, hard to get, and not available for long maturities. It is evident that in this field, where complete statistics are unobtainable, rumor and competitive exaggeration have had a free run.

Two kinds of credit have been employed in Germany, as in other European countries: (1) credit facilities for individual exports, and (2) balance of payments credits via EPU and via the swing margins of bilateral agreements. Balance of payments credits have been financed by the Bank deutscher Länder in their totality, credits to individual exporters to a limited extent, directly or indirectly.

The individual German exporter has at his disposal several sources of credit. First there is his regular banking connection. It is generally believed that the banks are very hesitant to extend anything but quite short-term export accommodation. The cost is high, in the neighborhood of 6 to 8 per cent and more. The exporter can furthermore take advantage of a standing offer by the Bank deutscher Länder, open since 1951, to discount short-term export drafts freely at rates equal to the discount rate prevailing in the importer's country. For the exporter this means a relatively cheap loan plus the advantage of not having to engage his credit line at his bank. The total amount of drafts so discounted does not appear separately on the statement of the Bank deutscher Länder, but it is believed to have ranged in recent years around the order of 1 billion DMark. This form of credit unquestionably contains a subsidy element.

Finally, the exporter can obtain funds from the Export Credit Corporation (Ausfuhrkredit A.G.). The total resources of this institution in 1953 amounted to 870 million DMark, plus 58 million reserved for trade with Yugoslavia. Of this total 600 million are supplied by the Bank deutscher Länder, the rest by the private banking system. The maximum maturity accepted is four years, with one additional year's stand-by period. Loans granted out of the contribution of the Bank deutscher Länder are made at a subsidy rate equal to the discount rate plus 1½ per cent. Other loans are at current market rates. Advance commitments for future loans are made for longer periods ahead.

At the end of 1953 credit commitments amounted to only 573 million DMark, slightly less than the year before, of which 456 million were actually outstanding. The number of loans was 411. The great bulk of the loans was for capital goods exports for which longer-term financing is especially important. Only one-third of the total, however, was for maturities in excess of two years.[1] The fact that by the end of 1953 the outstanding loans were below even the modest capacity of the institution throws a curious light upon foreign suspicions of the volume of Germany's long-term export financing and upon German complaints about the scarcity of such credit.

There are undoubtedly a good number of firms that can finance a certain amount of exports out of their own resources. Quite likely some of them can add a few years to the 4 to 5 years allowed by the Export Credit Corporation. But the generally tight cash position of German industry and the high cost of financing probably have kept this kind of credit within narrow bounds. All in all, therefore, and particularly when contrasted with annual exports of over 22 billion DMark, the volume and terms of export credit granted to specific firms seem to be modest and to offer little cause for alarm to Germany's competitors.

A second type of credit is that granted by the Bank deutscher Länder through its monetization of balance of payments surpluses. At the end of 1954 these consisted of a credit position with EPU of 489.0 million dollars and of credit balances with all but one of the 15 countries with which Germany was trading bilaterally of around 98 million dollars. There is some question, of course, how far these sums can be regarded as foreign exchange reserves and how far they have acquired the character of export credits. In the case of both the EPU and the bilateral countries the initial idea was that of a swing margin to take care of temporary fluctuations. Meanwhile, however, the amounts have been outstanding and growing for two or more years. With regard to several of the bilateral countries it is quite clear that what was to be a balance of payments credit has been employed for long-run development. The prospects of being able to use up these bilateral resources by means of an import surplus are usually limited. The EPU credit, which can be used to pay off any one of a group of countries accounting for nearly 70 per cent of Germany's trade, seems to fall more nearly in the category of exchange reserves. Yet if and when the EPU is liquidated, any then outstanding balances will probably be consolidated into three-year loans and may not be immediately usable for imports.

It seems clear, in any case, that without the willingness of the Bank deutscher Länder to finance the bilateral and EPU balances, Germany's exports would have been substantially smaller. In that sense they fall under the heading of export promotion through credit. It is only fair to say, however, that the Bank deutscher Länder has not been enthusiastic about its role. The credits have come about through force of circumstances far more than through foresight and design.

Export credit insurance. A comprehensive system of export credit insurance is one of the mainstays of German export promotion. It is privately organized through the Hermes Kreditversicherungs Aktiengesellschaft but backed by the federal government to the extent of 5 billion DMark. Except for this government guarantee the operation is not subsidized, since its premium receipts have met its losses so far. The risks covered are broad; they include the impairment of the export contract before delivery, e.g., through political upheaval in the importing country; the credit risk proper; transfer and convertibility risk; risk of moratoria; and war risk. Exchange depreciation risks are not included except in limited cases. The premiums vary widely. They are said to be somewhat higher than the rates in the British scheme, but this appears to be compensated by the freedom enjoyed by the German exporter to insure only a selected part of his total business. The exporter is required to share in the risk in a proportion varying from 15 to 50 per cent.[2]

There can be no doubt that the export credit insurance has contributed materially to the expansion of German exports. The volume of business insured at the end of 1954 was close to the ceiling of 5 billion DMarks set by the federal guarantee. The re-establishment of export credit relationships, after a total blackout of information for many years, could never have proceeded so rapidly without it.

Tax subsidies. The German tax subsidies for exports have created an even greater international stir than the export credit system, and perhaps with better reason. They are so complex, moreover, as to make evaluation very difficult. It is not surprising that startled competitors, faced with a sudden blossoming out of German exports, have suspected even more behind the subsidies than there probably is.

The tax advantages enjoyed by German exports have been the following:

1) Remission of the turnover tax of 4 per cent (for most products) which would be payable if the merchandise were sold at home. If the export takes place through an export dealer the dealer also receives a refund of the tax paid on the transaction between him and the manufacturer. This places him on a par, taxwise, with the manufacturing exporter.

2) Refund of 2.5 per cent (for most products) of the turnover tax presumed to have been paid on the materials entering into the product. It is believed that this is less

than the tax actually included in the price of most materials.

3) Deduction from taxable income of an amount equal to 3 per cent of export sales.

4) Deduction of a further 3 per cent, the tax on which, however, is only postponed and must be paid in ten annual installments thereafter. The amount deducted from income hereunder, together with that deducted under (3), must not exceed 50 per cent of total income from all sources.

5) Remission of tax on negotiable instruments (*Wechselsteuer*).

6) Remission of tax on insurance policies.

It has been calculated that the aggregate of the benefits under (1), (2), and (3) allows a manufacturing exporter to price his merchandise 11.575 per cent below the domestic price.[3]

Looking more closely into the conglomerate of refunds, remissions, and postponements, one discovers several peculiarities. The benefits relating to the turnover tax, items (1) and (2), are probably the most significant pricewise. They do not seem subject to much international criticism, however, because other countries do the same or more for their exporters, viz., the remission of the British purchase tax and of the French *taxe sur le chiffre d'affaires*. Taxes on negotiable instruments and on insurance policies, remitted under (5) and (6), are quantitatively unimportant. There remain, as the really controversial items, the deduction and postponement relating to corporation and income tax, items (3) and (4). While these can be used to lower the price, they are intended and reportedly are mainly employed to help build up capital. The amounts involved seem small, but the importance attached to them by industry and the effect which they seem to have had in certain cases suggests that they are valuable. They may help to explain the much more intense sales effort made by German industry in the export field, as contrasted with similar activities at home. As a gesture of international good will they have been scheduled to expire in 1955.

Retention quotas. At least four different schemes for the retention of foreign exchange proceeds by exports have been tried since the war. There have been (1) the foreign exchange bonus of JEIA, which expired February 1949; (2) the 20 per cent foreign exchange quota (*Devisenfreibetrag*) which was in effect from July 1950 to March 1951; (3) the 40 per cent dollar quota (*Einfuhranrechte*) initiated in April 1952 and abandoned in response to a request of the International Monetary Fund of May 4, 1953; and (4) the 4 per cent foreign exchange quota (*Devisenbetriebsfonds*) initiated in June 1951, which is scheduled to end in 1955. Some of the schemes have applied to all foreign exchange, others (the 40 per cent quota) only to dollars. Some have permitted the retained exchange to be negotiated (the 40 per cent quota), others have not, though this never made much difference as to what the exporter actually did. Some were generous about what could be imported with the exchange in question (the 20 per cent quota) and found that scandalous luxuries were bought instead of the hoped-for essential goods. Others set up stringent lists of permissible imports (the 40 per cent quota) and saw the value of the certificates issued go to zero. The multiplicity of the devices tried, together with the impossibility of discovering any bulges or kinks in the rising curve of exports at the time a particular scheme went into or out of effect suggests one conclusion: The practical results probably were small.

The most spectacular plan was the 40 per cent quota, which sought to stimulate dollar imports by permitting exporters to sell 40 per cent of their proceeds in the free market. The premium over the official dollar initially amounted to as much as 15 per cent. The plan therefore undoubtedly constituted a significant multiple rate practice and as such incurred the displeasure of the International Monetary Fund.

In practice the problem evaporated after the disappointment over the limited use that could be made of these dollars had caused them to drop virtually to par within less than a year. Many exporters who overspeculated finally allowed their quotas to expire unused.

The 4 per cent scheme still in effect (Devisenbetriebsfonds) is intended to enable exporters to acquire abroad equipment and materials that may be rapidly needed, without going through the official red tape. It may aid exporters by modestly increasing their flexibility in negotiations. A major incentive effect is neither intended nor possible within the scope of the plan.

Bilateral agreements. In addition to the bilateral agreements with European countries, which were dropped in 1950 in favor of EPU, Germany established a large number of similar relationships with other countries, of which 15 were still in effect at the end of 1954.* At that time all but one of these countries had a debit balance with Germany, and many of them were at or even above the limit of the swing margin. The sum total of the balances amounted to 98 million dollars. A year earlier it had been 201 million. In other words a good part of the swings had become more than short-term accommodation.

At the time they were made the agreements had been a convenient, perhaps a necessary means of re-establishing German exporters in foreign markets. Had Germany tried to deal with these countries on a dollar basis her partners would probably have discriminated against German exports in favor of countries with which they had bilateral agreements or whose goods were more competitive. The bilateral agreement was for Germany a means of protecting her exports. When German ex-

---

* The countries were Argentina, Brazil, Bulgaria, Chile, Czechoslovakia, Ecuador, Egypt, Hungary, Iran, Japan, Paraguay, Poland, Spain, Uruguay, Yugoslavia.

ports increased more than German imports and the swing margins began to be used, it was generally felt that a certain amount of this type of credit, financed by the Bank deutscher Länder, was justified to get back into business.

It is true that many of the countries receiving such credit from Germany were suffering from inflation and were offering their products at uneconomically high prices. Germany was not necessarily the loser, however. Inflation plus extreme shortages of foreign exchange often made the foreign importer willing to pay exaggerated prices for German goods. As a result exporters were eager to cultivate these markets. Sometimes this led to pressure upon the German authorities to expand the agreements, particularly when the purchaser country was able to dangle some major contract before the exporter's eyes. The bilateral agreements therefore served as instruments of export promotion in more ways than one.

As time went on, however, their potency in this respect appeared to diminish. The Bank deutscher Länder was visibly anxious to reduce its holdings of bilateral claims. The view was even heard that in some countries the bilateral mentality fostered by the agreements actually hampered German exports. The existence of the agreements seemed to set up a barrier to the use of convertible currency to pay for German goods. With the swing margins fully used, German exports would then be firmly limited by German imports. In other cases, however, the agreements still seemed to fulfill their original function of protecting German exports.

The bilateral agreements constitute a remarkable blind spot in the general German outlook upon convertibility. As long as they exist Germany will not be completely convertible even for nonresidents, whatever freedom of payments may be achieved vis-à-vis other countries. The recognition of this fact, which has been manifest in more recent public utterances of leading personalities, may be a first step toward their removal.[4]

Export surplus and terms of trade. The export promotion measures discussed so far have contributed in varying degrees to the German export and balance of payments surplus since 1951 (Table 29). This surplus has played a highly strategic role in the German economy. During periods when other impulses seemed to weaken it has helped to maintain and increase the level of activity, as for instance during most of 1953. It has swelled the flow of incomes and added to the liquidity of the money market. The 800 million dollars that went into the German economy in that way during 1953 have been a pillar of strength in an otherwise uncertain cyclical situation.[5]

The contribution of the export promotion measures has probably diminished with the passage of time. The foreign exchange retention schemes either have expired or will do so shortly. The credit lines of the Export Credit Corporation have dwindled almost to insignificance in comparison with the more than 20 billion DMark rate of annual exports in 1954. It was during the earlier years, therefore, and by getting exports off to a good start, that the various promotion devices had their main impact.

Another factor meanwhile appeared on the scene to give a decisive lift to the German export surplus. It was one not subject to policy but that fell like manna from the unpromising skies: the spectacular improvement in the terms of trade (Table 31). That liberalization may have played a modest role in this connection has already been mentioned. But the main cause has undoubtedly been the broad play of supply and demand, and Germany is very fortunate that since 1951 the scales have been tipped increasingly in her favor.

It has been observed that if the 1953 volume of trade had been conducted at the prices of 1951 the trade surplus of almost 3 billion DMark would have been replaced by a small deficit.[6] It is not to be supposed, of course, that the physical volume of trade would remain unchanged if its terms should revert to their 1951 level. Germany's export volume would improve, especially if the change in the terms of trade meant higher purchasing power for some of her customer countries. Her import volume would diminish through the play of free market forces that have been re-established in the domestic market. Yet in the latter respect expectations had better be cautious. The demand for raw materials, which bulk large among German imports, tends to be inelastic, because they are a small part of the price of the finished product. The price of imported stimulants is influenced more strongly by

TABLE 31: *Terms of Trade*

(Federal Republic and West Berlin, 1950 = 100)

Year	Quarter	Terms of Trade
1949	4	109.5
1950	1	103.2
	2	103.1
	3	101.6
	4	94.6
1951	1	95.0
	2	91.3
	3	94.1
	4	100.7
1952	1	99.7
	2	104.2
	3	113.4
	4	115.1
1953	1	113.7
	2	115.9
	3	116.8
	4	118.8
1954	1	119.6
	2	117.5
	3	113.8
	4	115.0

Source: Wirtschaft und Statistik.

internal taxation than by their world market price. Agricultural imports are subject to a stabilizing regime that would make them insensitive to foreign price changes. German demand for imports, therefore, may prove relatively inelastic in the face of a rise in prices. If so, the conclusion suggests itself that the German export surplus may be more volatile than its steady growth in recent years seems to imply.

Exchange Rate and Tariffs

Policies in the field of exchange rates and tariffs have played no very active role in the revival of Germany's foreign trade. Nevertheless some interesting and, in the case of the exchange rate, critical decisions had to be made that deserve to be recorded.

Exchange rate policies. When the Allies occupied Germany they fixed the rate for the Reichsmark at the grossly undervalued level of $.10, which was in keeping with the punitive spirit of those days. The rate was relevant mainly to troop pay and remittances, since other operations were negligible. When exports and imports again began to move the inappropriateness of this rate quickly became apparent, though it was less clear what level would prove satisfactory. Germany had been cut off from the free world for so long that her prices bore little relation to any international price structure. An exchange rate, for instance, that equated the German and the American price for coal would have greatly overpriced German wood products, and so on.

When exports were resumed the problem was solved by paying the German exporter the German ceiling price while selling the product for what it would bring abroad. Conversion factors were thus established for individual products and eventually came to govern German export and imports. Each product acquired its own private exchange rate. Shortly before and after the currency reform most of these rates were consolidated into a unified rate of $.30. That this drastic operation could be carried out without major repercussions upon the movement of goods and the level of prices was due largely to the artificial state of prices before the currency reform and to their turbulent movement thereafter. The $.30 rate could be regarded as appropriate at the prices prevailing immediately after the reform.[7]

The rapid rise of exports during the year following the currency reform, from a monthly rate of 60 million dollars to about 100 million, seems to suggest that despite the price increase in late 1948 the rate did not become a real handicap. For some goods, however, special rates were maintained until well into 1949.

The sterling devaluation of September 19, 1949, confronted the Federal Republic, formally established two days later, with a critical decision. To stick to the existing rate would probably have been fatal for exports. To devalue sharply meant to raise import prices and perhaps to throw the inflation-conscious German public into a panic. The issue was complicated by the fact that the Allies had reserved for themselves control over exchange rate matters but were naturally anxious not to prejudice the policies of the newly formed German government, whereas the latter was hardly as yet in a state to make delicate decisions. After prolonged deliberations a rate of $.238 was decided upon. The degree of devaluation therefore was 20.6 per cent, against 30.5 per cent for Great Britain. This choice probably was based not so much upon detailed price and balance of payments studies as upon the fact that it constituted a middle ground between the conflicting arguments from the export and the import side. The fact that it meant a return to the pre-1933 dollar rate, and avoided the appearance of simply following the British lead, may also have weighed.

At the time many observers expressed regret that Germany had not gone as far as the British. The relative stagnation of the German economy that continued until the spring of 1950 lent support to their case for the time being. The same can be said of the calmness with which the German public accepted the event, which seemed to argue that even a sharper cut would have provoked no panic. The rapid improvement of exports in 1950, however, and the price pressures generated by the Korea boom eventually proved the decision to have been a fortunate one.

No major events in the exchange rate field have occurred since. Some modest experimentation with multiple rate practices has been the only activity in the field. The first instance of what was, in effect, a multiple rate was the introduction of the 40 per cent dollar retention quota. The retained dollars began to be traded in June 1952 in the form of dollar import certificates (Einfuhranrechte), with a premium of 12 per cent. The premium reached a maximum of 15 per cent, as mentioned before, but virtually disappeared by March 1953. Soon thereafter the device was abandoned.

The other instance of multiple rate experimentation was the freeing of the "Brazil dollar" in September 1952. At that time the German exports surplus with Brazil had exceeded the 13.5 million dollar swing by a multiple. The Bank deutscher Länder, which had financed this spree, then decided to call a halt. Exporters to Brazil thereafter had to sell their Brazil dollars in a free market to German importers. A discount developed on the Brazil dollar which at first averaged 10 per cent or more but later dropped somewhat. The rate represented a mild *appreciation* of the German currency vis-à-vis Brazil, in contrast to most other multiple rate practices.

Tariff revision. During 1950 and 1951 a new and substantially increased German tariff went into effect. It is evidence of the dominant role of quantitative restrictions that this move in the tariff field went by practically unnoticed.

The tariff that was being superseded dated back to the

early days of the century. It had been a specific tariff, and its venerable age together with the ravages of inflation had undermined its protective strength. It would not be fair, therefore, to compare the *ad valorem* equivalents of the old tariff with the rates of its successor. Nevertheless there seems to be little doubt that the new tariff is more strongly protectionist than was the old even in its prime.

The tariff was prepared in anticipation of the Torquay conference of the GATT (General Agreement on Trade and Tariffs). It is reported that the rates were set somewhat high in order to gain room for bargaining but that the concessions that Germany found occasion to make at Torquay were not sufficient to bring rates down to the desired level. If this be true it would to some extent explain the gap between the old and the new tariff. In 1954 steps were initiated toward a unilateral cut in some of the rates, which went into effect early in 1955.

Nevertheless, with or without further cuts Germany cannot be regarded as a high tariff country as European tariffs go. Virtually no rates, except perhaps those for stimulants, seem to be above 40 per cent, and the average runs nearer 20 per cent. An OEEC study concluded that while the German rates were clearly above those of characteristic low tariff countries like Holland and the Scandinavian countries, it was difficult to make a decisive comparison as regards France or Italy. The core of Germany's protective arrangements today does not lie in her tariffs. It resides in the quantitative restrictions still maintained over much of her agricultural and a small part of her industrial imports.

Debt Settlement [8]

An important step in the reconstruction of Germany's international economic relations was the London Debt Agreement of February 27, 1953. With its recognition of prewar obligations it symbolizes a rejection of the practices that have undermined the international credit machinery. It makes a contribution, even though a small one, to the rebuilding of a world in which private enterprise can go to work.

The settlement involved some 13.5 billion DMark of prewar debts owed by German public and private debtors to predominantly private foreign creditors, and about 16 billion DMark of postwar debts owed by the new German government to the Allies, mainly the United States, for their postwar aid. As a result of the devaluations of the 1930's and other factors the 13.5 billion DMark prewar debts could be settled on the basis of 7.3 billion DMark without a scaling down of principal. Interest rates were reduced for past accruals (usually to two-thirds of the original rates) as well as for future payments (usually to three-fourths). Maturities generally were extended by 10 to 25 years.

The 16 billion DMark postwar debts were scaled down to 7 billion. This was made possible by the willingness of the United States to reduce its claim of about 13.5 billion DMark to 5 billion with an interest rate of 2½ per cent and amortization over 30 years. That concession, which was made very early in the game, was the cornerstone without which the rest of the agreement would not have been possible. While the concession is large, it would represent a fair recovery on what only shortly before looked like a very weak asset.

The total burden for Germany arising out of the agreement amounts to 567 million DMark annually for the first five years and will increase to 750 million when amortization payments begin in 1958. This may be somewhat more than Germany had expected to pay. Probably it is more also than the minimum with which she might have been able to get away. Responsible in part are the large EPU surpluses that Germany began to run up month after month during the negotiations. But there also seems to have been a real desire on the German side to reach terms that the creditors would regard as satisfactory. To this end Germany seems to have been willing to make financial concessions.

The initial impulse for the settlement originated on the side of the Allies. The Occupation Statute of 1949 contained a reference to external claims against Germany, and negotiations opened about a year later. The present settlement seems designed to contribute in several respects to the re-establishment of a healthy international credit atmosphere. The payments agreed upon, for instance, are in no way contingent on future events or conditions such as Germany's ability to earn surpluses. This unconditional character seems essential where private creditors are concerned, whatever the merits of escape clauses may be for intergovernment loans. Provision for consultation in case of difficulties, however, was made at German request. The agreement further avoids the creation of new blocked DMark balances (with special exceptions). To have permitted substantial payments in blocked currency would have created a barrier to future convertibility of the DMark, since these funds would always have hung over the market. Finally, as said before, it is not a stingy agreement. It conveys the impression that Germany made a good settlement in the hope of re-establishing her credit.

Whether Germany will receive or even want new foreign loans remains to be seen. At first blush it might appear that a country with tremendous investment needs, a poor capital market, and high interest rates would naturally be anxious to obtain foreign capital. Many individual German firms would indeed like to borrow at rates more nearly like those of Switzerland than those prevailing in the German securities market. But so long as Germany continues to have large balance of payments surpluses it is doubtful whether foreign loans would be in her interest, particularly from EPU countries. They would lead, in the first place, to still greater accumulation of foreign exchange or even of EPU credits, and then to a continuing interest burden. Their main virtue in the present situation would be to loosen up the capital market and drive down its exorbitant rates, but quantitatively this effect would probably be small.

Direct foreign investments—foreign firms coming in to operate in Germany—would be another matter. While the cost of such capital is high, if the enterprises prosper it is usually worth while in terms of the initiative, new ideas, and competition that are imported along with the capital. The liberalization of the transfer of earnings, which was one of the sequels to the debt settlement, has increased Germany's attractions in this respect.

Conclusion

Germany's foreign trade policies have been a mixture of liberal, forward-looking actions and of others less liberal and generous. It is fair to say, however, that the liberal side has predominated. Germany has cooperated with other European nations and in some phases has perhaps shown the way in rebuilding a free international economy.

This has involved the progressive surrender—as yet far from complete—of many of the techniques of trade policy developed during the 1930's: quantitative restrictions, exchange control, bilateralism, multiple exchange rates, and exploitation of foreign creditors. Born of the emergencies of their day, these techniques for a while threatened to congeal into a fixed system and to become the norm of international economic relations. Most of them have in common the grasping for an immediate advantage at the expense of undermining and eventually destroying the international mechanism as a whole. It has not been easy for Germany, hard pressed as she was, to surrender an important part of this protective as well as aggressive equipment. It has meant risks and sacrifices in the short run accepted for the sake of the long run, the courage to throw part of her scarce bread upon the waters.

The process still has far to go, and its ultimate consummation may never be complete. The techniques that are being
sloughed off, moreover, may be revived if the economic cycle
should again turn downward. Some of them would reac-
quire justification under such conditions, if used in moderation and cooperatively. Meanwhile, however, the fact that
Germany has found it to her advantage to drop them is all
the more significant in view of her very thorough experience
with them in the past.

CHAPTER 9

Population and Refugees

WHEN THE FACTS about Western Germany's new population structure began to unfold after the war they provoked some very pessimistic speculation. Combat losses and birth deficits of two wars, combined with the influx of refugees, seemed to have hopelessly distorted the age and sex distribution. To this was added the physical and moral damage suffered by the survivors and the loss of drive and stamina so noticeable during the precurrency-reform period. It was not surprising that the biological havoc alone came to be looked upon as a major obstacle to recovery.

Subsequent experience shows these fears to have been largely unjustified. Since the currency reform there has been no lack of vim and vigor. The age and sex structure has shown itself no effective block to a rapid economic build-up.

In some respects population developments have actually aided the recovery. For the future they may hold troubles, but almost certainly not on so serious a scale as was surmised shortly after the war. In this chapter we shall first take account of the growth and structural changes of the population and thereafter note certain changes in its qualitative features. Following this we shall deal with the role of the refugees in the population picture as well as in the economy generally.

Population Growth and Structure

The dominant fact about the population of Western Germany is its increase from 39.3 million in 1939 to 49.6 million in September 1954. This fabulous rise, most of which has taken place since 1945, has been almost entirely the consequence of an influx of some 10 million refugees. Together with a modicum of vegetative growth, the refugee tide has completely obliterated the numerical effect of combat and civilian war losses.

Immigration on such a scale was bound to produce a substantial rise in national income, given circumstances that were not too unfavorable. The discussion of these economic effects, however, since they are so intimately connected with the refugees, will be reserved for the sections devoted to the latter. Here we shall be concerned with the structural aspects of the new and enlarged population and with their implications for the revival.

The population pyramid of a healthy and growing nation—the graphic representation of the number of people in different age groups—looks somewhat like a well-grown Christmas tree, broad at the bottom, tapering off smoothly toward the top, its two sides (male and female) symmetrical. That of the United States is roughly of this shape. The German looks like some stunted, storm-whipped plant, with deep gashes marking the two wars, and a pathetic lopsidedness reflecting the disproportion between women and men.

The men now 55 to 75 years old have had their ranks thinned by the first World War, which pushed the death rate up from 15 per 1,000 in 1913 to 24.8 in 1918. The men now between 28 and 50 were similarly affected by the second war. The generation now (1954) 37 to 40, both men and women, is especially weak, having been born during the first World War when the birth rate dropped from 27.5 (1913) to 13.9 (1917). The number of men in this age group is approximately one-half, in relation to total population, of what it is in the United States. The age groups now 22 to 26 bear the scars of the low birth rate during the depression. They are followed by the crop of "Hitler babies" that is now swelling the labor force. These in turn are succeeded by the emaciated generation born during the war and by the only moderately broader group reared during the following years.

The net result of these distortions can be seen in Tables 32 and 33:

1) A preponderance of women over men, women representing 53 per cent of the total population but as much as 60 per cent of some age groups over 28.
2) An increase in old people of 65 and over from 7.3 per cent in 1939 to 9.3 per cent in 1951.
3) A decline (not visible in the tables) in the proportion of children under 10 years.

TABLE 32: *Western Germany's Population Structure*
(*in per cent*)

	1939	1951	1961 *	1971 *
Children, under 15	23.7	23.5	21.1–20.0	22.0–17.9
Working age, 15–64	69.0	67.2	67.9–69.1	64.4–68.6
(Male)	(68.6)	(65.5)	(67.4–68.6)	(64.2–68.6)
(Female)	(69.4)	(68.7)	(68.4–69.6)	(64.4–68.6)
Old people, 65 and over	7.3	9.3	11.0–10.9	13.6–13.5
Total	100.0	100.0	100.0	100.0

* Range given by alternative sets of assumptions as to future population growth. High figures in the "Working age" category imply assumption of lower rate of growth.

Sources: Sonne Report, p. 159; *Wirtschaft und Statistik,* December 1953.

From an economist's point of view special interest attaches to the proportion of persons of working age, i.e., between 15 and 65 years. This figure has shrunk only very moderately, from 69 per cent in 1939 to 67.2 per cent in 1951. This numerical result must be qualified, however, by pointing to the higher proportion of women, of men over 45, and of partly or wholly disabled persons. Nevertheless the figures are surprising and on the whole quite reassuring even for Germany's longer-run potentialities.

In the short run the economic potential of Germany's population is mainly determined by the proportion of the economically active, i.e., the labor force. On this group the war has left somewhat deeper traces, as can be seen from Table 33. The labor force (including registered unemployed), which had amounted to 51.3 per cent of the total population in 1925 and to 51.7 per cent in 1939, had dropped to 46.3 per cent in 1950 and had recovered to only 47.8 per cent by 1953. Several factors seem to have contributed to this drop. One of them is the decline in the working age ratio, but this is not the whole story. A further cause is the swelling of the ranks of the pensioners—heads of households outside the labor force, many of whom are disabled veterans and war widows. A third factor, and a particularly striking one, is the drop in the proportion of economically active women, which seems to run counter to common observation. The explanation for this seeming divergence between statistics and observation is that the drop has occurred in the category of "family helpers," which mainly represents farm population. Finally, there is the fact that the year 1939 was one of overfull employment, during which the prospects of drafting labor may have induced some who were on the margin of the labor force to seek convenient employment voluntarily.

The impression of a pronounced shrinkage in the economically active part of the population must be qualified, moreover, on several counts. In 1939 some 655,000 members of the labor force were in the armed services, to say nothing of the Labor Service and the numerous Nazi party organizations. A further 2,950,000 represented family helpers. Being predominantly agricultural their work was in any case not highly productive, and a large proportion of them was only very partially employed—the typical picture of an excess farm population that in the long run will move to the city. If one evaluates each member of this group at one-half of a regular worker and further deducts the armed services, the 1939 labor force ratio of 51.6 per cent is reduced to 45.8 per cent. Recomputed on the same basis, the labor force ratio for 1950 was 43 per cent

TABLE 33: *Occupational Structure of Population and Labor Force*
(in per cent)

	1939			1950			1953		
	Men	Women	Total	Men	Women	Total	Men	Women	Total
Total population in millions	19.3	20.0	39.3	22.4	25.3	47.7	23.0	26.0	49.0
Dependents	23.9	55.2	39.8	26.5	55.2	41.7			
Independents outside labor force	8.4	8.6	8.5	10.3	13.5	12.0			
Labor force *	67.7	36.2	51.7	63.2	31.3	46.3	64.4†	33.1†	47.8†
Total	100.0	100.0	100.0	100.0	100.0	100.0			
Labor force in millions	13.1	7.3	20.4	14.1	8.0	22.1	14.9†	8.6†	23.5†
Self-employed	18.6	6.9	14.4	18.8	7.6	14.8			
Dependently employed	71.3	52.3	64.5	76.6	60.3	71.0	77.7	63.2	72.2
Assisting family members	5.2	40.8	17.9	4.6	32.1	14.2			
Armed services	4.9	—	3.2	—	—	—			
Total	100.0	100.0	100.0	100.0	100.0	100.0			

* Including registered unemployed and armed services.

† Estimated on the assumption that in the labor-force categories other than "Dependently employed" no change has taken place since 1950, the date of the last census.

Sources: Bundesministerium für Arbeit, *Wohnbevölkerung und Erwerbspersonen* (Bonn); Sonne Report; *Wirtschaft und Statistik.*

and that for 1953, 44.6 per cent. Also to be considered, finally, is the widespread bootleg work done by pensioners. On the other side of the ledger must be counted the fact that a given labor force is probably less effective today than it was in 1939 because of the higher proportion of women and of people approaching retirement age, the great number of partly disabled, and the shortage of well-trained workers among the younger generation.

The labor force ratio, whatever its level, must in any case not be overrated as an economic factor. It is true, of course, that a low ratio means a heavier burden of nonproducers for each producer to carry. When a good part of the nonproducers are not children but pensioners, as is the case in Germany, the burden becomes especially severe. The pensioners are in large part maintained by the government, and the taxes required for their keep act as a disincentive in a way in which family expenses for children would not. But the importance of all this for the level and growth of per capita income is less than appears at first sight. Productivity and real income per head has recently been increasing in Germany by about 5 per cent per year. The adverse effect upon national income of a decrease in the labor force ratio of 10 per cent is made up in about two years at that rate. In other words, the economy has lost no more than the equivalent of two years of growth. Furthermore, the number of hours worked by a given labor force is flexible. The difference between a 48- and a 40-hour week is much greater than that between Germany's prewar and postwar labor force ratio. A general two-week vacation period, plus a few extra holidays, costs more man-hours than the entire distortion of the population structure. Finally, the labor force ratio is itself flexible. More women can work, and old people can work longer; both will probably do so if a labor shortage provides them with the economic incentives. All in all, these considerations suggest that the damage suffered by Germany's population need not be taken too seriously from an economic point of view.

It is conceivable that the real difficulties are yet to come. Population statisticians seem agreed that for the next 20 to 30 years only slow growth, if not stagnation, is the best that can be expected.* It remains to be seen whether with better housing, peace, and reasonable prosperity this relative pessimism will be warranted. But assuming it to be, what would a very slow rate of population growth mean for Germany? It is interesting to note that the working age ratio will rise above that of 1951 if the population as a whole remains constant, but will fall by 2.8 percentage points if a moderate rate of population growth prevails. From this angle, therefore, no major threat seems likely for many years ahead.

Nevertheless a slowing down of population growth may well deprive the economy of some of its natural impulses. The virtual assurance of widening markets has undoubtedly been one of the factors encouraging forward-looking investment. Rapid population growth is one of the strongest stimulants to autonomous as well as induced investment and to a production-oriented attitude. Consumer demand also would no longer be stimulated from this source, and labor would be less plentiful and hence less cheap. But *if* these handicaps can be overcome the prospects for better living standards will improve. No longer will part of the community's savings have to be diverted to equip the rising generations. It will be possible to concentrate investment upon equipping more effectively the existing labor supply. A more rapid increase in capital per worker will mean more rapid productivity gains.

* The Sonne Report (ECA Technical Assistance Commission, *Die Eingliederung der Flüchtlinge in die deutsche Gemeinschaft*) estimates total population in 1979 at 52.1 million, implying an annual rate of growth of less than 0.3 per cent. *Wirtschaft und Statistik*, December 1953, p. 538, estimates population in 1971 at 52.2 million on optimistic assumptions and at 48.1 million on pessimistic assumptions. The optimistic estimate involves an annual growth of somewhat less than 0.5 per cent.

A great many slips are possible, of course, between a cup and a lip twenty years apart. A stagnant population may develop economically harmful tendencies that might overshadow the potentialities for rapid gain—diminishing interest in work, inadequate savings, political feebleness. But it seems clear that there is nothing in Germany's present population structure or its future prospects that must inevitably lead to dire consequences.

Qualitative Population Changes

Germany's population has undergone a variety of changes that while not quantitatively measurable may be supposed to have left their imprint upon the economic life of the nation. The curious fact is that as one seeks to trace these effects one is driven to the conclusion that they have been very small.

One such change is the thinning out, through war and in small degree through Nazi taint, of the generation that should supply today's rising men in business, politics, science, and cultural pursuits. A shortage of top flight talent is indeed observable in the three last-named fields. Few German observers seem to believe, however, that the revival has been hampered by a shortage of competent and aggressive businessmen. The old men, together with the survivors among the young, have had enough strength to pull Germany out of her collapse. It may be added that these old men are by and large the same individuals who have been in charge all along—the tremendous upheavals of the recent past have brought no circulation of the elites.

The expulsion and murder of the Jews by the Nazis has deprived Germany of a population group representing an extraordinary concentration of intellectual power. It is hard to believe that such a blood-letting should not have left its traces. One can observe them, indeed, when one looks at German intellectual and cultural life today, as well as at certain fields of science, such as theoretical physics. But in the business world, where they were once so strong, the passing of the Jews seems to have left no irreparable gaps.

The wear and tear of the war and of the postwar starvation period might lead one to expect a permanent weakening of the physical and moral fiber of the population. During the last two war years the inhabitants of many major cities had few nights' sleep without interruption from air raid alarm. The three years thereafter were for most people a period of deadening hunger made barely tolerable by demoralizing black market dealings. These experiences may indeed account for certain features of German economic life today: the single-minded concentration upon material gain and the pronouncedly two-fisted manner with which it is pursued. A lack of drive is decidedly not among the results. It may be that the day of reckoning is still to come. Much is said today in Germany about the alleged spread of the "managerial disease," heart trouble. But statisticians seem to be of two minds about it, and in any case the cause is as likely to be the extreme exertion during the recent upswing as the wear and tear of the preceding years.

The thinning out of the middle generations creates the prospect that economic and political power some day may pass somewhat abruptly from a very old to a rather young generation. The tragedy which in 1888 caused power to pass from William I to his immature grandson William II may repeat itself on a multiple scale. Such a development may make for extreme dynamism but also for instability. Yet this is too vague a prospect to be regarded with much concern. It may some day have to be quoted as a contributory cause to a disaster or to a new flowering of energies, but it can hardly be cited as a source of prospective danger.

The lack of schooling of the generation that grew up under Hitler is even today regarded as a serious problem at all levels.

Skilled workers are scarce, competent young technicians less easy to find than they used to be. How grave a matter this may be it is impossible to say.

A number of compensating developments must also be mentioned. Germany today is free not only of the man-power drain of an army but also of the intellectual drain caused by the diversion of some of the best talent to a military career. Of politics the same can be observed. While in many other countries politics absorb some of the ablest people fully and a good many more part time, it can hardly be said to encroach far upon the present absorption of most of the German elite with money-making. Wartime losses have loosened a desire to recoup so passionate that it pushes aside most of the traditional German concern with noneconomic pursuits.

The conclusion is inescapable that whatever qualitative damage the German population may have suffered has not been a major obstacle to revival. Repercussions that may yet be to come will bear watching, but their impact, if any, is not likely to be directed toward the economic sphere.

The Refugees: Problems and Partial Solutions

The end of the war witnessed migrations on a scale such as the world has not often seen. While some 8 million displaced persons, who had been brought in during the war to do forced labor, quit Germany to go to their old homes or to new ones of their choice, most of the inhabitants of areas that had housed nearly 17 million Germans sought asylum in East and West Germany.[1] Four million went to the Russian Zone, eight million to Western Germany. Two million inhabitants of the Russian Zone fled to Western Germany over a longer period of time.

The expellees, those whose homes were outside the former Reich or in parts of the Reich east of the Oder-Neisse line, had to leave in consequence of inter-Allied decisions taken at Teheran, Yalta, and Potsdam. With a mercilessness surpassed only by the previous brutalities perpetrated upon many of these countries by the Nazis, they were forced out of Czechoslovakia (2.4 million), Poland (540,000), and the other satellite countries, as well as out of Silesia (2.7 million), East Prussia (1.4 million), Pomerania (1.2 million), and Brandenburg (130,-000) .* ² Those from the Russian Zone, known as immigrants, came in a continuous stream that fluctuated with the political climate of the zone. They all found themselves crowded into a country whose larger cities had lost 30 to 50 per cent of their houses. The bulk of the refugees inevitably had to be steered to where shelter could be found—to the rural districts. Among these the three states that lay closest to the points of origin of the wanderers found themselves saddled with well over 50 per cent of the refugees: Schleswig-Holstein, Lower Saxony, and Bavaria. Of the population of Schleswig-Holstein alone 32 per cent were refugees in 1951. There these unhappy people stayed, on farms, in camps, in air raid shelters, in every conceivable kind of temporary quarters—and waited (Table 34).

It soon became apparent that the refugee problem rivaled in

TABLE 34: *Number and Location of Refugees*
(in thousands)

	Expellees	Immigrants from Russian Zone	Total	Per cent of population
Schleswig-Holstein	742.2	131.5	873.7	35.8
Lower Saxony	1,755.0	382.6	2,137.6	32.0
Bavaria	1,893.1	249.5	2,142.6	23.3
Hesse	763.1	201.5	964.6	21.9
Baden-Württemberg	993.3	191.3	1,184.6	17.8
North Rhine-Westphalia	1,626.4	517.2	2,143.6	15.5
Bremen	61.3	26.6	87.9	14.9
Hamburg	146.6	85.3	231.9	13.8
Rheinland-Pfalz	233.4	71.6	305.0	9.7
Federal Republic	8,214.4	1,857.1	10,071.5	20.6

* Figures for all four zones and Berlin as of October 29, 1946.

Source: Bundesminister für Vertriebene, *Vertriebene, Flüchtlinge, Kriegsgefangene, heimatlose Ausländer, 1949–52* (Bonn, 1953), pp. 17, 21.

seriousness that of the repair of war damage and that the future stability of Germany would in good part depend upon its successful solution. The integration of the refugees came to be recognized as an important phase of reconstruction. Here was a large mass of people, destitute, at odds with their surroundings, without hope and without retreat, seemingly an easy prey to some new radical leader. Their abiding hope was of course for a change in the political situation that would allow them to return home. But even when they accepted the fact that their exile might be permanent, adjustment to the new surroundings was extremely difficult. Though they were Germans, they were not always well received in Germany. Seeing around themselves so many who had retained their property and station in life, they felt that it was they who had paid for the war. Religious differences as well as differences of temperament, education and background often aggravated these tensions under the crowded conditions of German life.

In its early phases the refugee problem might well have appeared insoluble. Indeed it is still far from a full solution and will probably never reach it. Nevertheless the problem has shown itself more manageable than it seemed at first, and less of a drag on reconstruction than might have been supposed. This is partly due to the measures taken to cope with it, but even more to the expansionary climate of the German economy.

The measures taken were, as might be supposed, the outcome of much study, deliberation, and political bargaining. Few topics have produced such a flowering of literature in postwar Germany as the refugee question. A variety of basic decisions had to be made. Could emigration be relied upon to relieve Germany of much of the added population? Should an effort be made to move the refugees to where there was employment (but for the time being no housing), or should employment be brought to the refugees? Should strictly economic criteria prevail in the development of the added man power, with all that this would mean in job changes, wasted training, and personal unhappiness? Or should these criteria be modified to permit a larger proportion of the refugees to resume their old occupations as farmers, artisans, and the like, even though these might be uneconomic? What priority should expenditures for refugees have over other claims on public resources?

The measures that were proposed were modest in relation to needs, and the execution often modest in relation to the proposals. Nevertheless a good deal was done for the refugees. These measures can be grouped under four main headings: (1) resettlement, (2) housing, (3) provision of jobs, and (4) legal status and social security.

Resettlement. The extreme disproportion in the regional distribution of refugees (in Schleswig-Holstein they represented 32 per cent of the population, in Rheinland-Pfalz 1 to 2 per cent) made some amount of resettlement imperative. The question was raised, of course, whether for some states the presence of a large number of refugees did not constitute an exceptional opportunity. But it proved to be a great deal cheaper to move the refugees to where there was employment than to build up a diversified economy in the often remote areas where they congregated. The first program, designed to move 300,000 refugees from the British and American zones to the French Zone, was initiated by the Allied authorities in March 1949. Previously the French occupation authorities had refused to accept refugees, on the grounds that France was not party to the Potsdam Agreement that had caused the dislocation. The program was thereafter taken over by the German government, which eventually committed itself to resettle 900,000 refugees. Till the end of 1952, however, only 470,000 had been moved.[3] Hand in hand with the resettlement program went a flow of individual migration that increased as the housing picture in the industrial centers improved and permits to settle there became more easily available. In 1954 it was estimated privately that all in all some 4 million refugees had moved from where they had first arrived, but that about an equal number still remained in less than optimal locations.

Both resettlement and private migration initially ran into opposition in the areas of immigration, which were themselves short of housing. Since part of the cost of maintaining the unemployed, aged, and sick fell upon the local communities and the individual states, the difficulty of securing agreement on regional redistribution was considerable. In the light of these problems the attainment cannot be judged altogether unsatisfactory. It is felt by many observers, nevertheless, that greater efforts would have achieved substantially more impressive results.

Housing. Upon the refugees fell the brunt of the housing difficulties. By September 1950 only 29.5 per cent of them had managed to become the principal occupants of a regular dwelling unit, as contrasted with 77.1 per cent of the local population. The rest lived as subtenants or in various kinds of emergency housing. The number of occupants per room was 1.75 for refugees as against 1.18 for the local people. By the end of 1952, 350,000 newly constructed dwelling units had been made available to refugees, equal to 40 per cent of the total low-cost housing put up till that time. Much of the financing, insofar as it came from official sources, was provided by the Immediate Assistance program and its successor, the Equalization of War Burdens Fund. Subsidies for purchase of furniture and for payment of rent were available from the same sources.

The housing program was an essential condition for the resettlement of the refugees. Like the latter it often moved more slowly than expected and caused further delays in the shifting of the refugees. Not infrequently bitter rivalry developed between the newcomers and the bombed-out members of the local population who likewise aspired to new homes. In absolute terms the achievements have been substantial, but measured against the needs they do not bulk overly large.

Jobs. Unemployment was heavy among the refugees. In April 1949 the expellees alone accounted for 37.9 per cent of total unemployment while representing only 16 per cent of the population. This disproportion was due partly to the unfortunate location of many of them and partly to their occupational structure. Particularly difficult was the case of the 300,-000 independent farm families and of the numerous independent artisans and tradespeople. Together these self-employed had accounted for 15 to 18 per cent of the refugee labor force prior to their expulsion from their homes. It was possible to argue that this was the moment to make a change that in the course of time economic processes would impose on many of them in any case—to move from the country to the city, and out of an old-fashioned artisan's shop into a factory. The present influx of refugees, it could be said, was basically no more than a tremendous acceleration and broadening of a movement that had been underway for many decades—from the cornfields of East Prussia to the coal mines and steel mills of the Ruhr. Large-scale re-establishment in their old jobs would merely aggravate already existing defects in the economic structure: too many farmers on too little land, too many artisans and storekeepers with too few customers.

Against these views it could be pointed out that for many of the older farmers and artisans the required change was beyond the limits of their adaptability. Unless they could be provided with the kind of work they knew, they were condemned to remain public charges and end their lives in bitterness and poverty. The Sonne Report, the most comprehensive set of proposals for dealing with the refugees, demonstrated the difficult nature of the balance that had to be struck between these two views.[4]

The measures taken to provide employment for the refugees encompassed a wide range. There were credits to refugees to re-establish their businesses, credits to facilitate the creation of new jobs, distressed area programs, and the like. The total assets of the Compensation of War Damage Bank (Lastenausgleichsbank), which deals mainly though not exclusively with refugees, had passed 150 million DMark in September 1952. A rural resettlement program was started for refugee farmers which by the end of 1952 enabled 40,000 farmers out of 300,000 to buy or lease a farm. Special tax privileges were granted to refugees to help them rebuild their capital. Legislation was passed that gave preferred or at least equal status to expellees in a number of occupations, from artisans to professional people and civil servants.

Nevertheless when all these efforts are added up they leave one dominant impression: What was done was significant and praiseworthy but still below what would have been technically possible had the government decided to make the refugees its top priority.

Legal status and social security. The treatment accorded to the expellees' claims to legal status and social protection has been undeniably generous. They are recognized as citizens regardless of their former nationality. Within the social security system they receive the benefits to which their past occupation and status would entitle them under the West German system, regardless of whether they were German nationals or ethnic Germans. Civil service pensions and the like are fully recognized. These rights have their root partly in the Basic Law (constitution), partly in the Expellees' Law, and also in the laws regulating the Immediate Assistance and Equalization of War Burdens programs.

Apart from the regular social security benefits available to the great majority of Germans, the refugees have been the main or sole object of a variety of special welfare and rehabilitation programs. Chief among these have been the Immediate Assistance and since 1952 its successor institution, the Equalization of War Burdens Fund. Under their provisions expellees and war victims generally have been entitled to continuing benefits for support of life and compensation for losses, a lump sum compensation, loans to facilitate integration into the community, compensation for home furnishings, and housing aid. Further benefits have been paid for education and in special hardship cases. Finally, the aid that many refugees have received from better placed relatives and friends has played an important role.

The present position of the refugees. From what has been said it is clear that the refugee problem has by no means been completely solved but has nevertheless been greatly eased. In 1954 it undoubtedly bulked much less large among Germany's preoccupations than it did a few years earlier. Unemployment was still nearly twice as high among the refugees as among the rest of the population, compared with roughly 2.5 times in 1949. But given the general reduction in unemployment this amounted to a substantial improvement. The refugees had not on the whole regained their old social or occupational status, but we have seen that to some extent these occupational shifts were imposed not by their lot as refugees but by the structure of the new German economy. There was still an extraordinary concentration of refugees in the three refugee states, but perhaps half of the relocation that seemed ultimately desirable had been accomplished. The large group of older people who could not adjust had aged further, insofar as they were still alive, and had in many cases reached the retirement limit. Their problem, otherwise insoluble, was on its way to what in Germany is referred to as a biological solution.

The most decisive manifestation of improvement from a political point of view was simply this: The sufferings of the refugees, be they great or small, had lost their seriousness as a political threat. Radicalization had been avoided, the refugee party was a well-established member of Chancellor Adenauer's coalition, and the fears that had prevailed some years ago had largely vanished.

The improvement in the refugees' lot was in good measure the result of government action on their behalf. To an even greater degree, however, it was simply the consequence of the general economic expansion. What the government at its various levels had done was substantial. Total expenditure on refugees during the three years 1949–51, including regular social security benefits, was estimated at 10.8 billion DMark.[5] Nevertheless this amount was still small in relation to needs. The German government had always maintained that the refugees were a consequence of the East-West split and that their burden should not have to be carried by Western Germany alone. But to this plea—which the refugees failed to support by appropriate signs of going communist—the United States had turned a deaf ear. The German government itself, in keeping with its general principle of not putting immediate social equity ahead of longer-run economic considerations, had never been prepared to give top priority to the refugee problem. Otherwise it would no doubt have been possible to do more for them even with the existing financial resources. On the whole, the policy pursued seems to have been justified by events. The rapid upswing of the economy made large-scale government action increasingly less necessary. As the refugees were absorbed into the expansion, much that the government had intended to do began to happen automatically. The number of refugees that moved from one state to another during the years 1950–52 without benefit of official resettlement planning was about 25 per cent larger than the number of those who moved under such guidance. Practically all who wanted to work were employed as soon as they arrived; in the industrial centers of North Rhine-Westphalia and Baden-Württemberg the demand for skilled labor was almost continuous. Much of the time the shortage of housing was the main limitation upon migration and the growth of employment. As housing and migration progressed the refugee problem eased automatically. The expanding economy had shown itself the best cure for the problem.

The Economic Consequences of the Refugees

In speaking of the refugees one cannot help being interested in the tremendous human problem they represent and in the policies and events that may lead to its solution. Yet from the viewpoint of this book it is their contribution to recovery with which we must primarily concern ourselves. When the refugees first streamed into the country as in a great wave, and then continued to come even after the first flood tide had subsided, it was inevitable that they should be regarded as a tremendous additional burden for the ruined German economy. The German government, which has to foot the bill for much of what is done for the refugees, continues to emphasize this aspect of the situation. But in public discussion it is generally accepted today that the refugees have on balance been an aid rather than a hindrance to recovery. Our own survey will confirm this view as far as national income and similar indexes are concerned. Moreover, the balance of forces seems to have shifted increasingly toward the positive side as the general recovery progressed. Concerning income per capita, however, there is reason to think that it would be higher today if the refugees were not there to share in the total. To believe otherwise would be to assume that without the refugees the German economy would not have been able to maintain high-level operations and would have slipped off into recession or stagnation for lack of demand.

The contribution of the refugees has been to the volume of population and labor force and to their structure and human quality, to the spirit of enterprise, to competition, and to the willingness to work. Moreover, the refugees have had an

impact upon such elements as the level of wages and the mobility of labor. We shall have to deal with most of these things
more briefly than the value of the contribution warrants.

Population and labor force. In 1953 the refugees (expellees
and immigrants from the Russian Zone together) numbered
almost exactly 10 million. A population increase of this kind
was almost bound to bring about an increase in national income, by one route or another. The new people had to be
housed, clad, and fed, and along with their demand for goods
they brought their man power, if nothing else, to augment the
supply. This was the most basic fact, which in importance
overshadows everything else. Time had to elapse until the
refugees' willingness to work could be matched by appropriate opportunity, but from the very start they made at least
some contribution to output.

Structurally the refugee population showed the same defects as the local, but usually to a lesser degree. The proportion
of persons of working age was somewhat better among them:
47.7 per cent (expellees only) between the ages of 14 and 44,
compared with 44.8 per cent for the population as a whole;
and 69.5 per cent for the ages 14 to 64, against 68.9 per cent
for the whole. The disproportion of the sexes was also slightly
less, particularly among the immigrants from the Russian
Zone, among whom men predominated. The labor force participation ratio was lower among the refugees than among the
total population: 42.5 per cent (expellees only, as of September 1950), against 46.3 per cent. This was due in part to the
fact that many refugees, located in rural areas where they had
no hope of employment, failed to register as unemployed.
Nevertheless, it is true that the occupational composition of
the refugees, with its heavy accent on formerly independent
farmers, militated against the attainment of a high ratio of
effective employment.

Qualitatively the refugees represented in many respects a

highly selected group. Among them were nearly 2 million Sudeten Germans, an alert people with an excellent educational background. Other groups were also especially well qualified in various respects. They had all been through a brief but ruthless process of natural selection. Many of the weak and unfit did not survive the rigors of expulsion and the long trek to safety. A second and more intensive process of selection was applied when the more enterprising migrated once more within Western Germany in search of jobs.

The refugees were under severe pressure to make good. To get employment they often had to take the least desirable jobs. Those who had been in the upper income brackets and who meant to stage some kind of social comeback had to work harder than most of the local population. While it is impossible to document the importance of refugee enterprise statistically, the individual cases that can be observed are impressive. The fluidity of the postwar situation and the gaps that partition had torn in the West German economy favored them. Some industries lost in the Russian Zone and the Oder-Neisse territories were largely rebuilt by refugees, often by the same men who had owned and operated the lost plants. Some industries altogether new to Germany were also built up by refugees who brought their know-how and their reputation. The most prominent case of this kind is represented by the Gablonz glass manufacturers, who have made a substantial contribution to Germany's export capacity.

The refugees intensified competition wherever they went. Well-established but perhaps somewhat staid local firms found themselves faced with aggressive upstarts who brought new techniques and new ideas. Fixed habits and attitudes had to be modified where they came into contact with those of the refugees. Though this meant much friction, it also brought fruitful impulses.

The refugees increased the mobility of the population as a whole. They had no local ties where they first landed and were

willing to move in response to market factors. The great outpouring of production from the Ruhr and other industrial
centers would never have been possible without a substantial
flow of population to the expanding industries. It is true that
there were enough bombed-out and uprooted natives of Western Germany to provide a sizable flow of this kind, perhaps as
large a one as could be accommodated, given the housing
shortage in the receiving areas. But for the longer pull the
refugees have undoubtedly facilitated the regional redistribution of man power that the changing structure of the German economy demands.

The refugees also left their imprint upon the level of wages.
This effect is probably much smaller than might be supposed
in the light of the great addition they made to the labor force
and particularly to the ranks of the unemployed. The reason
for its not being larger is the geographical maldistribution of
this unemployment. The industrial centers never experienced
a surplus of labor, particularly not of skilled labor. Because
the housing shortage limited the inflow of new workers, the
unemployment prevailing elsewhere did not act as a strong
depressant upon wage rates. Nevertheless the slow but steady
inflow of new man power probably did work in that direction.
The centralized wage policy of the German labor unions,
morever, and their intense concern with unemployment very
likely gave a weight to the availability of refugee labor that it
would not have had in a completely unregulated market. During a period when low wages meant higher profits and more
investment the downward pressure of the refugees upon wages
led to a more rapid expansion of plant capacity.

Finally, the refugees have played an undeniable role in
maintaining a high and expanding level of demand. The backlog of needs per capita has been greater for them than for most
other parts of the population. They have intensified the housing shortage to a point where it promises to serve as a prop to
activity for a number of years ahead. Their indigence, as it
were, has underwritten continued German prosperity.

There is some question, of course, as to how far such under-writing was required. Germany's replacement and investment needs were large even without the refugees. The economy has shown itself elastic in adjusting to changing conditions and has had exports to rely upon as a special prop. Serious deflationary tendencies, had they arisen, could probably have been miti-gated by appropriate stabilizing policies.

The coming of the refugees also had negative effects. The most important one, probably, had to do with productivity. The refugees came with their bare hands and had to be sup-plied with productive equipment. Public services and what has been called social overhead, like schools, roads, and hospi-tals, had to be provided, to say nothing of the immense added need for housing. To some extent the refugees could step into jobs left vacant by men who had died in the war. But for the majority capital had to be made available out of the current savings of the economy. No estimate is possible, but when we consider that the number of employed refugees is between 3.4 and 4 million, and remember the estimate made in Chapter 7 of capital requirements per nonagricultural worker of 12,000 DMark, it becomes clear that the total productive capital ab-sorbed by the refugees is high. In the absence of the refugees the savings of the economy could have been devoted far more intensively to improving the equipment of the existing labor force. Productivity per man hour would have risen substan-tially more. Such productivity gains would have been accom-panied, other things being equal, by an approximately equiv-alent rise in income per capita.

A compensating factor may be seen in the broader markets provided by the enlarged population. This may have facili-tated cost reduction in some industries. It can hardly, how-ever, have been of the same order of importance as the dilution of capital per worker made necessary by the refugees.

A second negative factor is the increase in the tax burden that was a consequence of the refugees. In 1950 it was esti-mated that the refugees received 40 to 42 per cent of social security benefits of all kinds, more than twice their share of the population. Thus, besides absorbing part of the national income in this way, they probably also held down its total because of the adverse effects of high taxation upon economic activity.

The impact of the refugees upon the balance of payments may also have been adverse. They increased the import needs of the economy probably more than in proportion to their number because of their marginal effect upon food imports. Up to a certain population level German agriculture probably could have met a high proportion of total food requirements. To feed additional mouths imports were required to an increasing extent. In 1949, on the basis of a relatively low volume of imports, the foreign exchange costs occasioned by the refugees were put at 450 million dollars annually.

There was a compensating element: Some of the refugee industries were highly export intensive, while others were important in economizing imports. To the extent that refugee labor contributed to keeping the wage level low, exports were further aided. In any case, whatever the net effects upon the balance of payments may have been they have evidently raised no serious obstacles to the achievement of equilibrium and even a large surplus.

The negative effects that we have observed do not in the least put in doubt the fact that the refugees have made a large positive contribution to the national income. They merely suggest that the per capita income would have been higher if the refugees had not come to share in the total. This follows almost inevitably unless one is prepared to attribute to the refugees an extraordinary importance in maintaining a high level of activity. Even so, it is not certain that the local population found its per capita income reduced substantially. The refugees as a group had to take the less desirable jobs and had a lower income per head. It is conceivable, therefore, that the local population, despite its higher tax burden, did not come off any worse than it would have without the refugees. This conclusion is highly tentative, of course, and needs to be qualified with respect to the inconvenience of crowded housing as well as in other respects. Nevertheless, in view of the residue of bitterness that one sometimes still encounters on both sides such speculations may not be without interest.

CHAPTER 10

Labor's Performance

LABOR'S CONTRIBUTION to the German revival has been of two kinds. One has been the steady effort of the German workingman that was the basic force behind the recovery. To appraise this performance we shall have to look into matters of working time and employment. The second has been the restraint practiced in wage demands, which has contributed to price stability, competitiveness of exports, and above all to the financing of the reconstruction. This will take us into the field of labor union policy.

Hard Work and Unemployment

Perhaps the most frequently heard explanation of the German miracle is the German capacity for hard work. No one who has observed German workers going about their jobs can deny that they work hard and long, if perhaps not very fast or imaginatively. It is somewhat surprising, therefore, to find that by their own high standards they seem to have worked less hard during the postwar period than before the war (Table 35). The 1938 figure of 49.7 hours per week was not reached again until November 1953.[1] Compared with the rest of Europe German hours are long but not exceptionally so. In 1952 they averaged 3.3 hours above France and 1.8 hours above Great Britain, were almost even with Switzerland, and 1 hour below the Netherlands.*[2] It must be noted, however, that the high proportion of women at work has pulled the average down somewhat for Germany.

* In manufacturing. Comparison with Netherlands for 1951.

Neither can substantial evidence be found to show that the intensity of work has increased. While there is no accurate way of measuring this, productivity can be used as a rough indicator so long as the chief determinant of productivity, the volume and quality of equipment, does not change. Owing to war damage, productivity after the war was low. By 1950–51, however, this damage had very largely been repaired, and in many instances improved equipment had been installed. An

TABLE 35: *Weekly Working Hours*

Year	Male	Female	All workers
1938	50.2	47.8	49.8
1946	40.5	35.4	39.5
1947	39.7	35.8	38.9
1948	42.9	39.8	42.2
1949	47.2	43.5	46.3
1950	49.0	45.2	48.0
1951	48.5	44.2	47.4
1952	48.5	44.7	47.5
1953	48.8	45.5	47.9
1954	49.5	45.9	48.6

Sources: *Wirtschaft und Statistik,* 1938; Bundesministerium für Arbeit, *Hauptergebnisse der Arbeits- und Sozialstatistik* (1953), p. 104.

increase in work intensity over prewar should therefore have shown up in a higher productivity index. In fact, the 1936 level of productivity was not significantly bettered until after 1951 (Table 25, p. 208). Quite possibly part of the failure to make a better showing must be charged to the greater proportion of old workers and women in the labor force as well as to the neglect of adequate training, but this can hardly alter the general conclusion.

Finally, an attempt could be made to test the willingness to work by comparing those of working age with the economically active population before and after the war. Germany's economically active ratio is influenced by so many special factors, however, which were pointed out in the last chapter, that a comparison with prewar would not be very meaningful. If made it would show a drop in the economically active group relative to the working-age group. Because of the same factors, a comparison of Germany's economically active ratio with that of other countries is apt to be misleading. Such a comparison could be made, if at all, only among countries of similar economic and population structure, since in countries with a strong agricultural sector the ratio tends to be pushed up by the numerous family helpers, while in countries with a high birth rate it is lowered by the large number of young children. For the year 1951 the comparison would show Germany with a ratio of 46.9 per cent slightly above the United Kingdom with 46.2 per cent and well above Belgium with 40.9 per cent (1947).

Even Germany's high ratio of economically active women provides at best a presumption of an exceptionally strong willingness to work. While the difference between Germany (33.1 per cent of the female population in 1953) on one side and Belgium (19.0 per cent, 1947), the Netherlands (19.5 per cent, 1947), Switzerland (25.9 per cent, 1950), and the United Kingdom (27.2 per cent, 1951) on the other is substantial, it is in large part explained by the German surplus of 3 million women in the working-age group.

Where does this leave the "hard work" thesis? A number of isolated facts that do not appear in any statistics can be cited in evidence of the work done in Germany since the war. For several years after the war people were busy in their spare time repairing damage to their homes and furnishings, to say nothing of the unproductive but immense labor involved in procuring food before the currency reform. Then and now a considerable number of people—in the city of Frankfurt one out of five—have been cultivating little suburban plots on which they grow fruits and vegetables. In the building industry unofficial bootleg shifts that add a few hours to the normal working day are said to be common. The readiness to work overtime is reported to be higher than it was in former years, and it must indeed be considerable in view of the fact that only 25 per cent extra (almost tax free) is paid for overtime. Among the pensioners as well as among the registered unemployed there are many who in fact have fairly steady employment. Businessmen and public servants worked to exhaustion for years after the currency reform and still keep hours that are long by any standard.

In the aggregate these things probably add up to a good deal of achievement that is never registered. But they are by no means all postwar developments. Overtime work, utility gardening, and extra hours of one sort or another have always been common in Germany. They cannot be cited as evidence of *unusual* postwar effort, except insofar as they may have become more widespread and more intensive.

The conclusion seems clear. The hard work of the German people is no myth, and it has contributed enormously to the rebuilding of the country. It has not, however, been something altogether exceptional either in German experience or on the contemporary European scene.

In the light of all the rebuilding that had to be done in Germany it may seem peculiar to ask whether this hard work was really necessary. But when we remember that most of the time Germany had from 1 to 2 million unemployed, the question appears not unreasonable. Had the unemployed been activated, it might be argued, the same results could have been reached with less effort per capita. We shall see that this hypothesis contains only a modest grain of truth. But the presence of fairly substantial unemployment during a period of intense effort is something that calls for an explanation. Are we to say that Germany recovered because of her hard work or despite her unemployment?

To understand German unemployment we must look at employment. During the six years from 1948 to 1954 employment rose from 13.5 million to 16.5 million, an average of nearly half a million a year, or about 3 per cent of the labor force (Table 36). This happened despite the fact that agriculture and the occupation authorities meanwhile released a total 800,000 workers. The exodus from agriculture, moreover, was not the typical long-run shift that occurs with rising productivity. It was simply the ebbing away of the wartime and postwar tide of refugees and hungry city people who had hired themselves out on farms to secure food and shelter, for during 1953 the man power in agriculture was still 12 per cent above 1938. Employment outside agriculture and the occupation, therefore, increased by 4.1 million from 1948 to 1954, an annual average of about 5 per cent of the existing employment outside those two fields. This is a very satisfactory performance by most standards. It was a key factor in the great upsurge of German production.

Worth noting also is the relative steadiness of the advance in employment outside agriculture and the occupation beginning in 1948, as contrasted with the apparent stagnation of total employment in 1948 and 1949. Once the currency reform had squeezed out the "phony" employment that existed so long as money did not matter, and had revealed the large underlying unemployment, the basic trend was always upward. Expectations of 3 million unemployed or more, which were widely advertised before the reform, proved totally unfounded. In appraising the significance of the actual unemployment these fears deserve to be recalled.

The advance of employment would have been sufficient to absorb within 2 to 3 years all the unemployment above a slow-melting structural core and to take care of any normal growth of the labor force besides. But this growth was far above normal, thanks to the integration of the refugees, the continued immigration from the Russian Zone, and the late return of war prisoners from Russia. During the five years 1948–53 the labor force increased by almost 4 million, an average annual gain of nearly 5 per cent. Here is the main reason

TABLE 36: *Employment*

(*in thousands, as of June 30 each year*)

	1948	1949	1950	1951	1952	1953	1954
Total employment excluding agriculture, forestry, the occupation	11,295	11,705	12,260	13,187	13,705	14,442	15,191
Employment in agriculture, forestry, the occupation	2,173	1,782	1,596	1,533	1,466	1,364 *	1,309
Total employment	13,468	13,487	13,856	14,720	15,171	15,806	16,500
Unemployment	451	1,283	1,538	1,326	1,240	1,073	1,007
Labor force, excluding self-employed and family helpers	13,919	14,770	15,394	16,046	16,411	16,879	17,507

* In part estimated.

Sources: *Wirtschaft und Statistik; Statistisches Jahrbuch; Analyse der westdeutschen Arbeitslosigkeit.*

for the agonizing stickiness of Germany's unemployment
figures, which refused to come down by more than 100–
200,000 per year (Table 37). The tendency toward wide—and
surprisingly regular—seasonal swings, which is apparent from
Table 37, has intensified the problem.

TABLE 37: *Seasonal Highs and Lows of Unemployment*
(*Federal Republic and West Berlin, in thousands*)

June	1949	1,283
February	1950	1,982
October	1950	1,230
January	1951	1,911
October	1951	1,214
February	1952	1,894
October	1952	1,028
January	1953	1,823
September	1953	941
February	1954	2,042 *
October	1954	821

* The high unemployment of the winter of 1954 was caused by an unusual
cold wave and was of brief duration.
Sources: *Wirtschaft und Statistik; Analyse der westdeutschen Arbeitslosigkeit.*

Perhaps this should be sufficient explanation. A country ex-
periencing a 25 per cent population increase within a few
years can hardly expect to have full employment during and
shortly after the process.

But for the policy makers of the period so detached an attitude was not easy to take. We have noted in Chapter 4 the
great debate over the policies that this unemployment seemed
to call for. On one side it was contended that mass unemployment required aggressive fiscal and monetary expansion. On
the other side it was argued that much of the unemployment
was structural and hence not removable by measures of this
kind, and that these measures, moreover, would seriously en-

danger the balance of payments and the stability of the currency. It is important to realize that while the first argument was correct, the second was the more immediately persuasive one.

All analysts of the employment situation agreed that some of the unemployment was not structural, and this part could have been alleviated by expansionary measures. It is because these measures were not considered safe that they were not adopted, and not because they were thought altogether ineffective. The marginal unemployment, in other words, must be attributed to the exigencies of monetary and fiscal policy.

Were structural elements nevertheless the reason why the spontaneous expansion of industry was so slow to absorb unemployment even over a period of years? German unemployment had two structural aspects. One was the limited ability of the German economy to absorb quite abnormal annual accretions to the labor force and large chunks of unemployment besides. From this viewpoint much though not all of the unemployment undoubtedly deserves to be called structural. The other aspect had to do with the geographic mislocation of many of the unemployed and with the limited capacity of some of them for regular work. In this sense the truly structural core of unemployment was probably smaller.

In either sense the structural character of the unemployment was probably less permanent than appeared at the time. Industrial expansion and internal migration have both helped to break it down. An estimate for early 1950 put structural unemployment at 800,000, another for mid-1950 at 600,000.[3] Both coming from the side of the labor unions, they are free from a suspicion of upward bias. To these structurally unemployed must be added some 200,000 who were unemployed while changing jobs. Contrasting the totals with the minimum unemployment figures of 820,000 reached in the course of 1954, it becomes evident that in the meantime substantial inroads had been made upon structural unemployment.

Experience so far suggests caution in putting the stamp of "structural" upon any major part of unemployment. Nonetheless there is some reason to think that further drains upon the remaining supply of idle labor will reveal an increasingly hard core. A survey of October 1952 indicated that of the 1 million unemployed covered, 350,000 were of limited employability and 65,000 virtually unemployable.[4] Physical defects were the reason in the great majority of cases. Moreover, among the fully employable over 70 per cent were unwilling or unable to relocate or commute over long distances to find employment. Very likely a good proportion of both groups will be drawn into employment if the reservoir of the fit and willing diminishes further. But the going will get harder.

An important factor in the attrition of structural unemployment has been the relatively high mobility of a large part of the labor force. This is an aspect of the general labor picture that deserves special attention. The volume of migration within Western Germany has been remarkable. During the three years 1950–52, 2.4 million persons moved from one German state to another.[5] A much greater number moved within states, although this often meant no more than that they had found a better apartment in the same locality. Finally, there was the continued inflow of refugees and others equal to about 50 per cent of the movement across state boundaries, and an outflow mainly of emigrants equal to about 25 per cent. About 40 per cent of those moving across state boundaries were refugees relocating themselves. Of the rest many were bombed-out people who had lost their roots in the community. Persons in the age brackets of 18 to 40 years accounted for over half of the total migration.

Very probably more would have moved and some would have moved earlier had housing been available. The desire to move was for a long time greater than the opportunity. From this resulted a popular feeling that mobility was highly restricted,

While geographic mobility was high, however, another type of mobility had tended to diminish: that between jobs. A variety of factors contributed to this result. Most important among these was the company housing that went with a job. In areas of extreme housing shortage this alone made a local move almost impossible. A second factor was the rising volume of retirement and other benefits provided by many employers outside the union wage contracts. Such benefits usually depended upon length and continuity of service and were lost through a change of jobs. A third factor reportedly was the growth of installment purchases, which in Germany are commonly secured with the buyer's salary. These are problems of labor relations and union policy, and to this subject we now turn.

Wages, Stability, and Investment

Looking back upon the years since the currency reform German labor can point with a good deal of satisfaction to a rapid and substantial increase in nominal and real wages (Table 38). Between June 1948 and November 1954 real weekly earnings advanced 92 per cent. Compared with prewar

TABLE 38: *Hourly Wage Rates of Industrial Workers*
(excluding miners, in Pfennig)

	Male	Female	All workers	Index of real weekly earnings,* all workers (1938 = 100)
1936			73.3	
1937			75.9	
1938			78.6	
1939			80.8	
Jun. 1946	94.3	57.2	88.7	
Jun. 1947	99.8	59.2	92.9	
Jun. 1948	106.5	63.5	98.5	66
Sep.	115.8	72.1	108.3	70
Dec.	121.6	76.4	113.1	72

TABLE 38 (*Continued*)

	Male	Female	All workers	Index of real weekly earnings,* all workers (1938 = 100)
Mar. 1949	126.2	79.1	116.1	77
Jun.	129.9	82.5	119.6	82
Sep.	131.7	83.8	120.7	88
Dec.	132.8	84.8	121.6	87
Mar. 1950	134.0	86.1	122.9	93
Jun.	135.5	86.5	124.4	98
Sep.	139.8	88.9	127.7	102
Dec.	146.9	94.1	133.9	103
Mar. 1951 †	150.7	96.0	136.7	101
Jun.	161.5	104.8	148.0	107
Sep.	162.9	104.2	148.8	105
Dec.	n.a.	n.a.	n.a.	n.a.
Feb. 1952	168.3	105.8	152.6	104
May	170.4	107.2	155.7	110
Aug.	171.5	107.3	156.5	113
Nov.	174.3	109.0	157.7	115
Feb. 1953	176.9	110.3	159.7	111
May	178.9	113.2	163.2	119
Aug.	179.0	113.3	163.2	122
Nov.	180.1	114.0	163.4	124
Feb. 1954	180.9	114.3	162.7	119
May	181.7	115.0	165.6	124
Aug.	183.6	115.8	167.3	126
Nov.	188.0	118.1	170.6	127

* Gross weekly wages divided by cost of living index, middle consumer group, without seasonal adjustment.
† Slight change in index for all following figures.
Sources: Statistisches Jahrbuch; Wirtschaft und Statistik.

(1938), labor earnings had improved by over 27 per cent. Nevertheless in contemplating its position at any one moment during that period labor had an uneasy feeling that it was getting a rather small share of the expanding pie. Business was making large profits, and from time to time labor made moderately successful efforts to cut in on these. But for a variety of reasons these forays remained within rather narrow limits of restraint and caution. Labor's suspicion, therefore, that its share in the national income continued to be modest was probably not unfounded (see Table 8, p. 53).

For the economy as a whole labor's muted and unaggressive policy has been an inestimable advantage. It has, in the first place, made a major contribution to the stability of the new currency. One may even say that at one critical juncture, when the success of the currency reform and of the free market policy hung in the balance, the day was won largely thanks to labor's restraint. If in the late fall of 1948 labor had made a determined effort to keep wages abreast of rising prices, both probably would have spiraled upward. The Erhard policy might have had to be abandoned, and the currency reform would have been a dubious success at best. But though labor protested bitterly and staged a one-day token strike, it allowed itself to be satisfied with a (not unsubstantial) raise of 15 per cent—in the face of a rise of about 25 per cent in the cost of living index. This forbearance was admittedly made easier by the fact that despite the price movement the post-currency-reform economy was an enormous improvement over what had gone before. It was further facilitated by the fact that the price rise centered on a limited range of goods, mainly clothing, shoes, and some foodstuffs, while many other items in the consumer's market basket were kept down by some form of control.

In the second place labor's restraint has helped to make and keep exports competitive. It is true that German wages have risen much more since 1948 than those of comparable European countries (Table 39). But they started at a low level, and productivity has increased considerably (Table 40).

The final and probably most decisive contribution, however, has been to the financing of the investment boom. By

allowing wages to lag behind profits, labor made it possible
for business to engage in large-scale self-financing. The inequality of the income distribution, favoring the higher incomes where proportionately more savings accrue, was the
essential condition of the high rate of investment. The development can be no more than illustrated by available data
but is nevertheless striking. In December 1948, six months
after the currency reform, the index of manufacturers' prices

TABLE 39: *Index of Hourly Wages (Manufacturing)*
in Germany, Belgium, and the United Kingdom,
1948–52
(1948 = 100)

	Germany *		Belgium †		United Kingdom	
	Nominal	Real	Nominal	Real	Nominal	Real
1948	100	100	100	100	100	100
1949	114	107	104	103	103	100
1950	121	122	106	105	107	101
1951	138	127	119	115	118	99
1952	149	135	122	n.a.	127	99
1953	157	n.a.	122	n.a.	134	n.a.

* Data of International Labour Office differ slightly from those presented in
Table 40.
† Men only.
Source: International Labour Office, *Yearbook of Labour Statistics, 1953.*

stood at 192 (1938 = 100) while hourly wages stood at 143.
The subindexes for basic materials and capital goods each
stood at 195. This gap has been the source of an exceptional
volume of profits and of financing capacity. In addition,
through the lift that it gave to profit expectations, it has also
strengthened the incentive to invest.

It is true that the gap between wages and prices does not
look nearly so large when one takes into account the low level
of productivity in 1948 and 1949. The cost of labor of prewar
productivity (computed by dividing the productivity index
by wage rates) was much above the actual wage level prior to

1951. In 1949, for instance, when the wage index stood at 150.5 and the productivity index at 82.3, the cost of an hour's work of prewar productivity according to this calculation was 182, as compared with a manufacturers' price index of 185. In

TABLE 40: *Wages and Productivity*

		Cost of living index	Hourly earnings *	Produc-tivity †	Index of labor cost ‡	Index of manufac-turers' prices	Index of hourly real wages
1936 §				100	100		
1938		100	100			100	100
1946		n.a.	110.4	n.a.	n.a.	n.a.	n.a.
1947		n.a.	116.0	n.a.	n.a.	n.a.	n.a.
1948	Mar.	127 ||				June 168	
	June	134 ||	129.8	n.a.	n.a.	Oct. 190	69
	Dec.	174 #				Dec. 192	
1949		166	148.8	82.3	182	185	84
1950		156	159.2	92.8	175	186	99
1951		168	182.7	102.6	192	221	104
1952		171	195.4	107.5	198	226	111
1953		168	203.9	113.3	196	220	119
1954		168	208.4	115.3 **	—	216	124

* Industrial workers, male and female, excluding miners.
† All industry, excluding electric power and construction.
‡ Wages divided by productivity, based on 1936 = 100 (efficiency wages).
§ 1936–39, per area of Reich.
\|\| Weights of 1946.
Estimated.
** First half of the year.
Sources: Wirtschaft und Statistik; Statistisches Jahrbuch.

1950 the comparison came to 166 for wage costs and 186 for prices. But since the productivity index probably understates true productivity in 1949 and 1950, because much labor was being diverted to repairing the plant, and since for other reasons the data are not fully comparable, these computations do not carry too much weight. They do not decisively challenge the fact that there was a substantial gap between wages and prices, though the gap undoubtedly was smaller than the unadjusted wage-price indexes suggest.*

The wage-price gap reached its peak at the end of 1948, six months after the currency reform. From then on it was whittled down through a gradual increase in wages and also through falling prices. The Korea crisis widened it once more. This time, however, labor was less inclined to practice self-restraint. Two rounds of wage increases, the first spearheaded by a strike in the building industry, the second by one in the metal trades, both in Hesse, lifted wages by an average of 19 per cent from June 1950 to June 1951 (Table 38). Thereafter wages moved up slowly, with real wages gaining somewhat faster owing to a slight drop in living costs. Weekly earnings benefited also from a lengthening of hours. The gap between wages and manufacturers' prices was almost closed by 1954. The accompanying gain in productivity suggested, however, that in terms of labor costs of constant productivity it still existed, although on a much smaller scale than in 1948. The shrinkage of the gap is confirmed by the rising share of labor in the national income for 1951 through the first half of 1953. Late in 1953, after wages had been relatively stagnant for about a year, this share again showed a small drop (see Table 8, p. 53).

It should be repeated that the price and wage data do no more than illustrate a phenomenon that was very complex and quite beyond the capacity of existing statistics to measure. The wage-price gap differed enormously from one industry to another; it was small or even negative for industries that remained under price control. The gap was influenced by the

---

* The productivity index is based upon 1936, the price and wage indexes upon 1938. A productivity index based upon 1938 would probably give lower figures for postwar productivity and thereby raise the cost of labor of prewar productivity (efficiency wages). Furthermore, the wage index is pulled down because it excludes the wages of local miners, which are among the highest in industry. The productivity index on the other hand, is pulled down by the inclusion of coal mining, where productivity has been 20 to 30 per cent below industry in general.

cost of imports, which on the whole had risen more over pre-war levels than German manufacturers' prices. It was further affected by productivity changes that were also different for different industries. It could give some broad indication as to the relative position of business and labor, but it was far too crude to serve as an argument for or against price cuts or wage increases.

There exists in Germany an interesting theory that by implication would seem to deprive labor of the credit for having aided capital formation through the moderation of its wage demands. According to this view neither wage increases nor higher taxes can reduce business profits once business has made up its mind how much investment it wants to undertake. If higher wages or taxes temporarily cut into profits the investment, instead of being financed out of profits, will be financed with bank credit. The resulting inflation will dilute the real value of the wages or taxes and restore profits to something like their original level. This theory does fit, in a general way, the German experience of 1948 and 1950–51, when the use of bank credit and idle cash for investment financing raised prices and profits. The reason why the "forced saving" mechanism worked so well, however, was precisely that labor did not immediately push for wage increases commensurate with the price rise. A more aggressive wage policy probably would have brought on an inflationary spiral as well as tighter credit controls, either of which would have interfered with investment. Continuing high investment would not have been possible in the absence of labor restraint.

Looking back upon labor's gains over a series of years the conclusion seems evident that wage restraint has paid off rather well. If after currency reform labor had pushed for and obtained a higher share in national income its immediate position would of course have improved. The improvement, however, would have been at the expense of long-run gains, since it would have meant lower profits, lower savings, and less investment, other things being equal. The benefits from a more rapid progress of national income are almost certain to outweigh, after some years, the gains that could have been scored through redistribution of income. When per capita income advances by more than 5 per cent annually, as it has done in Germany, it does not take many years for the gains from progress to outstrip those from redistribution.

It is true that Germany's progress has been achieved at the expense of a rapidly increasing inequality in the distribution of wealth. By enabling business to earn high profits and reinvest them, labor has in effect helped entrepreneurs to accumulate great wealth with extraordinary speed. Yet this fact, which is much stressed in German labor circles, presents no convincing argument against the wage policy that has been pursued. The virtually unilateral accumulation of wealth by entrepreneurs is inevitable unless and until labor begins to save substantially. Had labor obtained higher wages without saving part of them it would have reduced the formation of capital without in the long run changing the distribution of it. The wealth that was actually created in six years it would then have taken nine or twelve years to accumulate. Its distribution would not have been greatly affected thereby.

As long as business was willing to invest on a large scale— something that of course cannot be taken for granted—it would seem that labor's interests were best served by a continuation of its existing wage policies. Yet in 1953 and 1954 a growing impatience with these policies became apparent among labor strategists. It was being argued that circumstances were changing and demanding new decisions. Beyond that, however, the wisdom even of past actions was questioned and a basic change in approach urged by many. In the following analysis of the ideas and circumstances that shaped labor's action since the war we shall encounter some of the reasons for this dissatisfaction.

Union Structure and Policy

It is probably not surprising to discover that the wage action of German labor has only in part been the result of deliberate policy. In good part it has very clearly been shaped by fortuitous circumstances, by the mechanics of union organization, and by the attraction of competing objectives. Without serious exaggeration one can say that practically all of these factors have injected a downward bias into wage policy.

Union organization and wage demands. Immediately after the war labor unions and their officials enjoyed a position of special favor with the occupation authorities, insofar as one can use that term under conditions of nonfraternization. Because of the treatment of the unions and their leaders by the Nazis, and because of the resistance record of many union officials, they were practically the only group in whose anti-Nazi convictions the Allies felt able to place confidence. The unions thus were able to rebuild their organization fairly quickly. There emerged in October 1949 a single parent organization for all German labor, the German Federation of Labor Unions, comprising sixteen nationwide industrial unions.

The creation of a unified labor movement was viewed by observers of varying political persuasions as an improvement over the pre-1933 situation when several groups had been competing for membership. It promised greater strength through united action. At the same time it promised to be less completely identified with the Social Democratic party than the "free unions" had been, which represented the bulk of German labor before 1933. The presence in the Federation of the religiously oriented membership of the former Christian labor unions seemed to offer a counterpoise. With the Federal Republic still in its infancy these political aspects were regarded as primary. No doubt they still deserve to be so rated today, but the peaceful evolution of German politics so far has allowed that point to drift somewhat into the background.

The formation of a single top union organization was expected to increase labor's sense of responsibility. In this Germany has not been disappointed. The labor leadership, it is fair to say, has demonstrated remarkable statesmanship and breadth of vision. It has never lost sight of the interests of the economy as a whole, with its need for large-scale investment and financial stability, and has been mindful also of the repercussions of labor successes upon the weaker social groups— pensioners and refugees. The moderate reaction to runaway prices in the fall of 1948 was an example.

This sense of responsibility, however, has been something of a handicap in the pursuit of wage demands. Labor's immediate interests have sometimes had to yield to broader considerations. In the long run labor has almost certainly benefited from this attitude. The benefits, however, have been shared by all the community, while the short-run sacrifices have fallen only to labor. Far-sighted statesmanship can be irksome to its beneficiaries.

Unity of organization has further held back labor's drive for higher wages by allowing the attention of the leaders to be absorbed by matters far removed from weekly pay envelopes. It would be unfair to say that the labor leadership was chasing rainbows when it made codetermination its primary goal, but the pursuit of this objective probably did distract labor's energies from more immediate concerns. A less centralized organization, in which the leadership towered less remotely above the rank and file, might not have been subject to those temptations. That the size of the organization has encouraged a somewhat bureaucratic way of thinking and that this has not been conducive to vigorous wage-bargaining need scarcely be added. The interunion competition which characterizes the United States is very obviously absent from the German labor scene.

At the lower end of the labor hierarchy developments likewise have not favored an aggressive wage policy. The German union does not begin at the plant level; the place of the American local is taken, in most respects, by a works council. The works council is a small group of workers chosen by their co-workers to represent them before the management. It is altogether divorced from the union and does not deal with wages, but handles many of the routine tasks of a local such as grievances and working conditions. In effect the works council weakens the union by depriving it of many of the functions that make the union a real force with the men. At its best the works council is a block between the union and its members; at its worst—opinions differ as to how often this happens—it is a creature of the management.

The works council is not a new institution. It is a domesticated remnant of the revolutionary upheavals that followed the first World War. Abolished by the Nazis, it was revived after World War II and given added stature under the codetermination legislation. Works councils are generally credited with having made an important contribution to the good labor-management relations that prevail in Germany. At the same time, however, they have unquestionably acted as a drag on the unions' ability to pursue an active wage policy.

The lure of codetermination. The quest for codetermination has distracted, as said before, some of the union leadership's energies from a more determined pursuit of wage interests. In fairness it must be said that the conception was a bold and challenging one, though fraught with dangers for free enterprise. Three main thoughts seem to have started labor off on its campaign for codetermination. One was the realization that the unions had allowed the Nazis to take over the country without offering the kind of resistance that their strength and organization should have made possible. A material aid to the rise of the Nazis, in the eyes of labor, had been the support of big business. One way to prevent a recurrence, it was argued, was for labor to gain a strong voice in the councils of business.

A second motive was the desire for a living ideology. The strength of German labor had in the past derived largely from the intensity with which it adhered to its Marxist creed. Now the old belief in socialization was waning, but German labor could not conceive of itself without some ideological banner. Codetermination—the German word *Mitbestimmungsrecht* has much more punch—seemed to have the makings of a new faith.

The third motive, and the most concrete, was the desire for economic control. Union influence over the conduct of business, it was thought, would at the very least help to raise wages and to prevent price increases that would dilute these gains. More ambitiously, codetermination was looked upon as the road to full-scale economic planning with strong labor participation. It might even be turned into a "cold nationalization" of business. To give body to these ideas a comprehensive plan for the organization of all business in a rigid system of economic chambers and councils was put forward by the unions. The plan, if implemented, would almost certainly have meant the end of anything resembling a free economy in Germany. It might have proved a threat to parliamentary democracy itself.

As things turned out, labor got very much less codetermination than it had asked for, and what it got looks like a nearly empty shell. That, at least, has been the fairly general verdict so far. The possibility that the shell may contain a time bomb cannot be altogether discounted.

In the iron and steel industries, where codetermination had originally been introduced by the British, labor received at least in form a strong voice. The board of directors of each firm is divided evenly between representatives of the shareholders and of labor, with one neutral appointed by the two sides jointly. Half of the labor representatives are nominated by the union, i.e., are outsiders, the other half by the works council from among the plant working force, again with one neutral. On the managing board—the top executives of the company—there is a labor manager, with powers equal to those of his colleagues.

In all the rest of industry the degree of codetermination is materially weaker. The board of directors of each firm is still divided evenly, but the labor members are nominated by the employees not by the union. No labor manager sits on the managing board. This watered-down version of codetermination, which deprived the unions of any chance to play the role of coordinators of industry, was legislated over the heads of labor opposition.

According to the reports that circulate, labor's representatives so far have not given too good an account of themselves. Catapulted into an unaccustomed job, a higher social class—important in Germany—and sometimes into very high income brackets, many of them have not been able to hold their own with their new colleagues. Untrained in management problems, they have often failed to pull their weight in the conduct of business. The sarcastic description of codetermination as "boardroom privileges for labor" is not without its justification. The different outlook of their new associates, moreover, together with the inherent logic of their new responsibilities and perhaps the splendor of their positions have helped to turn many of labor's representatives into spokesmen for the management. Yet the unions, when it comes to wage talks, must step softly because "their men" are, after all, inside the companies. Business meanwhile seems to have taken the new set-up completely in its stride.

There are some indications that codetermination has had a beneficial effect upon labor-management relations. Management decisions can be interpreted to the rank and file more convincingly by the labor manager or the works council board member than by the company personnel director. Minor demands of the working force no doubt obtain a better hearing through the same conduct. But upon wages and prices code-termination seems to have left few traces.

Business may not enjoy the present idyl forever, of course. Labor may eventually develop a more effective group of representatives than it has now. If the Social Democratic party should some day form a government, codetermination may come to life. The consequences are hard to foresee and may hold a real threat to free enterprise. One must not forget that before things settled down to their present state the advent of codetermination had been viewed by many observers with considerable apprehension. There is no assurance that these fears may not some day find a belated justification.

Union methods and wage increases. The unions' wage policy has been further influenced—and very probably hampered—by certain peculiarities of approach. One is German labor's old habit of seeking to achieve its ends through legislation rather than through collective bargaining. In the past this has probably been an element of strength. Meanwhile, however, the unions have given their members so much by virtue of law—job security, vacations, maternity benefits, and the like—that they have little left to give by virtue of union membership. The result has been a somewhat lackadaisical attitude of many workers in membership matters. The unions' ability to bargain vigorously, and particularly the use of the strike threat, are correspondingly weakened.

A second source of bargaining weakness is the regional wage agreement, or perhaps rather the way in which this device has been handled by the unions. Wages are generally fixed by negotiations between a state-wide union and an employers' association, each agreement covering a wide geographic area. Differences in local conditions are taken into account by establishing certain differentials, but these often fall short of the true wage spreads. The unions had originally hoped that this device would pull the laggards up, but in practice it seems to have worked the other way. The extreme preoccupation of the unions with unemployment has forced them to pay special attention in their bargaining to marginal producers. The pay scale is very largely set according to what these can pay. The result is twofold: A downward bias is injected into wage bargaining, and the strong firms are put in a position where they can and often do pay wages far above the union scale. Their workers then tend to lose interest in the union, since a rise in the union scale does not necessarily mean a raise for them. That they are reluctant to strike under those conditions is obvious. The unrealistic union scale has become a serious problem for the unions. They have tried to protect the established differentials by special clauses in the wage agreement. Their effectiveness, however, seems somewhat uncertain.

Other factors. The factors mentioned so far constitute an impressive array of restraints upon an aggressive wage policy. To them must be added some others, in part historical circumstances, in part attitudes of the leadership and the rank and file, that have worked in the same direction. One has been the financial situation of the unions. The strike benefits paid by the unions have always been high. Without these, German workers cannot easily be persuaded to lay down their tools. During the critical second half of 1948 the unions found themselves virtually penniless owing to the currency reform. This fact cannot but have weighed in their decision to take a statesmanlike attitude, even when full recognition is given to nonmaterial motives. Subsequently the unions amply recouped their financial losses. Yet the preoccupation with the financial burdens of a strike seems to persist. Their critics say of the unions that they are now as rich as banks, and just about as daring.

Emphasis upon the avoidance of unemployment, as against the attainment of higher wages, is another restraining factor. Higher wages mean less to the average German worker than the security of his job. Union policy reflects this value judgment. The unions are also highly inflation conscious, which is understandable in the light of German experience. The thought that wage gains might lead to price increases deters aggressive bargaining, not only because of the danger of dilution but also through the fear of upsetting the economy. Labor is clearly aware that this economy, with its sensitive balance of payments, could not stand the kind of wage battles that American unions have been conducting. It is always easy for the opponents of higher wages to play upon the unions' sense of responsibility on this score.

There is also the influence of past experience to urge restraint upon the labor leadership. During the Weimar Republic the lesson was learned that rapid wage increases followed by wage cuts mean heavy losses of membership. This is a contributory reason why, in 1948 and after, it was thought safer to make haste slowly. During the Nazi period labor as a whole became imbued with the habit of stable wages. Benefits for labor had to be found in other directions—"Strength through Joy" and political intoxication. It is very probable that this contributed to labor's uncombative attitude after the war and to the concentration upon codetermination as a nonwage objective.

Conclusion. The foregoing account of the policies and circumstances that have shaped the action of German labor has emphasized their restraining effect upon wages. This emphasis, I believe, has been justified because wage restraint has been the most conspicuous result and because it has played such a key role in the German revival. But it must not be allowed to obscure other aspects.

Critics of German labor's policies are inclined to put a largely negative interpretation upon the unions' endeavors during the postwar period, and to blame them for not having effectively taken care of labor's pay envelope. Against this two things must be said. In the first place labor itself has probably gained more over a period of years from wage restraint than it could have from successive rounds of hard-fought wage increases. In the second place the German labor movement is not as exclusively wage-oriented as the American. It has other values which can to some extent be attained only at the expense of short-run wage gains.

It is true, however, that if labor did fairly well after all, the unions as organizations have suffered. To impress and rally the membership it is not enough for them to point to long-run increases in living standards. They must be able also to show immediate successes, and of these they have not scored many since the war. The works councils have further weakened the unions' position. Codetermination, upon which the leadership had set its heart, has been a disappointment. The political party to which the great majority of unionists belong, the Social Democrats, has found itself in a somewhat sterile opposition since the creation of the Federal Republic. In all, after getting off to a good start soon after the war, the unions have become a perplexed and disappointed group. They are among the tragedies of the reconstruction.

CHAPTER 11

The Political Bases of Revival

GERMANY'S ECONOMIC revival has been shaped in important respects by events in the political sphere. The electoral
victory of the Christian Democrats and their coalition partners
and the fact that they and not the Social Democrats formed the
government have decisively influenced economic policy. The
political stability enjoyed by the Federal Republic, remarkable for a defeated country, has been a boon to the economy.
In the international sphere Western Germany's rapid mutation from enemy to ally of the West has been the *sine qua non*
of the entire performance. This book being concerned with
the economics of the revival can pursue politics only so far as
they had economic consequences. To that extent, however,
they are indispensable to an understanding of what made the
recovery go forward.

CDU not SPD

When the Allies in 1945 began to encourage the formation
of political parties, two major and several minor groups crys-
tallized. Of the big two, one was the Social Democratic party
(Sozialdemokratische Partei Deutschlands) the other the
Christian Democratic Union. The first was in all respects the
successor of the party of the same name that had existed in
the old imperial Germany and in the Weimar Republic. It
had grown up in close contact with the labor movement,
steeped in class struggle doctrine, had carried considerable
responsibility and power in the Weimar Republic, had been

extinguished by Hitler, and was now revived and its powerful bureaucracy reconstituted.

The Christian Democratic Union was a newcomer. Its religious flavor, predominately Catholic, reflected not so much an increased religious sentiment as the fact that the Church was the only major institution that had survived the Nazi period relatively unstained. In contrast to the closely knit Social Democrats it was a loosely organized catch-all for a large range of predominately middle-class voters. Compared with these two giants the other parties were of lesser importance, except that the cooperation of some of them was needed to enable either of the big two to form a majority government.

The final vote that established the Christian Democratic Union and its coalition partners in the government, and made Dr. Adenauer chancellor, was extremely narrow. Yet the consequences of that decision for economic policy were far-reaching. It is true that neither side advocated any very extreme course and that the differences between the two sides could not be completely summed up in terms of left and right. But the Social Democrats were plainly to the left of center, and the government coalition about equally to the right. The result was a government with distinctly probusiness leanings. While this term falls far short of describing the many currents and crosscurrents that are always present in a great coalition, it does denote the government's outstanding characteristic in the economic field. This aspect was intensified by the necessity for the Christian Democrats to satisfy the demands of the Free Democrats, their main coalition partner, a party containing strong big-business elements.

The chief points on which the government differed from the Social Democrats were its tight monetary and fiscal management, implying a rejection of full employment policies; the free market policy; the tax privileges and reductions favoring the upper incomes; and the relatively smaller emphasis given to social considerations. It is a fair presumption that the

Social Democrats would have pursued full employment more aggressively, with a corresponding relaxation of monetary and fiscal policy, would have maintained price and distribution controls longer, would have gone in for more progressive taxation and something approaching "fair shares," and might have nationalized some basic industries.

These differences must not be exaggerated. It was to some extent a historical accident that the Christian Democratic coalition came to pursue certain policies in a fairly pronounced form. The early freeing of markets from controls, for instance (which predated the formal creation of the government), reflected the personal convictions of Economics Minister Erhard far more than those of many of his party friends. A goodly number of Christian Democrats remained on the fence about the free market policy until, its success having been clearly established, it became a vote-getting asset in the 1949 elections. The anticartel legislation, too, is largely the personal work of Erhard, pushed forward against the strongest opposition from within the government parties. A variety of measures hostile to a market economy, such as agricultural marketing controls and parity prices and the protection for numerous trades and professions, have been voted into law or at least proposed by members of the coalition. Likewise, the government parties cannot claim more than partial credit for the conservative monetary policies pursued by the Bank deutscher Länder. The creation of the Bank and the appointment of Dr. Vocke as its president were the work of the Allies, and the Bank was independent of the government in its policies. It is true, however, that these would hardly have been so effective had not the convictions of the Bank in currency matters been shared and strongly supported by Finance Minister Schäffer.

The Social Democrats, on the other hand, while professing adherence to full employment policies, were by no means rabid inflationists. Nor need they be suspected of seeking to maintain permanently the full array of controls that existed before the currency reform. Faced with the success of the free market policy, they have in fact taken to arguing that they, too, would have established something like a market economy. But given the bitterness of their early attacks on the Erhard measures, their full employment principles, and their basic antibusiness leanings, it is a fair guess that this is a bit of me-tooism and that things would have been substantially different in this sphere had they been in charge.

From this presumption of a major difference between the economic policies of the two parties it is not to be concluded, of course, that Germany would not have recovered under a Social Democratic administration. Policy is not everything, and there were many powerful factors that would have pushed Germany ahead by whatever route. But policy is obviously important. That the policies of the Christian Democratic government were particularly well designed to put Germany back on her feet has been the main contention of the earlier chapters of this book. It may be asserted with some confidence, therefore, that the political choice made by the German people contributed importantly to revival.

Political Stability

Since the annihilation of the Nazi regime Western Germany has enjoyed a remarkable degree of political stability. During the first four and a half years of the occupation there was the solidity of Allied Military Government. Beginning with the founding of the Federal Republic in September 1949, a coalition government took over with a meager majority which nevertheless lived out its four-year span to the next election. In that second contest the same government was returned with a crushing majority. The chancellorship and the key ministries of economics and finance have been headed by the same men throughout. In the international sphere, meanwhile, Germany has rapidly changed from foe to friend, and her relations with noncommunist countries have been uniformly good.

In a country that has lost a great war and had to throw overboard most of its past government institutions, stability like this cannot be taken for granted. One need only think of German experience after the first World War, when defeat and experimentation with a new form of government brought a succession of weak cabinets and repeated attempts at revolution. At that time conflict with the Allies over reparations finally brought the occupation of the Ruhr and the Rhineland and, partly in consequence, the final disastrous acceleration of the famous inflation.

The absence of such tensions, gyrations, and outbursts has been an obvious blessing for the post-World War II economy. It has helped business confidence and business planning. It has contributed to labor peace. It has enabled people to concentrate on the most urgent business: to get back on their feet economically.

The sources of this stability are numerous and worth analyzing. It is not sufficient to say that Germany was occupied and couldn't help being stable. During the immediate postwar period, of course, the occupation was the decisive factor. Without it, the government conceivably might have been seized by Communists. But most of the time Western Allies made an effort to remain neutral among the various democratic parties that eventually emerged. The presence of Allied troops no doubt did much to discourage extremists, but for the continuity of the Adenauer government the occupation is no adequate explanation. A succession of governments of differing shades would have been quite possible, had it not been for a variety of specific German factors.

In the first place the framers of the new German constitution, profiting from experience, had put an interesting safeguard into their document. It is the requirement for a "constructive vote of no confidence." The Bundestag cannot turn the executive out of office unless in expressing its lack of confidence it can also present a majority capable of forming a government. In the Weimar Republic, as well as in contemporary France, the extreme left and right sometimes joined forces to overthrow the executive without having any desire to govern together. This maneuver leads to perennial reshufflings of weak governments supported by center parties. In postwar Germany no alternative majority has ever appeared, and Dr. Adenauer has governed undismayed despite occasional setbacks.

In the second place the Germans were lucky in finding for their first chancellor a man of exceptional stature. Dr. Adenauer has given them what they want and most probably really need: strong leadership. Backed by a powerful bureaucracy he has conducted a government that elsewhere might be regarded as a little authoritarian. The appointed representatives of the people, the Bundestag, have not always had as much to say as might be supposed in a democratic country. No doubt political stability has thereby benefited.

It is not altogether the fault of the executive, however, if the expression of the people's will remains somewhat muted. Within the Bundestag, too, mildly authoritarian patterns prevail. Party-line voting is virtually compulsory. Party control usually rests with a small group, if not with a single man. There are no public hearings on pending legislation, and the people at large (not the very powerful lobbyists) have as hard a time being heard by the legislature as the legislature has with the bureaucracy. The Germans joke about all this, but there is no evidence that they want it differently.

The atmosphere is reminiscent, by all accounts, of the patriarchal spirit of government in the era before the first World War. The much used term "restoration" is not perhaps a very good description of the situation, but it conveys at least some of the flavor. In any case, if anything is being restored it is much more nearly the old paternalistic and authoritarian spirit of fifty years ago than the flamboyance and aggressiveness of the Nazis. The fact that a considerable number of ex-Nazis are in the cabinet and in the administration does not seem very significant. Unless a large percentage of Germany's ablest people were to be put in a dangerous isolation as social and political pariahs a readmission of former party members to high office was inevitable. It is doubtful that more than a very few unreconstructed Nazis are among them, although in the event of a new extremist government their careerist interests would probably again incline them to join whatever it may be profitable to join.

Here is probably the explanation of Germany's political stability that underlies all others: the absence of really strong conflicts. Without this, neither the skill of constitutional lawyers nor the strength of personalities and organizations would suffice. It is true that government and opposition have no trouble finding bitter words for each other. Their differences, however, while more than skin deep, do not go beyond what is bearable in a democracy. Both have in common a firm acceptance of this democracy. Both are antiextremist, against Communists, and against Nazis. On the right there is not, as there was in Weimar days, a large party rejecting the new state after the manner of the old German National party. This removes much of the tension that existed in the Weimar Republic even while the Nazis were still at the lunatic-fringe stage.

On the left, the Social Democrats have lost much of their old Marxist militancy. What they really stand for at present the party leadership has not made very clear, though it is fairly obvious what they are against. The Social Democrats today are groping for a new set of principles that will take account of present-day realities. The success of the free market policy has forced them to move in a liberal direction in their public pronouncements. The gains made by labor have taken much of the sting as well as the vote-getting power out of the old class-struggle doctrine. These things may not survive a new depression, but for the present the conflict between right and left seems mild in comparison to the past. For economic revival, this has been an ideal atmosphere.

The Political Void

The benefits of low political tension have worked in several directions. For one thing, political stability has been enhanced. For another, no great energies have been wasted in political battle. In present-day Germany able people devote themselves very predominantly to business. Neither politics nor, as formerly, the army absorbs an important share of the nation's elite. This concentration of talent can hardly have helped but speed up economic progress.

This single-minded devotion to economic betterment is not without certain ominous overtones, however. It implies a lack of concern with, or positive rejection of, political activities that is not wholesome in a country setting out for the second time in search of a solidly founded democracy. The lack of interest in politics is something that no observer of the contemporary German scene can help noticing. The high election turn-outs do not disprove it; they seem to be mainly a reflection of the German sense of duty and orderliness: The citizen must vote—and he does. But as for active participation in local party organizations, or even in civic affairs of any kind, there is very little. Party membership is low; the Social Democrats, who possess the most tightly knit organization, have less than one million members. In part this reflects, no doubt, the experience of denazification. People don't want to be caught a second time. But a more basic reason seems to be a positive lack of interest in political participation.

For this political void various explanations can be given. For one, German politics is still pervaded by an air of artificiality, a sense that everything is provisional. The country is still under occupation and without sovereignty. Bonn, the seat of government, has none of the earmarks of a permanent capital; Germany as a whole remained partitioned. Many Germans seem to feel that under such conditions politics is not worth while.

In the second place many Germans still are very far from having completed their personal reconstruction. Though income-wise many may be where they were before the war, or better, capital-wise this can be said of relatively few of those who had anything to lose. In the third place the nationalist fervor of the thirties has given way to a profound skepticism. To some extent this may just be the emotional exhaustion following years of whipped-up passion. In good part, however, it seems to be the disillusionment of people who have witnessed the successive bankruptcies of monarchy, democracy, and dictatorship, and who are no longer capable of believing in anything. Germany today is drained of all faith and ideals, and apparently even of its very capacity, formerly so strong, for attaching itself to some ideal—using that term without ethical connotations. The Nazis and Communists have discredited collectivism, restoration of the monarchy is not a serious issue, democracy looks like the regular outcome of lost wars—there seems to be nowhere to go.

As a final contributory explanation of the present political apathy, there is the long-standing German tradition of more or less authoritarian government. A nation of specialists finds it hard to believe that government is one activity where the principle of division of labor does not apply. It prefers to leave the function of governing to those who are "called" to exercise it. A nation of nonconformists whose heads do not easily fit under one hat unless knocked together by someone instinctively distrusts its capacity for democratic give and take and looks to some father image to maintain order and harmony. The present government fits these moods and needs admirably. Since it is a good government, Germany probably is as well governed as she could be. But what is to insure that there will always be a good government?

For some years ahead, quite likely, the Germans will remain relatively immune to high-sounding phrases and the harangues of a would-be dictator. But if such a man, on horseback or otherwise, perhaps during a depression, should somehow seize the government, there might not be many whose conscience would compel them to resist. Even without a dramatic apparition of this kind the present climate of political skepticism may not last. The old emotional need for some higher cause may reassert itself, and the existing void may be filled by some new political enthusiasm.

The East-West Split

If there is a single factor that has been more decisive for Germany's recovery than any other, it is the East-West split. This rent across the face of the earth is momentous for all the world, but whereas the greater part of humanity must look upon it as a catastrophe, for Germany it has meant the foundations of recovery. This is not a question of profiteering by calamity but of inevitable historical fact. If the wartime victors had remained united Germany would not so soon have ceased to be the universal enemy. The spirit of the Potsdam Conference and the heavy hand of the occupation would not have been lifted so quickly, nor would American aid have flowed so freely. The Korea boom, born of the East-West conflict, would not have come to the aid of the German economy.

Partition has been the price that Germany has had to pay. For East Germany this has been a disaster. Under Russian rule it is doing poorly in an economic way and miserably in every other. For Western Germany the economic loss from partition has been moderate and there have been some compensating advantages. The national and human consequences are of a different order, but how deeply they are really felt in Western Germany is a rather moot point. We shall revert to it presently. Prominence is also given in some German quarters to the loss of trade with the iron curtain countries. But since at its peak this trade was no more than 15 per cent of Germany's total trade, since German exports today are booming, and since the East's ability to deliver is questionable, this is not a matter of the first order.

Germany shares with all the rest of the world, of course, the political risks flowing from the East-West conflict. If World War III should be the ultimate outcome the temporary recovery will have availed her little. Yet this risk seems to have left the Germans strangely unmoved, as has the possibility that the East might swallow Western Germany by means short of war. One would have expected these fears to have had a deadening influence upon long-range investment and to encourage capital flight. If so, the effects have remained small. With impressive courage the Germans seem to have made themselves at home on the brink of the precipice and to have accepted the political risks as one accepts the risk of natural death. Their productive effort does not seem to have suffered. Up to the present, therefore, the East-West conflict must be entered as a major plus item in the balance sheet of the German revival.

As a result of her central position between East and West Germany has acquired great bargaining power. It is only fair to say that so far her government has not traded heavily upon this but has sided unequivocally with the West. The weight of the German power has been felt, however, in what the United States has been willing to do for Germany. Germany has not done badly by steering her course along the western shore of today's troubled sea. But the future holds anxious questions. Hasn't the West done so much for Germany that there is little left to do? Doesn't Russia today hold the key to all the things that Germany wants—reunification with East

Germany, return of the Oder-Neisse territories, eastern trade,
a more powerful international role, perhaps a secure peace?
Will not the balance of advantage for Germany come down
on the side of the East whenever Russia chooses to make her
bid?

The danger is a real one, but so far as it is possible to see
today the probabilities are against its materializing. Russia
can hardly afford to pay a big price unless she is sure of anchoring Germany firmly upon her side. Unless she achieves
that her concessions might merely create a Frankenstein on
her western flank. Most Germans, on the other hand, have a
very personal fear and hate of the Russians, born of experience. They are not likely to make a deal that would put them
in Russian hands. The main danger is that they might try
to outsmart the Russians and in doing so overreach themselves
and end up under Russian control.

At the same time, it is not true that the West has played
its last trump. In fact, the goal of a united Europe, the only
idea that in recent years has had any chance of arousing German enthusiasm, is still a possibility. The fate of the European Defense Community has weakened this chance. It presents the danger that its place as a potential focus of German
sentiment may be taken by a demand for reunification at any
price. This could lead Germany into ill-considered and premature moves toward a goal which, as things look now, probably cannot be achieved in the near future without extreme
risk. But on the whole this danger does not seem very acute.
For the present, at least, there exists a strong antidote against
it in the form of the curious and rather ambivalent attitude
of many West Germans toward reunification. This attitude,
on what is a key question of Germany's economic as well as
political life, is worth discussing in some detail.

Reunificaton

No political statement in Germany today is complete without some reference to reunification as the supreme goal. The
Social Democrats speak of it as an immediate goal, the government parties refer to it as something to be achieved after
and through integration with the West. Individuals often
speak of it as something that "must" come. About these asser-
tions, however, there is an air of unreality. A foreign observer
cannot help wondering whether a good deal of lip service is
not being paid.

There exists without doubt a strong and quite universal
feeling that something belonging to Germany has been taken
away and ought to be restored. This is intensified by the
knowledge of the inhuman conditions under which most
people in the Russian Zone live. Since almost everybody has
relatives or friends there, this cuts very close to home. From
an objective point of view, in fact, the plight of the East Germans is a much more forceful argument for reunification than
the belief that all Germans must necessarily live under one
government. Then there is also the desire to regain old markets or confiscated plants and property. For the refugees from
the Russian Zone this motive is particularly strong, though
the bulk of the refugees can cling only to the much more remote hope of a restoration of the Oder-Neisse territories or a
settlement with the non-German countries from which they
were expelled. If a depression should strike Germany's present
export markets these economic motives would gain weight.
Many people, finally, particularly Protestants and Social Democrats, see in reunification a chance to redress the religious
and political balance of the country, since East Germany is
strongly Protestant and also, probably, predominantly Social
Democratic.

There are strong undercurrents in the opposite direction,
however, although they rarely come to light. The government

parties and the Catholic population, which today has achieved numerical equality with the Protestants and hence effective predominance, would find their position weakened by reunification. Though one may credit them with enough national spirit to resist this line of thought, it cannot be completely without weight. Some people seem to think that reunification would impose an economic burden upon West Germany, even though it probably would also mean a great restocking and re-equipment boom. West Germany would undoubtedly have to finance East Germany, and in some industrial lines there would no doubt be an embarrassing excess capacity. The fear that reunification can only be achieved at the expense of political concessions that may eventually lead to communist domination scares many West Germans. Finally, the growing well-being of West Germany and the absorption with economic pursuits probably contributes to a diminishing interest in the subject. The reports of mounting bitterness among East Germans over what they consider West German neglect of their plight mirrors the rise of this attitude.

That a considerable majority of West Germans did not judge reunification a top priority so long as integration with the West appeared to be a possibility was shown by the elections of September 1953. In these the Social Democrats, who campaigned on a platform of reunification first, went down to resounding defeat. The dimming prospects for something approaching a united Europe may, as said before, lead to a change in this attitude. But the lack of interest and the perhaps unconscious resistance that have built up with part of the population suggest that a very violent move in that direction is unlikely under present conditions. Substantial changes, such as a major depression or some unforeseeable political constellation, would probably be necessary to produce a national outcry for reunification at any cost.

CHAPTER 12

Economic Consequences of German Mentality

OF THE FACTORS that have contributed to the revival, some partake of the nature of historical events or circumstances, some of policy, and some represent the response of the German people. Among the last are the willingness to work and save, the maintenance of labor discipline, and the acceptance of sometimes harsh government policies. One cannot help wondering how far this response was shaped by any special qualities of the German people. Was the German response something unique? Or would any other Western nation, given similar conditions, have performed equally? If the German effort deserves to be regarded as something special, is it possible to trace it back to definable national characteristics?

Some may argue that differences in national character, if they can be said to exist at all, are insufficiently marked to produce a materially different performance. Others may feel that the German mentality, though well defined, is not exceptional in its predisposition to high economic achievement. In the nature of the case a definite answer is impossible. In what follows, an attempt will be made to show that there seem to be a number of national characteristics that have shaped recent German performance. Most of them are positive, making for high performance. There are others, however, that may have had a retarding effect.

The proposed discussion implies an excursion into the fields of sociology and psychology. For an economist this is dangerous ground. He can do so only with apologies to specialists and with a caution to his readers that his approach will be that of a layman. He has to place reliance mainly upon the findings of others who are more at home in these fields.

It goes without saying that an investigation into national character has nothing to do with any assertion of racial differences. The history and environment of a nation are quite capable of conditioning it so as to give it a character clearly distinguishable from that of other nations. It further goes without saying that the existence of a national character does not depend on whether or not all nationals exhibit it. The question is one of averages and prevalent types. In referring to some German trait it will be understood that there are probably millions of Germans who do not possess it in the least.

In the voluminous literature on the German character,[1] two principal approaches stand out. One comes to its subject by way of political, social, and economic history. The other concentrates on contemporary sociological and psychological analysis. They are of course complementary. The present discussion draws on both but purports in no way to be a full-dress investigation of all aspects of the German mind. It aims only at those that seem to be relevant to German economic activity and to the recent revival in particular. The following are singled out: (1) attitudes toward material values, (2) motivations for productive work, (3) capacity for entrepreneurship and invention, (4) capacity for effective organization, and (5) motivations to save and invest. Of course there are others, but a discussion of these five should give us a good view of the German mentality insofar as its economic capabilities are concerned.

Material Values

It is generally thought by social scientists that a strong orientation toward material values is essential for good economic performance. A society dedicated purely to the pursuit of truth and beauty or to the contemplation of the life hereafter is less likely to reach high levels of production than one that stresses material welfare. Germany has the pronounced orientation in this direction that is characteristic of modern Western civilization. As in other countries, however, there are important competing noneconomic values. Without imputing anything like exclusive economic orientation to the United States and Canada, the countries that today have achieved the highest standards of living, it is probably true that Germany's concentration in this direction is less intensive.

Germany's conversion to a strongly materialistic civilization has come late. In the early 19th century, when industrialization was well under way in Britain and France, Germany was still the nation of poets and philosophers, with numerous feudal characteristics. Though the change since then has been fast and thorough, some of the older values have been maintained. The aristocracy, often rich but less often economically active, has always been the highest social and to some extent political layer, whose way of life was imitated by the successful alumni of the middle classes. A career in the army or in the public service has ranked socially above a business career, at least up to the first World War. These two services have absorbed a good deal of talent that otherwise might have left its mark upon the economy. Even academic and artistic distinction can, in social esteem, rival business success.

The class barriers separating different educational and occupational levels have set up values that seem at least in part to be noneconomic and to interfere with full concentration of effort upon economic pursuits. Great satisfaction is derived from belonging to an "elevated" group, as indicated by the ostentation of titles signifying such membership. It is much more difficult than in the United States, however, to jump these barriers; material success is decisive only when on a large scale. Finally, there seems to be still another competing set of values: the strong German ethical sense, the metaphysical preoccupation with the meaning and philosophy of things, and to some extent the religious orientation of the German people.

Yet social and moral values that appear to compete with wholehearted economic orientation often do, directly or indirectly, stimulate economic activity. The most familiar instance, of course, is that of Protestant ethics, which is generally credited with having contributed greatly to the rise of capitalist civilization. Another instance is class consciousness, which may stimulate economic performance not for pecuniary reasons but as part of the class spirit. The rigid class system also helps in another way: Though it may stifle attempts at betterment, it drives people to really desperate efforts when they think themselves in danger of sinking. Loss of status is an utter calamity and can often, though not always, be staved off by greater economic effort—when such effort makes it possible to send children to school or university, to maintain social contacts, standards of living, and the like. In the postwar period, when refugees and bombed-out people often had to begin from scratch, this orientation played a great role.

Since the second World War the move toward economic values—the growing "Americanization" of Germany—has accelerated. Diversity of values remains, but as we have seen even that does not seem to stand in the way of concentration on economic effort. It only means that not all of this effort is economically motivated. Things would be different if among the noneconomic values there were some that kept their devotees from engaging in commercial pursuits, such as an aristocratic injunction against going into trade. Feudal remnants of this kind play no part in the contemporary German scene. We shall presently see that, on the contrary, work of all kinds is something almost sacred in Germany.

Work

The performance of work has very evident ethical connotations in Germany. A strong sense of duty prevails, in part perhaps a Prussian heritage. Work is a "task" (*Aufgabe*) not just a job; whoever works "produces" (*schafft*), he is not merely getting through with what he has to do. People take a craftsman's pride in their work. Work is a kind of privilege; the workman who sells his labor to his employer is the "recipient" of work (*Arbeitnehmer*), while the boss is the "giver" (*Arbeitgeber*). Idleness meets with social disapproval, unemployment tends to become a stigma. People who work overtime do not hesitate to make this fact known to their friends; there is no effort to hide the lamp with the midnight oil behind a screen of gentlemanly leisure.

Without denying the sincerity of the individual who devotes himself to his job, one must of course remain aware that this ethical exaltation of work has resulted from a process of rationalization on the part of society. This is the implication of Max Weber's thesis—Protestant society succeeded in convincing itself that what it wanted to do anyway was also good for its soul. In other communities and ages people with equally strong religious or ethical preoccupations but different inclinations have found that the demands of the Christian religion were best met through the idleness of contemplative monks or beggars. One must look, therefore, to the internal and external pressures that have pushed the Germans toward their exaltation of work.

One need not seek far to discover at least some of the facts of life that taught the Germans to become industrious. Much of the soil of their country is poor, the winters are long and severe in large parts of it, there is little opportunity for dozing under trees and reaching up into the branches at mealtime. The climate is invigorating. A rapidly rising population has continually pressed against the margin of resources.

With their strong physique it was natural for the Germans to develop into steady, vigorous workers.

These external pressures are of course not all of the story. Observers of the German temperament believe it to be dominated by a strong emotional drive and to be less effectively controlled by judgment than that of some other nations—"the primacy of will over reason," [2] or the "urge to produce" (*Schaffensdrang*).[3] Goethe's Faust is the symbol of this drive. The result of this constellation is a lack of balance—of *mesure* —and a tendency to go overboard in one direction or another. It is often true also of their work. The Germans throw themselves into it, frequently to the point where it turns into an obsession. Work then becomes its own reward. Many Germans think of themselves as working "for the sake of the job" (*um der Sache willen*). It would be more accurate to say that they work because they cannot help it.

In many cases this compulsive urge to work seems to be connected with a sense of insecurity that some observers regard as a basic German characteristic. This insecurity may have many roots—the aforesaid lack of balance, the difficulty many Germans have in getting along with their fellow men, their tendency to worry over matters of conscience, the experience of the genuine hazards of war and peace in Germany. Whatever the causes, which the sufferer normally is unaware of, he finds intensive work an excellent antidote. It enables him to lose himself, and its material rewards fortify him against some of his troubles. Success alleviates inferiority feelings and promises security and happiness for the future.

Resort to intensive work as a means of overcoming fear and perplexity produces a figure familiar in Germany (and not altogether unknown in the United States). It is the man who forever prepares for the future, putting aside money for future enjoyment that he never spends or accumulating time for a vacation he never takes. He can never enjoy the present because he is uncomfortable unless he is preparing for the future. Insecurity may be one of the roots of still another aspect of German work performance: the compulsive adherence to fixed rules and methods. There is a strong inclination to devise a system for doing even the most casual sort of work. This is a great source of strength wherever the situation calls for a systematic approach, but it can at times also create friction and rigidity and stifle imaginative adaptation.

The opportunity to drive himself and his subordinates presents an outlet to still another well-recognizable characteristic: the cult of hardness. "Hard work" (*harte Arbeit*) [4] in German means hard in the sense of "not soft" rather than of "heavy." Whether we trace this pride in hardness to the military temperament and the Prussian legacy or, as some authors do, to psychoanalytical factors, its existence cannot be denied. It goes hand in hand with—compensates for—a certain sentimentality and a tendency, according to some, toward self-pity. Both reflect strong egocentric elements in the German make-up that find their expression in the frequent claim to being misunderstood and the concomitant difficulty of seeing the point of view of others. To prove one's masculinity and toughness through hard work is no doubt one of the most positive ways of coping with this psychic problem.

Apart from the amount and intensity of the work done, its quality, too, is influenced by the German social and psychological make-up. German thoroughness favors high quality work; some experts connect it with the German inclination to the tortured plumbing of philosophical depths and to the tendency to carry things to extremes. The pride taken in workmanship and the stigma attaching to sloppy work have already been mentioned. The importance attached to high standards of workmanship is also evident in the elaborate system of apprenticeship training and in the profusion of technical schools, both of which have helped to endow Germany with a very high-grade labor force.

Entrepreneurship and Inventive Capacity

Emphasis on material values and willingness to work hard to attain them are no doubt the most essential prerequisites of a successful industrial civilization. But there are others. An important role is played by capacity for entrepreneurship and technological invention. Whether the entrepreneurial faculty is highly developed in Germany and whether the existing system makes optimum use of the available supply of talent is hard to say. It took Germany a relatively long time to pick up the example set by Great Britain since the Industrial Revolution. But once she did progress was rapid, and the entrepreneurial figures that appeared were as impressive as those of any other European country. One may suspect, however, that the relatively low social mobility existing even today would hamper the free flow of talent to places of maximum usefulness. The existence of competing social values may also be an impediment, although far less today than in the past.

As to the intensity of entrepreneurial performance, what was said about work as an obsession applies here with particular force. Businessmen, being generally free to fix their own hours, can give full vent to the drive to work. Observers seem to agree that with regard both to the length of hours worked and the inconvenience accepted—night travel, Sunday meetings, and the like—the businessmen of few other nations can compete with the Germans.

In addition to the previously mentioned sources of this drive, the German businessman's behavior may reflect a tendency of imitators and latecomers to carry things further than the originators. To the British, who originated modern business habits, a business life tended to remain a part of more general existence. Other phases of that existence continued to have their claims. The German businessman, and perhaps even more the American, discovered that business could become an almost exclusive way of life. The German may also have been pushed in that direction by his lack of balance and by a certain international inferiority complex. The latter is attested to by the passionate intensity with which the German businessman throws himself into export promotion, contrasting sharply with his rather relaxed selling methods at home. As a latecomer he did of course have to run harder, but he continued to run after his initial handicap had been wiped out.

The disinclination of German businessmen to compete aggressively in the home market is interesting in several respects. It is of course perfectly natural for businessmen to combine in restraint of trade where the law does not interfere, since it means higher profits. The German penchant for order and organization also works in favor of cartelized markets. But the tendency toward cartels and similar protective arrangements may have deeper roots. In general these devices imply a surrender of opportunity in return for security. The possibility of conquering a bigger market is given up, or at least reduced, for a safe share. A sense of insecurity may also play a role, therefore. So may the importance of class status, which makes it more urgent to protect the existing position than to pursue the possibilities of elevation. In the case of labor this psychology takes the form of a preference for stable employment at modest wages over rising wages with some risk of unemployment.

Finally, as pointed out in an earlier chapter, the high value placed in Germany upon wealth as against income, compared with their relative valuation in the United States, promotes the cartel spirit. There is a strong tendency to protect the book value of an investment after its earning power has become impaired. A cartel is an easy way of doing this. The prevalence of family firms is important in this connection.

This array of psychological factors may be presumed to have contributed in some measure to the heavy cartelization of German industry prevailing in the past. That such cartel-ization has not, on the whole, caused business initiative to atrophy seriously is probably in good part due to the com-pulsive drive to work which pervades German economic life. The restraint of competition has meant, however, that this drive has been concentrated more upon problems of produc-tion than of selling. This emphasis upon technology, to the detriment of distribution, is something that has often been noted by American observers of German business practices.

Technological inventiveness has at all times played a great role in Germany's economic success. Its main characteristic seems to have been not brilliant intuition but systematic and thorough investigation. In the past Germany has been particularly strong in basic research, although that has not been generally true since the war. The systematic approach—doing things by some rule, perhaps rather rigidly—often tends to slow down progress, but in science it is likely to pay off in the end. The German capacity for minute specialization, an-other fruit of the lack of balance and the tendency to carry things to extremes, is of course tremendously helpful in re-search.

The emphasis on the production side of business just alluded to frequently results in a rapid practical exploitation of the fruits of research. This is evidenced by the technologi-cal up-to-dateness of many German concerns. Certain traits exist, on the other hand, at least among one sector of German business, that slow down the introduction of innovations. One is the tendency to operate by fixed rules, schematically, which breeds an unwillingness to accept change. Another is the already mentioned high regard for capital values. Many German businessmen find it difficult to accept the fact that obsolescence can make equipment valueless while it is still in working order, and that such equipment ought to be scraped. The proportion of firms operating with outmoded equipment is probably high by American standards, although

perhaps not by European. The gap between the technologically leading firms and the laggards is said to be wide.
Restriction of competition once more is the answer to which
the backward firms find themselves driven. It ought to be
added that in view of the near capacity operation of the capital goods industries during most of recent years there has
been a physical limit to the speed of modernization.

Capacity for Organization

Organization and discipline are part of the strength of
German economic performance. German talent for organization is famous the world over. This talent seems to spring
in part from a deeply felt need for order and system. Quite
possibly it reflects an effort of the German mind to protect itself against the vagueness of its basic emotional drive. In part
it also seems to be the traditional means the Germans have
employed to facilitate human relations. Many Germans lack
the easy, well-adjusted give and take and the ability to compromise that in countries with a democratic tradition make
for smooth human relations. They develop friction easily
and tend to respond with disproportionate violence to minor
provocations. The high estimation in which formal honesty
is held, which forbids the small pleasantries and deceits that
grease the social wheels, adds to the problem. In the absence
of self-discipline, therefore, order and discipline must be imposed from the outside. The Germans have developed to a
high pitch of perfection the capacity both for imposing order
and for gladly submitting to it. Their history, their religion,
and apparently their temperament all predispose them to this.
In this environment the art of deploying large masses of people and materials has come naturally to businessmen, while
discipline, reliability, and precision have become habitual
with labor. As a citizen the German is accustomed to accept
the decisions of his government, and the government knows
that it can count on a great deal of patience and acquiescence

on the part of the citizen. All these things have helped the revival.

It is true that the same traits may also have negative economic implications. Emphasis on order creates an attitude favorable to cartelization. Strong government authority may stifle the self-reliance of the citizen. These debits must be entered against the credit item due to order and organization.

Saving and Investment

Germans tend to be economical. In the more distant past they were frugal because they had very little. It was then that the Prussian tradition of starving oneself rich (*grosshungern*) was born. Today, out of better incomes, they continue to achieve savings ratios that permit high investment and rapid advance.

When war and inflation had for a second time wiped out most savings it was widely said in Germany that consumer saving was dead for a long time to come. Very soon, however, the old habits or compulsions reasserted themselves. In the last few years the seemingly ineradicable habit has revived even among the lower income groups. One may surmise that one of the motivating factors is the strong urge to provide for the future, born of a sense of insecurity. Like an animal instinct it continues to function in the face of repeated disappointments. Also at work may be the possessive quality of the Germans which some diagnosticians consider to be marked. It finds expression, apart from the accumulation of savings, in a preference for durable over fleeting sources of enjoyment —for furniture, books, a family home. Postwar patterns of consumptions tend to confirm the existence of this preference, but more concrete factors such as replacement needs are no doubt more immediately responsible.

It is interesting also that most German economists seem to feel fairly confident that a businessman's profits will in large measure be ploughed back into his business. They are aware that modern economic doctrine has shown saving and investment to be two very different acts. In postwar Germany, however, the two seem to have been closely tied together. Here, too, one can trace the drive that keeps a businessman working all the time with all the means at his command.

Postwar Psychology

War and collapse have intensified some of the old incentives and have created new ones of their own. The Germans were under no illusion as to what awaited them after military resistance broke down—witness the bon mot current at the time: "Enjoy the war while you may, the peace will be terrible." This realistic attitude was helpful and contrasted sharply with the reluctance of some of the victor countries to acknowledge the depth of their wounds and act accordingly. It was no doubt infinitely better to gain even a Pyrrhic victory than to lose the war, but such a victory created psychic problems that Germany was spared.

The initial effect was of course a profound shock. But economic life went on, though before the currency reform it moved mainly in uneconomic channels. In fact, the failure of the state to take care of its citizens in the paternalistic way to which they were accustomed probably helped them to develop increased self-reliance. During this hard period many people learned to fend for themselves by methods they had not dreamed of before.

When currency reform and decontrol allowed economic life to return to its normal channels a tremendous surge of energy burst loose. Businessmen reminiscing of that episode refer to the "intoxication of normalcy." In this new atmosphere the characteristic German drive to work was intensified in a variety of ways. In the first place the concentration upon material values grew sharply. The economic bases of existence had to be rebuilt before other interests could again claim attention. Cultural pursuits, politics, and social life had to take a back seat while all energies were bent upon taking advantage of the new economic opportunities.

In the second place there were large numbers of people who had to begin virtually from scratch. These were the refugees, the bombed-out, and many returning soldiers whose livelihood had disappeared. Their plight was all the more desperate because, apart from their real economic problem, they faced the loss of their class status. It is true that under the impact of common misery class distinctions for a while tended to lose their sharpness. But as things got better the old system tended rapidly to be restored even though many of the old faces had disappeared. The combined threat of destitution and degradation drove many of these people to extraordinary exertions.

Important in the process of recovering a lost position is the German emphasis upon wealth as against mere income. Many formerly wealthy people have been able to re-establish their position in terms of income and, to some degree, of living standards. To recover the capital wiped out by bombs or inflation has been more difficult. The typical answer of the upper-class German to the comment that he seems to be back to prewar standards is that "the substance is still missing." Only when that is replaced will the recovery be complete and status fully regained.

In the third place it is perhaps not too much to say that the German need for order has played an important role in the revival, particularly during its earliest phases before the currency reform. When many factories were only piles of rubble, when there was neither fuel nor raw materials, and when a day's wages did not buy a day's food, it would have been natural for owners and workers alike to give up on their job, concentrate on the black market, or just bemoan their fate. This was not what they did. In the great majority of cases they proceeded to dig through the rubble until some tools and machines had been brought to light. They pieced these together until at least a few functioned again. Though the immediate positive results might be small, owner and worker alike derived satisfaction from feeling that things were being put in order.

Some observers of the postwar scene also believe that the intensity with which many people have thrown themselves into their work has helped them to forget some aspects of the recent past of which they do not like to be reminded. It is perfectly true that many people show a strong reluctance to talk about the Hitler period. For those Germans to whom that time does not represent the "good old days"—and people who look back upon it with pleasure are probably not a majority—the recollection seems to be so painful that many apparently would like to repress it. Evidence of this can be found, for instance, in the absence of serious literature dealing with the problems of the Hitler period. In fact, the apparent reluctance to think about these matters may be acting as a block to creative intellectual activity of any kind. If a man finds it emotionally impossible to write or think about the things that have been the central experience of his life he can hardly hope to produce serious writing and thought on any subject. Exclusive concentration upon material pursuits may be one of the mechanisms by which many Germans succeed in pushing painful recollection out of mind.

What conclusions seem to follow from our analysis of German mentality? We have found a number of traits that make for high economic performance and that were particularly valuable in a situation like that faced by Germany after the war. Reverting to the terms used in an earlier chapter, we may say that the German mentality is strongly production oriented.

At the same time, however, we have encountered traits tending to suggest that the Germans, after restoring their prewar standard of living, would slow down and move forward only quite gradually. The emphasis on putting things back in order, on the recovery of class status, the preference for security over higher profits and wages, all seem to point in that direction. This is, in fact, the way in which many Germans have envisaged their revival—first a rapid return to "normal" and then transition to the stability and the very slow growth characteristic of Western European economies. Foreign observers, too, have sometimes felt that the Germans would be better at reconstruction than at breaking new ground.

It is perhaps too early to judge, but present trends certainly do not indicate that the German revival is encountering a ceiling at the old level. For most Germans that level has already been passed in terms of income if not of possessions of all kinds. Income nevertheless continues to rise rapidly. So far, therefore, it seems that the retarding elements are being overcome, perhaps by the very momentum of the revival itself and by the factors making for continued high performance.

CHAPTER 13

Allied Aid and Occupation Policy

IN A BOOK ABOUT the German revival written by an American it is only proper that mention of the American contribution should come at the end. Yet this is rather clearly a case of last but not least. The policies of the Allies were decisive for Germany's fate. Without the positive contribution particularly of the United States the German recovery would have been agonizingly slow, its final outcome dubious, and certain only the long years of hardship that the German people would have had to endure.

The core of this contribution was the aid which began to flow almost immediately after the defeat. But important also was the influence brought to bear by the Allies upon almost every phase of the recovery. Many of the occupation policies have already been mentioned in preceding chapters —the currency reform, the support of free markets and liberalized trade, the channeling of counterpart funds into critical sectors, and the help given to political stability. In most of these chapters only minor emphasis was given to the presence of some degree of Allied sponsorship. But it is no more than fair to stress at this point that in many key policies Allied intiative or support played a role.

Revival was not, of course, the keynote on which the Allies began their occupation. In the hour of victory quite different ideas had been held. The reversal came gradually, and to each of the three Allies in different degree. Some of the original concepts were abandoned very late, and these remnants proved hard to fit into the changing general framework.

In analyzing the policies of the occupation, therefore, the first thing to be studied is their general evolution.

THE EVOLUTION OF ALLIED POLICY

When the United States took over control of its zone in Germany it did so with what appeared to be a clearly defined economic policy. This policy was expressed in Joint Chiefs of Staff Directive 1067 of April 1945. The policy was based in many respects upon the ideas formulated by Secretary of the Treasury Morgenthau, although JCS 1067 had already poured a considerable amount of water into the original Morgenthau acid. Some of the same ideas, further watered down, were written into the Potsdam Agreement of August 1945.

The overriding aim of Allied economic policy at that time was to prevent Germany from ever again making war. The principal means was to be the large-scale dismantling of German industry and the creation of a predominantly pastoral economy. JCS 1067, which for two years remained the law for American military men in Germany, instructed the military governor that "except as may be necessary to carry out [your basic] objectives, you will take no steps (a) looking toward the economic rehabilitation of Germany or (b) designed to maintain or strengthen the German economy." It was not the fault of the drafters that the occupation authorities came to place increasing emphasis upon that part of the injunction beginning "except . . ."

American policy toward Germany at the outset of the occupation, therefore, was nothing if not deliberate, and it was very clearly designed to keep Germany down. Yet less than a year and a half later enough of a change had taken place to enable Secretary Byrnes to say, in his speech of September 1946: ". . . the United States has no desire . . . to deny the German people an opportunity to work their way out of [their] hardships so long as they respect human freedom . . ." In 1947 the decision was made to include Germany in the European Recovery Program, whose principles and purposes bore no visible resemblance to those of Potsdam. In 1950, finally, at the Brussels Conference the first steps were taken to put the Germans back into uniform. How did this 180 degree shift come about?

The two main causes are evident. One was the East-West split, which changed not only the politics but also the economics of the situation. The other was the inherent unworkability of the Morgenthau ideas, or what has been called the return to their senses on the part of the Allies. Both contributed to the reversal of Allied policy that we are to trace.

EFFECT OF THE EAST-WEST SPLIT ON ALLIED POLICY

At Potsdam it had been agreed that Germany would be treated as an economic unit, that is, each of the four zones would share its output with the other three. The Level of Industry Plan adopted in March 1946, which severely cut down German industrial capacity and provided for dismantling of all facilities above the specified level, rested on the assumption that such interzonal supplies would be forthcoming. When supplies from the Russian Zone remained but a dribble the Western Allies announced that they would have to raise the ceiling on capacity so as to enable West Germany to compensate for this shortfall through a higher output of its own. This removed the threat of dismantling from a significant sector of German industry and constituted a major economic advance.

As Russian truculence increased, Germany's value in Allied eyes as an economic and political bulwark continued to mount. Apparent Russian designs upon the European democracies helped to bring on the Marshall Plan. The blockade of Berlin forced the Allies to pour additional resources into Germany and to underline their commitment there. Finally, after the outbreak of the Korean War the erstwhile inconceivable happened: The Allies, who five years ago had known no more important goal than German demilitarization, proposed to rearm their former enemy.

MORGENTHAU AD ABSURDUM

Of the Morgenthau Plan it has been well said that it presented the astonishing spectacle of the chief financial officer of the world's economically most successful nation disregarding what appeared to be obvious facts about the German and European economies.[1] It should have been self-evident that Germany could not live without industry and that Europe could not live—at least not well—without Germany. Yet the Morgenthau Plan, though it referred to these realities, treated them as illusions and even argued that the destruction of German industry would be a blessing for the rest of Europe.[2] That the plan was formulated and in good part accepted must be attributed mainly to wartime passion and the prevailing expectation of unemployment and vast excess capacity.

The first taste of practical occupation responsibility did away with some of the more extreme concepts. Action to "maintain or strengthen the German economy," banned under JCS 1067, just could not be avoided. Reluctantly perhaps, but quite inevitably, the Allies found themselves assuming all the responsibilities of government. People had to be fed, transportation had to be got back in motion, coal had to be dug. The idea that it would be possible to let things take their natural downward course proved quite illusory. Soon the Allies even found themselves importing food for the conquered population. The "disease and unrest" formula and other loopholes in the top-level directives covered these reversals of policy.

It did not take the Allies long to realize that this kind of occupation was an expensive proposition. And while the cost of achieving the original goals of the occupation seemed to be going up, the goals themselves were becoming questionable in the light of the East-West split. Allied policy therefore shifted increasingly in a constructive direction. In July 1947 a new directive of the Joint Chiefs of Staff (JCS 1779) made a self-supporting economy the chief goal of American economic policy for Germany. In August 1947 the Revised Level of Industry Plan lifted the level to which industry was to be reduced by dismantling from the 50 to 55 per cent of 1938 stipulated in the first plan to an estimated 70 to 75 per cent. The stage for entry into the Marshall Plan was set.

At a purely human level, too, constructive forces tended to prevail. Of the members of the American occupation forces it was reported time and again that they found it constitutionally difficult to tolerate continued breakdown and disorder. Their inclination was to pitch in, fix things up, and get them going again. The national gift of improvisation came to their aid in these endeavors.

THE THREE ALLIES

To speak of "Allied policy" in Germany is permissible only by way of contrasting it with the total lack of common purpose between the three Western powers and the Russians. In their stand against Russia the Western Allies were united, but otherwise they often went their own ways.

It has been said that in the zonal division the British got the industry, the French the agriculture, and the Americans the scenery. There is enough truth in this observation to illuminate some of the problems that arose for each ally out of the economic geography of his zone. The British, who had the Ruhr, controlled the industrially strongest zone. The area was weak in food, however. This deprived the British of the powerful position they might otherwise have held among the Allies. Lacking the resources that the United States was able to pour into its zone, the British had to lean more and more upon the American ally and accept his leadership. Thus they found themselves involved more deeply than their own matter-of-fact approach might have carried them in the numerous policies energetically pursued by the United States to re- form Germany and the Germans. On one issue, however, the British stood firm: They turned a deaf ear to United States and French pleas for federalism and ran their zone on a cen- tralized basis. In the subsequent merger of the zones this proved an element of strength for the political and economic leaders of the British Zone.

While the record of the occupation bespeaks a fair-minded attitude on the part of the British, it is hardly surprising that they were acutely aware of the threat of future German com- petition. The dismantling policy, therefore, put them in an ambiguous position. Since most of the industry was in the British Zone most of the dismantling inevitably had to occur there. The ostensible purpose, agreed upon by all the occu- pying powers, was to limit Germany's economic potential and to provide reparations. Yet dismantling also served, or so it was then thought, to weaken Germany as a competitor in world markets. For a fair appraisal of the British position it is important to remember also that in the debates leading to the first Level of Industry Plan the British argued for almost twice the steel capacity that was finally allowed.[3] The United States was at that time a far more enthusiastic dismantler. With the coming of the Marshall Plan, perhaps even before, this enthusiasm turned into its opposite. It was mainly then that the British, by sticking to their old line, exposed them- selves to the accusations that have at times embittered their relations with the Germans.

The problems of the French were different. Their zone was economically weak but approximately self-supporting in food—at least the French made it support itself. Far more than the two other Allies the French were concerned with protecting themselves against future German aggression. Clemenceau's complaint about the "twenty million Germans too many" seemed to have been satisfied by partition, but even Western Germany, if revitalized, could be dangerous. This not unreasonable concern led the French to support whatever measures would weaken Germany: separation from Germany of the Ruhr and the Rhineland, extreme decentralization, and reduction of steel capacity to a virtual trickle of 3 million tons. The French had not been invited to the Potsdam Conference and did not consider themselves bound by the agreements arrived at there. They consequently felt free to run their zone according to their judgment, which at times differed noticeably from that of their allies. It was due mainly to the conflict with Russia, which welded the three Western powers together and overshadowed their differences, that French occupation policies did not lead to more pronounced friction with the two other powers.

The United States had the easiest job among the three powers, or at least the most clear-cut. With no sense of commercial rivalry, with the fear of renewed German aggression diluted by 3,000 miles of ocean, with huge funds and the willingness to use them, the United States could concentrate fully upon whatever job it wished to accomplish in Germany. This very freedom of action, however, presented a difficulty. Lacking an overriding motive United States policy in Germany was in danger of falling prey to inconsistencies, of running to extremes, and of making abrupt turns. That these dangers were on the whole minimized, if not altogether avoided, was largely due to the strong central direction provided by General Clay and High Commissioner McCloy.

In its relation with the two other powers the United States occasionally found it difficult to gain acceptance for some particular policy. Both the French and the British seemed to harbor only moderate enthusiasm for endeavors like deconcentration, decartelization, and civil service reform. But in most respects the United States had a strong voice, as befits the party that foots the bill—to say nothing of the leading role that the U.S. was assuming in world affairs generally. In matters affecting Germany's foreign exchange position the three powers had in fact agreed on the principle of weighted voting within the High Commission, in accordance with the financial contribution of each of them. Though this method was reportedly never used, its availability was probably not without effect. When one speaks of Allied policy, therefore, one in fact is referring to policies often very predominantly shaped by the United States.

MILESTONES OF DE-OCCUPATION

If the first two years of the occupation witnessed the great reversal of initial plans, the following saw rapid progress on the newly charted course. The American occupation authorities appeared to have reached the conviction that a long occupation would be bad for both sides. "Permanent or short" was the alternative formulated by one of the leading figures. And indeed the dismantling of effective occupation proceeded at a sometimes breath-taking speed.

It is interesting to observe some of the milestones in this process, particularly those that mark important economic developments. The first was no doubt the Stuttgart speech of Secretary Byrnes (September 1946) in which he paved the way for a constructive occupation policy. This was followed on January 1, 1947, by the fusion of the British and American zones, which permitted a more rational use of German productive capacity. In May 1947 an embryonic German government appeared in the form of the Bizonal Economic Council, with modest powers in the economic field. In February 1948 more vigorous life was injected into this body.

The currency reform of June 1948 and the incipient flow of Marshall Plan aid were major turning points in the economic situation. Shortly before the currency reform an important political step had been accomplished: The authorization had been granted for the preparation of a constitution that would form the basis for a German government. At the moment, therefore, when the economy was about to take off on its long upward surge, political deliberations began that ended with the establishment of the Federal Republic of Western Germany in September 1949.

With this last action the Allies surrendered a substantial share of their power in Germany. Under the occupation statute issued at the time, they voluntarily turned back to the newly founded republic all powers not contained within the limited range of "reserved powers." These latter were designed principally to safeguard the economic and political reforms in which the Allies were interested, to provide military security, and to forestall German policies that would make necessary greater United States subsidies to Germany. From the point of view of the Allies this was a generous concession, even though they realized that it was only one further step along the road to German sovereignty.

To the Germans the reserved power nevertheless represented a severe limitation of their freedom of action.[4] From then on the Allies found themselves under steady and very skillful pressure to grant greater freedom. The Petersburg Protocol of November 1949, which the Allies readily concluded, was the first instance. Its signing saved several large plants from dismantling, eased restrictions on shipbuilding, and strengthened Germany's international relations in return for Germany's cooperation in the (for her) unpleasant matter of forced exports of Ruhr coal.

The free and equal form in which these discussions were conducted did much to enhance the prestige of the new German government. Negotiations for a more fundamental revision of the occupation statute soon got underway, but before these had progressed very far the outbreak of the Korean War imposed a reappraisal of the situation. At the Brussels Conference of December 1950, which was concerned with the strengthening of Europe's defenses, the decision was taken to rearm Germany. Thus, while the occupation statute was revised in March 1951, with important gains for Germany in political sovereignty and the easing of economic restrictions in return for a formal acknowledgement of Germany's foreign debts, events already had moved further ahead.

At Brussels it had been recognized that in order to make rearmament acceptable to the unenthusiastic Germans, and to make Germany an equal partner in the defense effort, the occupation statute would have to be replaced by something less unilateral. A peace treaty was impossible owing to the attitude of Russia. A set of Contractual Agreements was to be its substitute. After prolonged negotiations, in which the Allies made great efforts to avoid any semblance of a dictated peace, these agreements were signed in May 1952. Had they been ratified—their connection with the ill-fated European Defense Community Treaty prevented this—they would have ended the occupation and re-established a slightly qualified German sovereignty. Though the failure of the EDC left the Contractual Agreements without effect, they indicate that the Allies were then ready to restore full sovereignty to Germany.

The *de facto* dismantling of the occupation powers proceeded even more rapidly than their legal surrender. Already, before the establishment of the Federal Republic, negotiation and suasion had largely displaced more direct methods. The list of reserved powers maintained thereafter looked formidable, but appeal to them was a double-edged weapon. It would have meant the discredit of the German government and the destruction of the good relations laboriously built up. In the interests of helping to establish a self-reliant and respected government the Allies repeatedly assented to actions that on their merits they would rather have vetoed. The history of the occupation presents an interesting study in the inevitable self-limitation of the power wielded by a democratically minded occupation.

FOREIGN AID AND OCCUPATION POLICY IN ACTION

The occupation confronted the Allies with an extraordinary range of tasks. They had to take over the administration of a disrupted country where everything required detailed control. They intended, moreover, to rebuild that country, to reform it in some measure, and to pursue various other goals incidental to the successful termination of the war. It is in these tasks, which go beyond administration and which may be regarded as the truly constructive aspects of the occupation, that its main impact must be sought.

Allied contributions to the economic rebuilding of Germany were of four kinds: (1) the addition of resources, very predominantly American, through foreign aid, (2) domestic investment through counterpart, (3) certain policy actions, chief among them the currency reform and trade liberalization, and (4) the basic reforms that the Allies sought to implement, centering around decartelization and deconcentration. Efforts to reform the people and the body politic, although they were an important part of occupation policy, are not on the whole germane to our inquiry.

In some fields the Allies, besides pursuing their dominant constructive goals, found themselves compelled to carry out certain restrictive policies. While they added resources to the German economy through foreign aid, they also withdrew them through reparations, restitution, occupation costs, and other channels. While they pushed counterpart investment they also dismantled. They stimulated trade through liberalization but at the same time put tight controls on East-West trade. Moreover, with the shift in the goals of occupation and in the balance of power the importance of some of these policies and purposes also changed. Reform, which originally had had high priority, lost ground as compared with reconstruction. We shall observe some of these shifts and crosscurrents below.

FOREIGN AID AND FOREIGN BURDENS

The total aid received by Germany from the three Allied governments amounted to roughly 4.4 billion dollars, which includes 200 million pounds sterling (800 million dollars at the old rate of $4.03) given by the United Kingdom and 15 million dollars by France.[5] When the Allies took over they were very far from expecting to have to subsidize the defeated enemy on such a scale, although it was realized that some relief might be necessary. The Potsdam Agreement sought to create a Germany that would be self-supporting at a very low level. It was assumed at that time that this would be possible even after very considerable dismantling for reparations.

What Did Foreign Aid Contribute?

Soon it became clear, however, that in Western Germany starvation would occur on a large scale unless massive aid were supplied. Treatment of Germany as an economic unit, as provided at Potsdam, would have improved the situation somewhat. It is quite doubtful, however, whether the Russian Zone, under the conditions prevailing there, could have supplied much food to the West even had the Russians been willing. To avoid disease and unrest, therefore, GARIOA aid (Government and Relief in Occupied Areas) was called into existence.

All told, GARIOA and some pre-GARIOA aid involved outlays of about 1.7 billion dollars, to which the British and French contributions of 200 pounds and 15 million dollars, respectively, must be added. These amounts were spent largely on foodstuffs, with a small part going for agricultural supplies, seed and fertilizer, and petroleum products. Almost no industrial raw materials or equipment were brought into the American Zone and very little into the British. The operation, in other words, was oriented mainly toward relief and not toward reconstruction. The possibility of acquiring urgently needed industrial supplies depended upon the development of Germany's exports, which were increasing at a snail's pace.

Under the Marshall Plan, which succeeded GARIOA, emphasis in import programs shifted to industrial supplies, mainly raw materials. This new approach was facilitated by better domestic food production and by Germany's increasing ability to buy foodstuffs in Europe with the proceeds of her exports. Together with the currency reform and the lifting of price and distribution controls, the Marshall Plan sparked the revival of Germany's industrial output. Total ERP and post-ERP aid, including certain other funds and allowing for drawing rights granted and received under the two Intra-European Payments Plans, amounts to almost 2 billion dollars up to October 1954.[6]

A quantitative appraisal of the role of foreign aid in the German revival is not easy. At a maximum, annual deliveries never exceeded 1,155.2 million dollars. Even during the peak year 1948–49 they were less than 5 per cent of German national income. As a contribution to total resources, therefore, aid though not insignificant was by no means a major factor.

As a contribution to investible resources over and above minimum consumption needs aid was much more impressive. At its 1950 peak counterpart investment was equal to 9 per cent of gross investment. One cannot, of course, say that it *added* this much to investment. In its absence the Germans might have tightened their belts still further and somehow might have squeezed out more investment from their own meager output. But since without the aid-financed imports German production would probably have been a great deal lower, this is not very likely.

The main contribution of foreign aid, however, was to Germany's balance of payments—there it was decisive. As late as 1948, 64 per cent of imports were financed by aid. Over the years 1947–49, 57 per cent of imports were so financed. Had there been no aid during the early postwar years large numbers of people would simply not have survived. After the currency reform absence of aid might not have meant starvation, but it would have compelled Germany to push her exports at all costs to secure a minimum of imports. These would have had to consist largely of foodstuffs. Industrial recovery would have been held back for lack of raw materials and other supplies. By providing key commodities at a critical time foreign aid probably helped to increase output by a multiple of its own value. The help given was more significant qualitatively than quantitatively, so to speak, because for Germany the difficulty of procuring foreign goods was greater than indicated by their mere money value. Here lies the key to a proper appraisal of the role of foreign aid.

Offsets to Foreign Aid

The conclusion that the main impact of aid was qualitative becomes more significant if we consider various burdens that were imposed upon Germany's resources by the Allies. These burdens in the aggregate seem to add up to a figure considerably in excess of the aid received. On a purely quantitative calculation, therefore, it might appear as if the Allies had made no net contribution to German revival. The error of such a conclusion is revealed by considering the qualitative features of aid and burdens respectively.

The burdens in question are of widely different kinds. A few of them cost Germany scarce foreign exchange, a greater number drew only upon domestic resources, which could be spared more easily. Some were felt immediately, others were spread over many years. Some, finally, arose out of Germany's position as an occupied country and the Allies' obligation to carry out certain functions of government, while others, on the contrary, reflected a return to normal international relations. They all deserve attention not only because they did tend in greater or lesser measure to offset foreign aid but also because they were usually connected with important Allied policies.

Reparations. In contrast to policy after World War I Germany was required to pay reparations not from current output but from her existing stock of capital, mainly by dismantling of industrial equipment. For this decision there were several reasons. One was to avoid the financial difficulties caused by reparations after World War I. Another was to make it possible for Germany to exist with a low industrial potential, something that would have been difficult if a large export surplus had had to be generated to finance reparations. A third was to protect the United States from having to finance indirectly, through aid, the reparations that other countries were to take out. Total reparations were to be arrived at by calculating the industrial capacity required to give Germany a minimum standard of living. The surplus of peacetime industrial capacity over this minimum limit, plus any general purpose equipment in war plants, was to be dismantled and shipped out as reparations.

Between 1946 and 1950 numerous reductions were made in the number of plants originally chosen for dismantling (see pp. 369–72 below). In the final count the value of reparations equipment shipped from Western Germany to 18 recipient nations came to the modest sum of 708.5 million DMark at 1938 prices. To this must be added an indeterminate amount shipped to Russia and Poland, which in view of the early stoppage of such shipments probably did not exceed a small fraction of the other figure. In appraising the total it must be borne in mind that in many cases other installations and buildings were destroyed as part of the dismantling process, thus raising the cost to Germany; that the valuation was based upon rather severe depreciation standards; and that at current prices the value of the equipment was usually twice the 1938 figure. The usefulness of the equipment to the receiving countries may in many cases have been quite debatable.

The loss of much of this equipment was not felt by the German economy at the time. There were neither raw materials nor fuel to operate all plants to capacity. The losses began to be felt as capacity operations were approached, when they had to be replaced out of domestic resources, usually in a much modernized form. Major foreign exchange costs were not involved at any time.

External assets. A second type of reparation was the distribution, if one may call it such, of Germany's foreign assets. Countries at war with Germany had usually taken over German property within their reach, such as branches of German firms, patents and trademarks, merchant vessels, and German participations in local enterprises. Most of the countries in question showed no inclination to share their windfalls with other reparations claimants, and no serious attempt was made to persuade them. All that could be done was to ratify the *fait accompli.* The total of these external assets retained as reparations was 260 million dollars at 1938 prices.[7] To allow for subsequent price increases and for a probable degree of underreporting by the vesting governments, competent observers have frequently employed a figure of 1 billion dollars. A few countries have meanwhile returned to Germany the assets under their control, and in some others, including the United States, legislation for their return has been proposed.

The loss of these assets was a serious handicap to Germany and particularly to her foreign exchange position. Trademarks and foreign branches would have speeded the recovery of exports had they still been at Germany's disposal. Some of the assets could have been liquidated at the time of greatest postwar need. But, given the fact that they were widely dispersed among a large number of reparations claimants, there was little chance of collecting on them either for the benefit of Germany or for that of the powers who were paying for aid to Germany.

External restitution. During the war a large amount of equipment and other goods had been removed by Germany from countries she had occupied. Some of this was taken by force, some by means ostensibly legal but hardly reflecting the real desires of the occupied country. The Allies decided upon the full restitution of all goods that had been taken by force insofar as identifiable. Goods taken by other means were restituted only if they were not required in order to maintain the minimum industrial capacity fixed for reparations purposes. The total thus returned from the American Zone alone was valued at upward of 70 million dollars at 1938 prices, or about twice that at postwar prices. The economic effect of these external restitutions was analogous to that of dismantling and reparations removals.

Internal restitution. To make material amends insofar as possible for the persecution of Jews and other minority groups, a broad internal restitution and general indemnification program was undertaken by Germany at Allied request. The full amount ultimately payable by the federal government is expected to reach 8 billion DMark.[8] Of this total, indemnity payments in the form of pensions to persecutees or their heirs will eventually account for 3 billion DMark. The agreement with Israel for resettlement assistance to Jewish victims provides for a further 3 billion in the form of goods delivered to Israel over a period of 12 years. Restitution claims against the defunct Reich and other lesser items make up the remaining 2 billion DMark. In addition to these sums payable by the Federal Republic, restitution by private parties of property acquired from persecutees or compensation therefore had reached 371 million DMark by May 1954 in the American Zone alone.

All payments not made in kind are in DMark without transfer obligation. Since 1951 the resulting blocked DMark have been negotiable at discounts ranging from about 50 per cent at the beginning to small fractions in 1954. Sales of blocked DMark by their recipients have not required any direct foreign exchange outlay by Germany. Indirectly they may have involved an exchange loss, because they have discouraged the purchase of DMark for investment at the official rate. More recently, when the exchange position of the Bank deutscher Länder had become more liquid, the transfer of small sums at the official rate was permitted.

Occupation costs. The Allies levied occupation costs upon Germany to cover those parts of their own expenditures that could be paid in DMark. Costs involving foreign exchange payments, however (from the German point of view), including troop pay (for United Kingdom and United States troops), food, and similar items, were not assessed against Germany. Some of these foreign exchange expenditures were actually spent on German goods, and the resulting dollar income from them, together with that from the local expenditures of the soldiers, became a major factor in Germany's dollar balance of payments. The annual occupation-cost levy, fixed at 7.2 billion DMark, constituted a considerable outlay for the federal budget and for the German economy. It ought to be observed, however, that occupation costs must in large measure be regarded as a substitute for defense expenditures. Germany, for whom the Allies were performing this normal function of government, was getting her defense relatively cheaply. In 1951–52 she was paying less in relation to her national income than any of the three occupying powers. All the installations built by the Allies with occupation money will, moreover, eventually fall to Germany.

Coal exports. Prior to her entry into the Schumann Plan Germany had been required to export a certain amount of coal to other European countries. Coal was very scarce in Germany, and the enforced exports at times undoubtedly held back the German recovery. Moreover, since the controlled domestic price was well below the average European price, and since the Allies would not authorize a higher export price such as employed by Great Britain, less foreign exchange was received than might have been. At the prices prevailing in 1950–51 the loss was 4 to 5 dollars per ton; on exports of 23 million tons that meant a sum of 100 million dollars or more. Insofar as the shortage could be mitigated by importing coal from the United States, the cost per ton was about twice the export price of German coal.[9]

Foreign debt. As one of the conditions for the establishment of the Federal Republic the new German government had to acknowledge its responsibility for the prewar foreign debts of the Reich. In addition Germany was liable, in principle, for the full amount of the net foreign aid received up to July 1951. Finally, there was the large volume of old private debts, short term as well as long term.

In the London Debt Agreement payments of 567 million DMark per annum up to 1958 and of 750 million DMark thereafter were agreed upon. (For details see Chapter 8.) The settlement was made possible mainly by the action of the United States in reducing its claims on aid account, then at 3.2 billion dollars, to 1.2 billion. In the light of Germany's recent exchange surpluses this concession was probably more generous than it need have been. Even so, the foreign exchange obligations assumed by Germany are considerable.

Ten per cent counterpart. For certain parts of American aid Germany, like other countries, was required to turn over to the United States ten per cent of the resulting counterpart.

The total supplied by Germany was 279 million DMark or 67 million dollars. This amount was not large, and most of it was spent on programs of value to Germany.[10]

Conclusion. The sum total of the amounts payable by Germany, then, exceeds the aid that Germany received. This accounting has nothing to do with the question of equity, for no payment by Germany, however high, could compensate the world for the cost of Hitler's war. The problem is simply whether and how far the Allies undid the effects of aid by simultaneously throwing present and future burdens upon Germany. The answer given earlier, that the qualitative impact of aid was decisive, undoubtedly stands. Aid at a critical time provided resources of a kind that would otherwise have been very hard for Germany to obtain. Except for the coal exports and the loss of external assets none of the demands made upon Germany had a negative impact of a similar kind. These burdens could either be met out of domestic resources that were not critically short, or were spread over time and could be met after Germany got back on her feet. Some of them were no more than substitutes for the normal costs of a sovereign government. With neither aid nor burdens Germany would have fared a great deal worse.

A second question is whether the United States did not foot part of the bill for the German commitments by having to plough in more aid or by recovering less of it. Here it must be noted that a good part of the equipment dismantled for reparations, the external assets, and the coal shipments went to countries that were also receiving American aid. Their needs were probably reduced by these receipts, and to that extent the aggregate need for American aid was not increased. But with regard to the recovery of aid given to Germany it is quite clear that the United States lost something by her willingness to see Germany assume other obligations. Without this willingness the United States would not, at the London

Debt Conference, have had to reduce its claims upon Germany so sharply in order to make possible the resumption of private debt service. Had the United States been prepared to crowd out other creditors she might have recovered almost her full investment in aid.

Very probably this restraint, though not inexpensive, has been worth while in terms of over-all American objectives. The sacrifice, in fact, had considerable leverage. By helping to put the German debt on a paying basis it restored large capital values and improved the international credit atmosphere. It facilitated the assumption by Germany of internal and external burdens that in the aggregate greatly exceed the sacrifice. All in all one may say that American aid to Germany was an operation satisfactory to all concerned.

INVESTMENT AND PRODUCTION: HELP AND HINDRANCE

In the field of domestic investment and production, as in that of foreign trade and finance, the multiplicity of Allied purposes led to activities that sometimes appeared to be at cross-purposes. The dominant goal was to push investment and output. Counterpart fund programs and efforts in special fields such as coal and transportation were the key instruments. But on the other hand, and to some extent at the same time, the Allies were dismantling German plants and also maintained controls over certain kinds of production. It will become apparent from the following account that the area of constructive effort greatly exceeded that of repression and that instances of real conflict were on the whole minor.

Counterpart Investment

Most Germans, when asked what American aid had done for them, will reply unhesitatingly that the United States gave Germany power plants, mining equipment, and similar investment items. They are right, but in a rather abstract sense that is probably quite far from their minds. Technically what the United States gave were imports, or the money with which to buy them. The sale of these goods to German consumers generated DMark counterpart, and with this counterpart the power plants and other investments were built. The counterpart was German money, identical in all respects with that created by the German banking system. Had Germany had ample foreign exchange reserves she could with no great risk of inflation have created an equivalent amount of money. But her foreign exchange position was in fact very tight. Imports therefore could not have been brought in freely in the absence of aid. Under such conditions the creation of money for investment would not have been possible without inflation. It was by supplying the means for imports to forestall the inflationary effect of added investment expenditures that the United States made possible the building of power plants and, in a sense, "gave" them to Germany.

The counterpart resulting from foreign aid thus became an important factor in the German investment picture. In countries where a less conservative monetary policy allowed money to be created readily in response to the needs, real or fancied, of business or the government, counterpart did not have quite this role. There, a lack of it could always be made up by new money creation. In Germany, where currency stability took top priority, such practices were looked upon askance. Counterpart therefore acquired a significance that it did not always have in all the other Marshall Plan countries.

Ownership of the counterpart funds was vested in the German government. For their expenditure, however, United States approval was required. This made counterpart funds an important instrument of persuasion. The same arrangements existed, of course, in other Marshall Plan countries. In Germany, however, the unwillingness of the government to consider money creation as an alternative to the use of counter-part funds, plus the exceptionally tight handling of the funds by the American authorities, lent them special bargaining power.

The volume of funds disposed of through past and current counterpart programs is surprisingly small considering the large amount of aid to Germany. The sum total of pro-grammed expenditures in Western Germany as of November 1954 was 5 billion DMark, of which only 3.5 billion was invest-ment expenditures. In addition there were programs totaling 2.2 billion DMark for West Berlin. The modesty of the sum is explained by the fact that much of the non-Marshall aid did not generate counterpart for these programs. Much of the counterpart that arose, for instance, from GARIOA aid was employed for general occupation purposes, including the DMark costs of the Berlin airlift and subsidies for the feeding of the Berlin population during that time.

For the years 1949–53 counterpart investment averaged 3.5 per cent of gross investment. Even during the peak year 1950, as noted before, the proportion did not go beyond 9 per cent. The real significance of the counterpart funds, like that of foreign aid, was qualitative: They represented the chief *masse de manoeuvre* of investment planning. A certain amount of such centralized planning, as has been pointed out in Chapter 6, was required to compensate for the distortions of the Ger-man capital market and because of other reasons. The basic materials industries, mainly coal and steel, and the electric power industry were unable to finance themselves out of profits or to attract outside capital because price ceilings kept their profits low. These industries needed special assistance. Counterpart investment programs responded to the need. After an initial attempt to spread the money widely the pro-grams were increasingly aimed at the areas in question. After the outbreak of the Korean War the desire to aid defense-supporting industries added weight to that decision.

The Battle for Coal

No other industry received so much concentrated attention from the Allies as coal mining. Success on this front was so necessary and the obstacles so great that the battle for coal became one of the most dramatic stories of the occupation.

It did not take the Allies long to discover that coal was the most important commodity in Germany. Coal was the key to transportation, power, and production. At the same time coal was extraordinarily resistant to all efforts to stimulate its output. Even after the currency reform, when all other production shot ahead far beyond expectations, coal continued to lag behind the most modest goals.

The industry was beset by a whole congeries of difficulties. The Nazis had overworked the mines, trying to get the most out of them without regard to conservation or maintenance. The equipment was in poor condition, inferior seams were being worked and much effort had to be diverted to development, the labor force had grown too old, and turnover and absenteeism remained high owing to lack of housing. Management was without a strong incentive to push current output so long as the future ownership of the mines was left uncertain by the deconcentration procedure.

The Allies worked hard on the problem as one patent solution after another fell short of expectations. At one time more pit props seemed to be the key to the puzzle, at another food packages to the miners. Slowly and painfully daily output inched upward until in November 1950, when the general production index had passed its 1936 level by 40 per cent, coal output at last touched the 1936 average. At that point the postwar coal shortage seemed to have been overcome, even though productivity was still one-third below prewar.

The outbreak of war in Korea created a new shortage. Once more Americans and Germans concentrated on the problem, with an apparatus of committees and study groups that no other industry had been able to attract. In this second battle miners' housing appeared to be the key to the problem, and that was the direction in which counterpart funds were deployed. It was not until a year later that victory became assured.

Transportation

Transportation was a second field in which the Allies made a special effort and exerted considerable influence. The campaign was less spectacular and sustained than in the case of coal, and it occurred earlier, but without it German recovery would have gone more slowly. Transportation had been hit harder by Allied bombing than almost any other sector of the German economy. What the Allies missed the Wehrmacht blew up as it retreated. Of railway bridges across waterways more than 70 per cent were down, blocking both rail and water transportation. Some 17,000 switches, 3,150 railway bridges, and 2,600 miles of track were out of operation.[11] But even during the fighting the engineers began to put up emergency bridges. After the capitulation the repair work continued, because an efficient occupation could not operate without transportation. The engineers raised ships and barges that blocked the rivers—some 1,700 had been sunk in the Rhine alone. They continued to restore bridges. In addition the Allies provided gasoline for motor transport, which was at that time often the only means of communication for isolated towns.

When the first emergency had been overcome and the damage counted, rolling stock proved to be one of the biggest transport bottlenecks. Less than half of the freight cars existing in Germany in 1936 were still found within the four zones of occupation and in serviceable condition at the end of 1945. A comprehensive program for freight-car building and repair was put underway in Czechoslovakia and Belgium until the worst of the shortage was overcome. After 1947 the main Allied contribution in the transportation field tapered off.

Dismantling

The dismantling program has often been cited as the outstanding example of Allied policies at cross-purposes. While the United States was pouring billions of dollars into Germany for reconstruction, plants were still being torn down. Among the Germans dismantling has caused more bitterness than almost any other Allied activity. A survey of the facts suggests, however, that the importance of the matter can easily be exaggerated.

The original number of plants selected for dismantling under the 1946 Level of Industry Plan was about 1,500. Their elimination was expected to cut heavy industry to 50 to 55 per cent of its 1938 level. The equipment, insofar as it was not specifically military, was to be removed for reparations. Equipment usable only for military purposes was to be destroyed; the buildings were to be left standing or destroyed depending on whether or not they could be employed for peacetime purposes.

Little more than a year after the first Level of Industry Plan had been announced a revised plan was put into effect, on the grounds that the three Western zones would need a higher industrial capacity if they could not count on supplies from the Russian Zone. It may be noted that current production in almost all fields at that time was still much below the ceiling set by the first plan. The new plan reduced the number of plants to be dismantled to 859. This list was again combed through by various United States government committees to avoid the dismantling of plants that might help the Marshall Plan. The result was a further reduction in the list of plants subject to dismantling to about 700. Still further cuts were made in November 1949, two months after the establishment of the Federal Republic, again saving several important plants. Meanwhile the actual dismantling had proceeded so slowly that decisions to preserve certain plants never seemed to come too late.

The value of equipment removed for reparations to countries other than Russia and Poland was placed by the Inter-Allied Reparations Agency at 708.5 million DMark at 1938 prices, plus an amount sent to those two countries that was probably quite small. Allowing for a near doubling of prices since 1938, for an especially severe depreciation schedule applied by the Allies, for the loss of some buildings, and for original installation costs, one arrives at an estimate of the order of 2 billion DMark.[12]

The total loss to Germany from dismantling was undoubtedly much in excess of the gains to the recipients of reparations. The bitterness caused by dismantling is all the more understandable when one recalls the strong emotional attachment that many Germans feel for their places of work, and the passionate intensity with which they devoted themselves to rebuilding them after the war. Yet the real effects cannot have been very great in comparison to the volume of investment that was meanwhile taking place in Germany. At the time when most of the plants were dismantled many of them were idle for want of raw materials, power, or essential repairs. Later, when output began to push against the limits of capacity, an annual rate of gross investment of 17 billion DMark far outweighed the dismantling loss. While the frequently mentioned fact that dismantled plants were replaced with the most up-to-date equipment does not imply the absence of a loss, it does point to an important compensating factor.

Limitations of Industry

Even after dismantling had come to an end, German industry remained subject to certain limitations and prohibitions imposed by the Allies for security reasons. A last major easing of these restraints took place through the Agreement on Industrial Controls of April 1951, but many lesser instances have occurred since then. Limitations on shipping, aluminum, and numerous important chemicals have been dropped, others liberalized. The prohibition on every kind of military equipment has been maintained, including all aircraft. The range of output of industries with pronounced war potential, such as electronics, remained subject to control. These limitations are perhaps not very important, but they have had their effects. Without them Germany no doubt would today be building airplanes once more. German technical skill might be making strides in atomic research. Yet for the welfare of the German economy these are undoubtedly very minor handicaps.

POLICY CONTRIBUTIONS

The Allies initiated or laid the foundations for several major policies that were later successfully carried on by the German government. Chief among these were the currency reform, import liberalization, and the creation of the essential conditions for political stability. The role played in the German revival by these policies and conditions has already been traced. The present account of specific Allied contributions would not be complete, however, without some explicit reference to them.

The backing given to political stability was probably the most basic contribution of this kind. The presence of the Allies insured that no extremist group could move effectively against the precariously established democracy. At the same time they provided protection against dangers from abroad.

The currency reform was likewise a basic factor. It was, in fact, the *sine qua non* of the revival, no matter how generously one may appraise the recovery that preceded it. There is general agreement in Germany that so drastic a reform could only have been carried out by a military dictatorship. No democratic German government would have been able to wipe out so ruthlessly money and savings which, however dubious their purchasing power, were still regarded by their owners as genuine wealth.

Credit for keeping the new currency stable, nevertheless, goes largely to the German side. While the Allies exercised supervision over fiscal and monetary policies, the initiative very quickly passed to the Germans. One may even question whether the advice given by the Allies was always altogether fortunate, particularly as regards their easy money proposals during the period of relative stagnation in 1949 and early 1950. But Allied pressure for expansion was never applied so massively as to push the German policy makers off their cautious course. Evidently the United States government was not sufficiently of one mind on this point to push very hard.

Trade liberalization is the third Allied policy contribution that deserves mention. The concept fitted in so well with the ideas of Economics Minister Erhard and was so energetically taken over by the German government that its Allied origin has become somewhat obscured. There can be no doubt, however, that the original impulses toward liberalization of European trade came from the ECA, and that the American authorities in Washington and Paris had decided to make Germany into a test or showcase of liberalization.

When the first liberalized trade agreements were concluded in 1949 JEIA was still in full control of German trade. United States officials were responsible for all trade negotiations. It was with the liberalization features of these first agreements that the initial steps toward full liberalization were taken. For some time Germany was substantially ahead of other Marshall Plan countries, as indicated by her large passive balances in 1949. The pressure upon the partner countries to reciprocate, however, powerfully reinforced by the OEEC, gave impetus to the entire movement. It seems certain, as noted before, that liberalization among the Marshall Plan countries was a major factor in the recovery of German trade.

In the field of trade policy, as elsewhere, American intervention was no altogether unmixed blessing. While the United States gave in the intra-European sector, it took away in the East-West sector. Nevertheless, it would be wrong to attribute to the United States primary responsibility for the low level of trade with either the Russian Zone or with the iron curtain countries.

As regards the Russian Zone, the decay of East-West trade was the result of Russian action much more than of Allied. There had been two trade agreements, signed in 1947 and 1948, but the blockade of Berlin and the Allied counter-blockade closed all channels except illegal ones. After the lifting of the blockade a new agreement was signed. The volume attained under it was disappointing, however, since East Germany apparently had little to sell, and efforts in 1950 and 1951 toward formalizing a further agreement remained fruitless.

As regards trade with the iron curtain countries, it is true that the weight of United States–imposed limitations has probably been felt more severely by Germany than by most other European countries. Germany's trade ties with the East had been close. Her long frontier made supervision more difficult and caused the measures taken to control traffic—including at one time the intervention of M.P.'s—to become more irritating. Yet the damage to Germany can easily be overestimated. Trade with the East at its prewar peak never amounted to more than 15 per cent of Germany's total trade. Under postwar conditions it would have been limited to a vastly lower figure by the inability of the iron curtain countries to deliver exports. With all their efforts bent toward industrialization they were sometimes suffering shortages of the very foodstuffs and raw materials that had been their typical export products. What Germany lost through American restrictions on East-West trade was no more than the ruins of her prewar trade.

BERLIN

The greatest single undertaking of the Allies was the saving of Berlin. Berlin gave them their most spectacular victory in the cold war. Economically, however, the city has been a heavy liability to the Allies as well as to the Federal Republic.

The dramatic story of the Berlin airlift is well known. The Russians had blockaded the city in retaliation against the currency reform. They evidently expected that this maneuver would compel the Allies to withdraw and to surrender the city. When the Allies first began to supply Berlin by air many doubted that they would be able to hold the city. The success of the airlift was an impressive demonstration of the Allies' technological superiority and of their determination not to yield. This victory strengthened the position of the United States throughout Europe. Since that time Berlin has continued to pay political dividends as a symbol of resistance, as an observation point toward the East, and as a showcase of West German living standards for the inhabitants of East Germany. In addition it has provided an escape route for hundreds of thousands of fugitives from communism, many of whom might not have been able to cross the zonal frontier to the West but could not be prevented from departing via the Berlin enclave.

On the economic side, however, Berlin was a heavy burden. The problems faced by the city were far greater than those confronting the Western zones. Before the war Berlin made a good part of its living from its special position as capital and economic nerve center of Germany. This position was now gone and with it the income and employment from government, banking and insurance, entrepôt trade, and numerous other services. Furthermore, Berlin's industries had been dismantled with ruthless thoroughness by the Russians in the two months during which they had the town to themselves. Counting losses from war and dismantling, Berlin in July

1945 had perhaps no more than 20 per cent of its prewar industrial capacity.[13] This meant that whereas Berlin would have to expand her industries greatly above prewar in order to become viable, she had to start building them up from a pitifully low level. Finally, Berlin had lost a large part of her markets. To the East the zonal boundary strangled the flow of trade. In the West fears that a new blockade might prevent Berlin suppliers from delivering held down orders. Altogether the obstacles loomed enormous.

The bleak outlook led to a flight of productive factors to the West. Businesses shifted their head offices and did most of their new construction in the new location. Young people, faced with heavy unemployment in Berlin, tended to move West where wages and job prospects were better. Berlin threatened to become a city of old people and chronically unemployed.

It took some time for the United States and Western Germany to react constructively to this situation. Before the currency reform West Berlin had received its share of aid as and when it was needed. During the airlift period the goods flown in served as aid. The counterpart realized from their sale was largely employed to subsidize the relief expenditures in the city budget. This rather substantial help, together with the excitement of the times, tended to obscure the fact that economically the blockade did succeed in almost ruining Berlin. While in the three Western zones the production index was passing 90 per cent of 1936, in Berlin it dropped from about 40 to 20 per cent. The rapid curtailment of aid after the blockade brought Berlin face to face with disaster.

After long delays and deliberations Berlin in December 1949 was formally included in the ECA counterpart investment program. This implied a corresponding cut in the counterpart that could be spent in the three Western zones. To provide employment while the investment program got under way, a work relief program financed with GARIOA funds was undertaken. As time went on additional investment programs were formulated. In addition a variety of ingenious financing devices were developed to meet the working capital needs of business for new-order financing, for equity investment, and for other purposes. These special programs came mostly out of GARIOA counterpart funds, which could be handled more flexibly than ECA counterpart. By November 1954 the sum total of all Berlin programs amounted to 2.1 billion DMark and actual disbursements to 1.8 billion. To this must be added a sum of about 670 million DMark turned over to the city during and shortly after the airlift.

Berlin also received large-scale assistance from the Federal Republic. Berlin is not a part of the Federal Republic, owing to Allied action in suspending the provision of the Basic Law (constitution) that would have made Berlin a tenth state. Nevertheless Berlin is united with the Federal Republic as regards the tax and monetary systems; most federal legislation is also applied in Berlin. After prolonged pulling and hauling the primary responsibility of the Federal Republic for the deficit of the Berlin budget was established. Annual payments under this head were considerably in excess of half a billion DMark. In addition there is a variety of tax and other subsidies designed to help Berlin industry. All in all the annual cost of Berlin to the Federal Republic probably exceeds 1 billion DMark.[14]

While the contributions of the Federal Republic exceed those of the United States, the latter have a special significance. They have been designed to promote industrial expansion in Berlin, which is essential if the city is to overcome its handicaps. The investment programs have been mainstays of capital formation. This is indicated by the fact that while the gross savings of the Berlin economy have been no more than about 5 per cent of the city's "national" income in 1952 and 1953, investment (including that financed by outside aid) has averaged about 20 per cent. The financing of new orders has also been helpful in attracting business to the city.[15]

In recent years Berlin has become the main beneficiary of counterpart operations in Germany. Despite this concentration of effort progress has been slow. The index of industrial production in West Berlin by September 1954 had reached only 92 per cent of 1936, against 182 for Western Germany. The number of unemployed was 177,000 out of a labor force of about 1 million in December 1954. For 1953 the balance of payments of the city still had a deficit of 1 billion DMark, equal to about 15 per cent of the gross "national" product. All these figures show how far recovery in Berlin has lagged behind that of the Federal Republic. Nevertheless there has been progress, and even fairly rapid progress, considering the low starting point. As the economy of Western Germany approaches capacity operations Berlin's chances improve, because its role all along has been that of the marginal supplier. In this ultimate recovery the American contribution will have played a leading role.

REFORM

With the start of the occupation each of the Allies initiated broad programs of political and economic reform. The United States, with probably more of the reformer's zeal and certainly with more money, led the way. In the light of hindsight it is easy to point up the weaknesses of some of these schemes. They assumed a little too readily that what was good for the United States was bound to be good for Germany, and they underestimated the ease with which a leopard can be made to change its spots. Yet, though today one is bound to feel rather uncertain about the depth and durability of the imprint left by most of the specific programs, some trace of the human quality of the American occupation still remains in Germany.

In the economic field the principal aim of reform was the liberalization of the German economy through the limitation of concentrated economic power and the removal of restraints of trade. The main policies undertaken to that end were deconcentration and decartelization, and limitation of the practice of trade licensing. These policies were implemented by means both of general legislation and of direct action against certain industries or enterprises.

The initial impulse toward deconcentration and decartelization seems to have come from a belief widespread in the United States at the end of the war that German cartels and trusts were a major military threat. In numerous books and other publications and in hearings before a Senate committee it was argued with more force than evidence that these organizations had played a key role in the restoration of Germany's military potential after the first World War. It was further argued that they had sought, in some cases successfully, to weaken the American economy in preparation for World War II.[16] The breaking up of trusts and cartels was viewed as a necessary security measure. This idea found expression in a passage of the Potsdam Agreement reading, "the German economy shall be decentralized for the purpose of eliminating the present excessive concentration of economic power . . ." The same sentiment inspires the preamble to Law 56, the general deconcentration and decartelization law of the American Military Government of February 1947. Three of its four clauses refer to concentrations of economic power as a military and political threat. Only the fourth touches obliquely on their possible adverse economic implications. As time went on, this rationale was to yield almost completely to the standard American antitrust view that monopolies are bad for purely economic reasons.

The Three Big Antitrust Cases

While antitrust action in general was to be governed by Law 56 and its British and French counterparts, some cases that were too big or too urgent to be handled with the rest were dealt with by special laws. These cases concerned the I. G.

Farben trust, the coal, iron, and steel industries, and the banking system. A fourth case, the government-owned UFA film monopoly, is of lesser interest.

I. G. Farben. The I. G. Farben combine comprised the dominant majority of the German chemical industry and had vast international ramifications. It was a favorite target for critics of German industrial concentrations. Under the action taken by the Allies it was broken up into four successor companies, rather fewer than the United States would have wished. The reform was made relatively simple by the fact that the stock of the original concern was widely held and that controlling interests did not exist. Hence there seemed to be no danger that the break-up of the organization might be nullified by a continued concentration of stock ownership. To prevent control by the banks—in Germany, where most stocks are in bearer form, banks customarily vote shares deposited with them for safekeeping—the new securities were cast in the form of registered stock.

The I. G. Farben break-up is undoubtedly the most successful among the major operations in this field. It seems to be generally agreed that the four successor companies do operate as separate entities and that they are viable. Whether they compete actively, whether they are superior in efficiency to the old organization, and whether they will stay apart once Allied control lapses are mute questions. The aim of impeding bank voting of stock has in part already been frustrated by arrangements between the depository banks and the stockholders.

Coal, iron, and steel. The break-up of the coal-steel complex presented far greater problems than that of I. G. Farben, because concentration of organization here was reinforced by concentration of ownership. The 12 steel companies that formed the core of the system were for the most part controlled

by the families of the founders, many of them with close personal ties, or by other dominant stockholders. These 12 companies controlled 90 per cent of German steel output and 55
per cent of Ruhr coal output. The largest company alone controlled almost 50 per cent of steel and 30 per cent of coal. Since
the companies needed for their own steel production only
half the coal that they controlled, they had a dominant voice in
the European coal market upon which some of their competitors depended. Both steel and coal companies were tightly
cartelizèd through their respective joint sales agencies.

To break up this great concentration of power the Allies,
after the most difficult negotiations involving the German government, the labor unions, and others, set up 28 independent
steel companies. No steel company was allowed to control
more than 75 per cent of its own coal requirements. Fabri-
cating facilities were separated from steel production. A number of new sales agencies were established to insure competitive marketing. Steps were also taken to prevent one stock-
holder from controlling more than one firm. Complex ex-
changes and sales of large blocks of stock became necessary to
accomplish this end. The difficulty of finding buyers in an
illiquid economy became one of the main factors slowing down
the reorganization. Some familiar names, like that of Krupp,
were shut out altogether from their old business. To guard
further against concealed concentration, controls were established over interlocking directorates and bank voting of stock.

Despite all these efforts grave doubts exist regarding the
present effectiveness and future stability of the new set-up.
It is true that in principle, according to the reorganization
plans laid down, any further organizational changes fall under
the jurisdiction of the coal-steel community. But it is rumored
even now, and not very confidentially, that present competition in the German coal-steel industries is less than perfect.
In the second place many German observers question whether
all of the 28 companies will prove viable should the going get

difficult. It may well be that the advantages of vertical integration tend to be overestimated in Germany. But the spectacle of the small unintegrated companies precariously poised somewhere up in the coal-steel industry structure, exposed to price pressures from above and below, is somewhat alarming. In practice the issue may never come to a test. Not many observers would bet heavily on the survival of the new arrangements after Allied control disappears.

The banking system. The reorganization of the banking system must be viewed at two levels: the commercial banks and the central banking system. The three large commercial banks became a target for reorganization because, with their country-wide branch system, they did wield great economic power and because it was believed that somehow a centralized banking system had enabled Germany to finance the war more effectively than a decentralized one would have. Initially the United States insisted upon breaking up each of these banks into as many units as there were states, which made 33 banks out of three. Later it became apparent that such small banks were suited neither to the needs of reconstruction nor to the task of attracting funds from foreign lenders. A partial reconcentration was then sanctioned, and the eleven successors of each bank were reduced to three. It is widely reported that the successor institutions of each bank cooperate closely, and rumor is looking ahead to the day when further reconcentration may take place. The deconcentration of the commercial banks has probably been the least effective of the major Allied efforts.

At the central bank level the old Reichsbank with its branches was replaced by a group of eleven Land Central Banks, one for each state, together with the Bank deutscher Länder as a central institution. This system, which seems to have been modeled on a somewhat literal interpretation of the Federal Reserve system, has worked well. The reason, as in the case of the Federal Reserve, appears to be that the system has evolved along lines rather different from those anticipated by the sponsors. Instead of becoming the loose organization that it was intended to be, it has developed strong central tendencies. Monetary policy has been made in the Bank deutscher Länder, not in the eleven Land Central Banks, even though these central decisions are strongly influenced by the presidents of the eleven banks who form the board of the Bank deutscher Länder. The reorganization has not therefore basically altered the realities of central banking in Germany. With the merging of three of the states, and the consequent reduction in their number to nine, a like reduction occurred in the number of Land Central Banks.

The General Decartelization and Deconcentration Law

Apart from the special cases mentioned so far, antitrust action was to be handled under general legislation embodied in U.S. Military Government Law 56 and similar laws in the two other zones. Great difficulties had to be overcome in order to reach this measure of agreement among the Allies. The legislation therefore did not go into effect until early 1947. Meanwhile a large and somewhat mixed staff in the United States Military Government had been gathering material and was thirsting for action. When the time had arrived, however, General Clay had come to the realization that widespread application of the law would interfere with the economic revival. Instead of authorizing the expected frontal attack he cut back program and staff, an action which led to some commotion.[17] Only limited deconcentration measures were eventually carried out under Law 56.

In addition to deconcentration Law 56 also provided for decartelization. It declared all cartel agreements to be null and void. Later on all participants in such agreements were required to serve notices of termination on their partners. By the end of 1948, 1,100 agreements had been ended in this manner. Several cases of illegal cartel activities were prosecuted both by Allied and German authorities. In recent years, however, only limited use has been made of the powers available under the law, presumably because frequent prosecutions under an Allied law might intensify opposition in Germany to the anticartel law that Economics Minister Erhard is pushing. When a German law satisfactory to the Allies is passed Law 56 and its British and French companion pieces will lapse.

It is perhaps worth noting that the final stages of the American antitrust campaign were conducted almost entirely in the name of achieving a stronger and healthier German economy. The anticartel features of Allied legislation have probably helped to stimulate competition, although they have by no means established it throughout the economy. Numerous cartel-like arrangements are believed to be operating more or less underground. Their effectiveness in restraining competition, however, is diminished by the fact that legally enforcible contracts, upon which German cartels used to rely, are at present ruled out. Whether these gains for competition will be preserved depends in good part on the German legislation that is to supplant Allied law.

Taking all measures together, one cannot help concluding that the effort of the United States to remake Germany in its own antitrust image has met with rather limited success. The outlook, moreover, is for a reversal of at least some of the major reforms. It may be reckoned as a gain, however, that the climate of German opinion today is probably less predominantly procartel than it was between the two wars. Credit for this goes in the main to men like Economics Minister Erhard, but United States antitrust policy may claim its share. The interest lies in the fact that these same measures of deconcentration were initiated shortly after the war for the purpose of weakening the German economy's war potential. A variety of considerations can be adduced that may help to explain, if not altogether to justify, the apparent inconsistency. But it is not surprising if some German observers seem almost to have resigned themselves to the conclusion that trust busting is an American principle equally applicable whether the goal is to weaken or to strengthen the German economy.

Trade Licensing

A third though less spectacular phase of the reforms pushed by the United States was the attempt to outlaw trade licensing. Tradesmen, artisans, and small storekeepers play an important economic and political role in Germany. Under Hitler these groups were given protection by a system of trade licensing that in effect allowed those already established in a trade or business to keep down the number of newcomers. During the depression of the thirties there was some economic justification for this practice, particularly because the system did make for high professional standards. After the currency reform, with the entire economy expanding, with millions of refugees to be absorbed and other adjustments to be made, free entry into trade and business seemed eminently desirable. In the fall of 1948, therefore, the American Military Government abolished all trade licensing except where required for the protection of public health and safety. Even where these were involved, only the competence of the applicant was to be considered, as established by a governmental agency and not by his future competitors, and without reference to his financial condition or to the "economic need" for the new business. The number of new businesses increased very substantially following this action.

The two other occupying powers, however, showed no inclination to follow the American policy. In their zones, therefore, trade licensing remained in effect. In the American Zone the ban on licensing has been subjected to a succession of legislative assaults, against which the United States has been fighting a rear-guard action. Through the pressure of middle-class elements, which form an important part of the political strength of the Adenauer government, much of the freedom gained in 1948 has been whittled away. Some compensating advantage may be found in the fact that the licensing system restrains the proliferation of marginal retail stores, a process that would tend further to increase the cost of distribution.

CONCLUSION

Although we have dealt here only with economic reform, it must be emphasized that the center of gravity of the Allied effort was to the side of political reform. Through demilitarization and denazification the Allies sought to eradicate the sources of past evil; through democratization and reorientation, and through reform of education, the civil service, the judiciary, and other things they endeavored to lay the foundations for a democratic German future. A full discussion of those efforts is beyond the scope of this book, and little is to be gained by summary judgments on topics that are still controversial. By way of conclusion, however, something that applies to political and economic reform equally may be said on the general problem of remaking Germany by force of occupation.[18]

A military occupation, no matter how democratically inspired, is in effect a dictatorship. As such, can it instill the kind of values for which the United States stands? Operating through command, can it hope to found a democracy? Symbolizing might, can it establish a belief in right? As the representative of a foreign and until recently hostile power, can it hope to make any impact at all upon the minds of the defeated? General Clay and High Commissioner McCloy tried to ease these inner conflicts by rapidly turning responsibility back to the Germans and by exercising restraint in the use of their powers. But fundamentally there seems to be no solution.

Things were made more complex by repeated reversals of policy. Nonfraternization was followed by such a notable instance of fraternization as the exchange of persons program. Dismantling was followed—sometimes accompanied—by aid for reconstruction. Demilitarization ended in rearmament. Granted that these changes of direction were imposed by circumstances, they could not fail to make the Germans skeptical.

Receptiveness to Allied reforms was probably at its height immediately after the war. The collapse had left the Germans stunned and limp, and many would no doubt have gone far in adopting foreign ways. But this opportunity did not last. Soon old habits were resumed, old institutions revived, minds were beginning to close. The Allies were not prepared for the immensity of the job; they lacked detailed plans and had no common policy. When these things had gradually been worked out conditions were already far less favorable. After the currency reform German self-confidence rose in step with the index of production. While most people continued to welcome the occupation, thanks to the Russian threat, their willingness to listen to Allied precepts diminished.

Yet precepts are not the only way of influencing people. The Germans might close their ears to what they considered Allied preaching, but they could not insulate themselves against Allied example. This example, true enough, was overlaid with the forms of military authoritarianism. Nevertheless the democratic and humanitarian core came through at many points. Particularly could this be said of the American contingent. From the generous gesture of Marshall aid to the easy-going and friendly ways of the ubiquitous G.I. a continuous demonstration impressed upon large numbers of Germans a way of thinking and acting new to them but not unattractive. Germany is today regarded by many observers as the most "Americanized" country in Europe. This shows up in the emphasis on material progress, the worship of efficiency, the general tempo of business. It is confirmed by the reaction of the G.I.'s, who seem to prefer Germany to other European countries. Various factors no doubt contribute to the German attitude, but the demonstration of American ways through the occupation probably rates high among them. Whether all the influences that have been brought to bear will succeed in helping Germany to create a stable democracy and in anchoring her firmly on the side of the West only time can tell.

REFERENCES

CHAPTER 1. THE "GERMAN MIRACLE"

No references

CHAPTER 2. SOME PRINCIPLES OF ECONOMIC
DEVELOPMENT

1. "Notes toward a Theory of Derived Development," *Proceedings of the Third Conference of Central Bank Technicians* (Havana, Banco Nacional de Cuba, 1952), vol. 2.
2. R. F. Harrod, *Towards a Dynamic Economics* (London, Macmillan & Co., Ltd., 1948), lecture 3; E. D. Domar, "Expansion and Employment," *American Economic Review*, March 1947, vol. *37*, no. 1, pp. 34–5; "The Problem of Capital Accumulation," *ibid.*, December 1948, vol. *38*, no. 5, pp. 777–94; William Fellner, "The Capital-Output Ratio in Dynamic Economics," *Money, Trade, and Economic Growth: Essays in Honor of John Henry Williams* (New York, Macmillan Co., 1951), pp. 105–34.

CHAPTER 3. THE COMEBACK OF PRODUCTION AND INCOME

1. Colin Clark, *The Conditions of Economic Progress* (2d ed., London, 1951), p. 195.
2. *Wirtschaft und Statistik*, June 1954, p. 265.
3. Institut für Demoskopie, *Die Einkommensverhältnisse im Bundesgebiet 1952* (Allensbach am Bodensee, 1952), pp. 21–2.
4. Simon Kuznets, *Shares of Upper Income Groups in Income and Saving* (New York, National Bureau of Economic Research, 1953), p. 46.
5. K. Elsholz, "Die Sozialen Leistungen in der Bundesrepublik," *Bulletin des Presse- und Informationsamtes der Bundesregierung*, Bonn, January 15, 1954, pp. 70–1; A. Oel, "Die Sozialleistungsempfänger im Bundesgebiet," *Sozialer Fortschritt*, February 1953, p. 37.
6. William Fellner, "The Capital-Output Ratio in Dynamic Economics," in *Money, Trade, and Economic Growth*.
7. Cf. John H. Adler, "Some Comments on Mr. Pazos' Paper on Economic Development and Financial Stability," *Proceedings of the Third Conference of Central Bank Technicians*, vol. *1*.

CHAPTER 4. MONETARY POLICY AND FISCAL POLICY

1. Bank deutscher Länder, *Monthly Report*, March 1949.
2. Office of the U.S. High Commissioner for Germany, *Report on Germany*, September 1949–January 1952, p. 32.
3. Bank deutscher Länder, *Report for the Year 1952*.
4. The best source for American policy during this period is the Office of Military Government for Germany (U.S.), *Monthly Report of the Military Governor*.
5. Eduard Wolf, "Geld- und Finanzprobleme der deutschen Nachkriegswirt-

schaft," *Die deutsche Wirtschaft zwei Jahre nach dem Zusammenbruch* (Berlin, 1947), p. 215.

6. Verwaltung für Finanzwesen des vereinigten Wirtschaftsgebiets, *Entwurf eines Gesetzes zur Neuordnung des Geldwesens* (Heidelberg, Springer Verlag, 1948).

7. For a detailed description of the reform, see Bank deutscher Länder, *Report for the Years 1948–1949.*

CHAPTER 5. THE FREE MARKET POLICY

1. Cf. Walter Eucken, *Grundsätze der Wirtschaftspolitik,* ed. by Edith Eucken and K. Paul Hensel (Bern, A. Francke A. G. Verlag, 1952); Leonhard Miksch, "Zur Theorie des Gleichgewichts," *Ordo: Jahrbuch für die Ordnung von Wirtschaft und Gesellschaft,* ed. by Walter Eucken and Franz Böhm (Godesberg, Helmut Küpper Verlag, 1948), vol. *1,* see also vols. *2–6;* Alfred Müller-Armack, *Wirtschaftslenkung und Marktwirtschaft* (Hamburg, Verlag für Wirtschaft und Sozialpolitik, 1947); Wilhelm Röpke, *Ist die deutsche Wirtschaftspolitik richtig?* (Stuttgart, W. Kohlhammer Verlag, 1950); Ludwig Erhard, *Germany's Comeback in the World Market* (New York, Macmillan Co., 1954); *Wirtschaft ohne Wunder,* ed. by Albert Hunold (Erlenbach-Zürich, Eugen Rentsch Verlag, 1953), especially articles by Franz Böhm, Ludwig Erhard, Walter Eucken, F. A. Hayek, Friedrich Lutz, Leonhard Miksch, Wilhelm Röpke, Alexander Rüstow, and Otto Veit. For criticism, see Hans Peter, *Freiheit der Wirtschaft* (Köln, Bund Verlag G.m.b.H., 1953).

2. Cf. Henry C. Simons, *Economic Policy for a Free Society* (Chicago, 1948).

3. *Wirtschaftsverwaltung* (Frankfurt am Main, Verwaltung für Wirtschaft, 1948), no. 1, p. 20.

4. Der wissenschaftliche Beirat bei der Verwaltung für Wirtschaft des vereinigten Wirtschaftsgebiets, *Gutachten* (Göttingen, Otto Schwarz & Co.), April 18, 1948.

5. Harold Rasch, *Kartelle und Kartellpolitik,* "Schriften der Industrie und Handelskammer" (Frankfurt am Main, 1953), no. 2.

6. *Report on Germany,* pp. 157–62.

7. *Finanzen und Steuern,* vol. *1,* no. 27, p. 137.

8. K. Elsholz, *Bulletin der Bundesregierung,* January 15, 1954, no. 9, p. 65.

9. Bank deutscher Länder, *Monthly Report,* February 1954.

10. U.S. Economic Cooperation Administration, *Western Germany Country Study* (Washington, D.C., February 1949).

11. *Lebensfähigkeit und Vollbeschäftigung* (Bonn, April 1950), prepared under the leadership of the Institut für Weltwirtschaft an der Universität Kiel.

CHAPTER 6. INVESTMENT AND ITS FINANCING

1. A. K. Cairncross, "The Economic Recovery of Western Germany," *Lloyds Bank Review,* October 1951, p. 30.

2. Gesetz über den Kapitalverkehr, September 2, 1949.

3. Housing Premium Law, March 17, 1952.

4. Cf. Helmut Meinhold, "Die Kapitallenkung und ihr Einfluss auf die Kapitalbildung," *Kapitalbildung und Kapitalverwendung* (Berlin, Duncker und Humblot, 1953), p. 145.

5. ECA Technical Assistance Commission, *Die Eingliederung der Flüchtlinge in die deutsche Gemeinschaft* (Bonn, Bundesministerium für Vertriebene, 1951), p. 174.

6. Bundesministerium für Wohnungsbau, *Der Wohnungsbau in der Bundesrepublik Deutschland* (Bonn, 1951), p. 46.

7. Wohnungsbaugesetz, April 24, 1950.

8. Office of the U.S. High Commissioner for Germany, *Handbook of Economic Statistics;* and Bank deutscher Länder, *Report for the Year 1953.*

9. *Report on Germany,* pp. 51–2.

10. Kreditanstalt für Wiederaufbau, *Annual Reports,* 1949–53.

11. Gesetz über die Investitionshilfe der gewerblichen Wirtschaft, January 7, 1952.

12. Kuratorium für das Industriekreditbank-Sondervermögen Investitionshilfe, *Annual Report,* 1952–53.

13. Erstes Gesetz zur Förderung des Kapitalmarktes, December 15, 1952.

14. Zweite Bekanntmachung des Ausschusses für Kapitalverkehr, September 2, 1950.

15. Bernhard Benning, "Bankkredite und Kapitalmarkt," *Fünf Jahre Wirtschaftspolitik der Bundesrepublik Deutschland* (Bonn, Deutscher Industrie und Handelstag, 1953), no. 25.

CHAPTER 7. INDUSTRIAL STRUCTURE, IMPORT NEEDS, AND EXPORT CAPACITY

1. *Reparationen, Sozialprodukt, Lebensstandard* (Bremen, Friedrich Trüjen Verlag, 1948), *3,* 44. Referred to as the Harmssen Report.

2. Ifo-Institut für Wirtschaftsforschung, *Fünf Jahre Deutsche Mark* (München, 1953), p. 48, based upon Länderrat des amerikanischen Besatzungsgebietes, *Statistisches Handbuch von Deutschland,* 1928–44 (München, Franz Ehrenwirth Verlag, 1949). Other estimates range from 59 per cent of manufacturing production (Economic Cooperation Administration, *Western Germany Country Study,* Washington, D.C., February 1949, p. 39), to 64.2 per cent of value added by industry (Harmssen Report, *3,* 70.)

3. Jürgen Eick, *Die wirtschaftlichen Folgen der Zonengrenzen* (Hamburg, Union Verlag, 1948), p. 35.

4. Harmssen Report, *3,* 83.

5. K. Padberg and A. Nieschulz, "Produktion, Verkaufserlöse und Betriebsausgaben der Landwirtschaft im Bundesgebiet," *Agrarwirtschaft,* December 1953, p. 365.

6. Milton Gilbert and Irving B. Kravis, *An International Comparison of National Products and the Purchasing Power of Currencies* (Paris, Organization for European Economic Cooperation, 1953), p. 32.

7. Colin Clark, *The Conditions of Economic Progress.*

8. Hans Röper, *Rationalisierung durch Typenbeschränkung* (Frankfurt am Main, Rationalisierungs-Kuratorium der deutschen Wirtschaft, n.d.), p. 5.

9. Otmar Emminger, "Deutschland's Stellung in der Weltwirtschaft," *Kieler Vorträge* (Kiel, 1953), N.S., no. 4.

10. Waldemar B. Hasselblatt, "Industrieproduktion und Rohstoffeinfuhr," *Weltwirtschaftliches Archiv* (Kiel, 1954), vol. 2, no. 73, pp. 244–69.

11. *Reparationen, Sozialprodukt, Lebensstandard, 3, 38.*
12. Bank deutscher Länder, *Monthly Report,* November 1953.

CHAPTER 8. FOREIGN TRADE POLICIES

1. Ausfuhrkredit Aktiengesellschaft, *Geschäftsbericht, 1953.*
2. Adolf Bötte, "Die Garantien und Bürgschaften des Bundes zur Förderung der Ausfuhr," *DWD-Sonderblatt* (Köln, Deutscher Wirtschaftsdienst G.m.b.H.), June 1, 1953.
3. J. Esser and H. C. M. Stumm, *Die heutige Steuerbelastung der gewerblichen Wirtschaft* (Bonn, Institut Finanzen und Steuern, 1953), p. 131.
4. Economics Minister Erhard, quoted in *Frankfurter Allgemeine Zeitung,* July 21, 1954, p. 11.
5. Chapter 2 of the United Nations Economic Commission for Europe, *Annual Survey for 1953,* underlines the great importance that exports have had in maintaining activity.
6. Bank deutscher Länder, *Report for the Year 1953.*
7. Alfred Jacobs, *Gutachten über die Kaufkraftparität der deutschen Mark* (Bremen, Bremer Ausschuss für Wirtschaftsforschung, 1948), p. 51.
8. See Hermann J. Abs, *Das Londoner Schuldenabkommen* (Frankfurt, Süddeutsche Bank A.G., October 29, 1952); Hans J. Dernburg, "Some Basic Aspects of the German Debt Settlement," *Journal of Finance,* September 1953, *8,* 298–318; U.S. Department of State, *Report of the Conference on German External Debts, London, February–August 1952* (London, August 8, 1952).

CHAPTER 9. POPULATION AND REFUGEES

1. Statistisches Bundesamt, *Statistisches Taschenbuch über die Heimatvertriebenen* (Wiesbaden, 1953), p. 3.
2. *Statistisches Taschenbuch,* p. 3.
3. Bundesminister für Vertriebene, *Vertriebene, Flüchtlinge, Kriegsgefangene, heimatlose Ausländer, 1949–52* (Bonn, 1953), p. 20.
4. ECA Technical Assistance Commission, *Die Eingliederung der Flüchtlinge in die deutsche Gemeinschaft.*
5. Bundesministerium der Finanzen, *Flüchtlingslasten und Verteidigungsbeitrag* (Bonn, 1951).

CHAPTER 10. LABOR'S PERFORMANCE

1. Bundesministerium für Arbeit, *Arbeits und Sozialstatistische Mitteilungen,* May 1954, p. 234.
2. International Labour Office, *Yearbook of Labour Statistics, 1953* (Geneva, 1954).
3. Rolf Wagenführ, 'Zur Analyse der Arbeitslosigkeit in Westdeutschland," *Vollbeschäftigung, Ergebnisse einer Arbeitstagung* (Köln, 1950), p. 80; and R. Nimptsch, *Überbevölkerung, Bevölkerungsausgleich und Arbeitsmarkt* (Köln, 1952), p. 34.
4. Bundesanstalt für Arbeitsvermittlung und Arbeitslosenversicherung, *Die Schichtung der Arbeitslosigkeit* (Nuremberg, 1953).
5. *Statistisches Taschenbuch über die Heimatvertriebenen,* pp. 9–10.

Chapter 11. The Political Bases of Revival

No references

Chapter 12. Economic Consequences of German
                     Mentality

1. Karl Bednarik, *Der junge Arbeiter von Heute* (Stuttgart, Gustav Kilper, 1953); Eugen Diesel, *Die deutsche Wandlung* (Stuttgart, J. G. Gotta'sche Buchhandlung Nachfolger, 1931); Nathan Leites and Paul Kecskemeti, "Some Psychological Hypotheses on Nazi Germany," *Journal of Social Psychology*, vols. *26, 27, 28*, article in four parts; Erich Fromm, *Escape from Freedom* (New York, Farrar and Rinehart, Inc., 1941); Willy Hellpach, *Der deutsche Charakter* (Bonn, 1954); Richard Müller-Freienfels, *Psychologie des deutschen Menschen und seiner Kultur* (2d ed., München, 1930); David Rodnick, *Postwar Germans* (New Haven, Yale University Press, 1948); Wilhelm Röpke, *Die deutsche Frage* (3d ed., München, 1948); Helmut Schelsky, *Wandlungen der deutschen Familie in der Gegenwart* (2d ed., Stuttgart, 1954); Werner Sombart, *Der moderne Kapitalismus* (Leipzig, Duncker und Humblot, 1902).
2. Müller-Freienfels, *Psychologie*, p. 80.
3. Hellpach, *Der deutsche Charakter*, p. 171.
4. Leites and Kecskemeti, "Some Psychological Hypotheses," p. 92.

Chapter 13. Allied Aid and Occupation Policy

1. Gustav Stolper, *German Realities* (New York, Reynal & Hitchcock, 1948), p. 13.
2. Henry Morgenthau Jr., *Germany Is Our Problem* (New York, 1945), pp. 30–47.
3. B. U. Ratchford and W. D. Ross, *Berlin Reparations Assignment* (Chapel Hill, N.C., University of North Carolina Press, 1947), pp. 134, 141.
4. Press and Information Office of the German Government, *Germany Reports* (Bonn 1953), p. 23.
5. For the contributions of the United Kingdom and France, see U.S. Department of State, *Report of the Conference on German External Debts, London, February–August 1952*, p. 10. For the United States' contribution, see Department of Commerce, *Foreign Grants and Credits* (Washington, D.C., June 1954).
6. Office of the U.S. High Commissioner for Germany, *Handbook of Economic Statistics*, August 1954.
7. Inter-Allied Reparations Agency, *Report of the Assembly* (Brussels, June 1951), p. 19.
8. Margaret Rupli Woodward, "Germany Makes Amends," *Department of State Bulletin* (Washington, D.C., July 26, 1954), p. 128.
9. Bundesminister für den Marshallplan, *Bericht der deutschen Bundesregierung über die Durchführung des Marshallplanes, October 1949–March 1951* (Bonn, 1951), p. 94.
10. Foreign Operations Administration, *Local Currency Counterparts* (Washington, D.C., June 30, 1954), p. 10.
11. Bundesminister für Verkehr, *Die Verkehrspolitik in der Bundesrepublik*

Deutschland, 1949–1953 (Dortmund, Verkehrs- und Wirtschaftsverlag, 1954), p. 20.

12. Inter-Allied Reparations Agency, *Report of the Assembly,* p. 15; also G. W. Harmssen, *Am Abend der Demontage* (Bremen, Friedrich Trüjen Verlag, 1951), p. 26.

13. Richardson Wood & Co., *Proposals for Furthering the Economic Development of West Berlin* (n.p., 1952), p. 2.

14. *Germany Reports,* p. 57.

15. Berliner Zentralbank, *West Berlin's Economic Development in 1953* (Berlin, 1954), pp. 4–6.

16. Joseph Borkin and Charles A. Welsh, *Germany's Master Plan* (New York, 1943); Darel McConkey, *Out of Your Pocket: The Story of Cartels* (New York, 1947); Charles R. Whittlesey, *National Interest and International Cartels* (New York, 1946); Wendell Berge, *Cartels, Challenge to a Free World* (Washington, 1944); Henry Morgenthau Jr., *Germany Is Our Problem,* pp. 36–7; *Cartel Practices and National Security,* Hearings before a Subcommittee of the Committee on Military Affairs, United States Senate (Washington, D.C., December 20, 1944).

17. Lucius D. Clay, *Decision in Germany* (New York, 1950), p. 331.

18. Cf. E. H. Litchfield, "Political Objectives and Legal Bases of Occupation Government," *Governing Postwar Germany,* ed. by E. H. Litchfield (Ithaca, N.Y., Cornell University Press, 1953), p. 8.

INDEX

Abs, Hermann J., 391
Adenauer, Konrad, 157, 279, 315, 318, 319, 385
Adler, John H., 388
Advisory Council of academic economists, 121
Agreement on Industrial Controls, 371
Agriculture: exodus from, 292; agricultural reconstruction, 203 ff.; structure, 194 ff.
Aid, Allied. *See* Allies
Aid, to private business, 171, 175
Airlift, Berlin, 374
Allies, 348 ff., 352; Allied aid, 39, 344 ff., 354 ff.; authorities, 142; Military Government, 317; evolution of policy, 345 ff.; anticartel features of Allied legislation, 383
Americanization, 331, 386
Amortization allowances, 166
Antitrust action, 382; three big cases, 378 ff.
Arbeit, Bundesministerium für, 391
Arbeitsvermittlung, Bundesanstalt für, 391
Arms burden, 217
Ausfuhrkredit A. G., 245
Ausgleichsforderungen, 70

Balance of payments, 88, 107, 235, 356
Bank deutscher Länder, 76, 77 ff., 146, 159, 219, 236, 245, 246, 247, 252, 257, 381, 382, 388
Bank for International Settlements, 91
Banks, 70, 187; commercial, 180; mortgage, 181; savings, 180, 181; bank credit, 74, 88, 177 ff.; reserve requirements, 70, 76, 78, 84, 90, 98; acceptances, 76; structure and practices, 180 ff.; system, 381 ff. *See also* Bank deutscher Länder, Bank for International Settlements, Berliner

Zentralbank, *Grossbanken*, Investment, Land Central Bank, Reichsbank, Compensation of War Damage Bank
Basic Law, 278, 376
Bednarik, Karl, 392
Benning, Bernhard, 390
Berge, Wendell, 393
Berlin, 195, 374 ff.
Berliner Zentralbank, 393
Bilateral restriction, 230 ff., 240, 251 ff.
Bizonal Economic Council, 120, 351
Black market, 64 ff., 122
Blocked DMark, 237, 361
Böhm, Franz, 389
Bonn, 321
Borkin, Joseph, 393
Borrowers, 185
Bötte, Adolf, 391
Brussels Conference, 346, 352, 353
Budget, 130; federal, 141 ff., 361; surpluses, 78, 80
Bundestag, 318, 319
Businessman, American and German, 335
Byrnes, James F., 345, 351

Cairncross, A., 91, 155, 157, 165, 389
Capacity: reserve, 87; industrial, 200
Capital, 22; -output ratios, 24, 54 ff.; marginal productivity, 54; per worker, 58, 211; price of equipment, 59; market, 124, 155, 168 ff.; Market Law, 190; formation, 129; issues control, 160; Issues Committee, 184; misallocation, 164; -poor country, 190; social, 210; volume of, 210; per capita, 215; account, 237; movement, 243
Capital Issues Committee. *See* Capital
Capital Market Law. *See* Capital, First Capital Market Law

YALE STUDIES IN ECONOMICS